Handbook of Behavioral Assessment *edited by Anthony R. Ciminero, Karen S. Calhoun, and Henry E. Adams*

Counseling and Psychotherapy: A Behavioral Approach *by E. Lakin Phillips*

Dimensions of Personality *edited by Harvey London and John E. Exner, Jr.*

The Mental Health Industry: A Cultural Phenomenon *by Peter A. Magaro, Robert Gripp, David McDowell, and Ivan W. Miller III*

Nonverbal Communication: The State of the Art *by Robert G. Harper, Arthur N. Weins, and Joseph D. Matarazzo*

Alcoholism and Treatment *by David J. Armor, J. Michael Polich, and Harriet B. Stambul*

A Biodevelopmental Approach to Clinical Child Psychology: Cognitive Controls and Cognitive Control Theory *by Sebastiano Santostefano*

Handbook of Infant Development *edited by Joy D. Osofsky*

Understanding the Rape Victim: A Synthesis of Research Findings *by Sedelle Katz and Mary Ann Mazur*

Childhood Pathology and Later Adjustment: The Question of Prediction *by Loretta K. Cass and Carolyn B. Thomas*

Intelligent Testing with the WISC-R *by Alan S. Kaufman*

Adaptation in Schizophrenia: The Theory of Segmental Set *by David Shakow*

Psychotherapy: An Eclectic Approach *by Sol L. Garfield*

Handbook of Minimal Brain Dysfunctions *edited by Herbert E. Rie and Ellen D. Rie*

Handbook of Behavioral Interventions: A Clinical Guide *edited by Alan Goldstein and Edna B. Foa*

Art Psychotherapy *by Harriet Wadeson*

Handbook of Adolescent Psychology *edited by Joseph Adelson*

Psychotherapy Supervision: Theory, Research and Practice *edited by Allen K. Hess*

Psychology and Psychiatry in Courts and Corrections: Controversy and Change *by Ellsworth A. Fersch, Jr.*

Restricted Environmental Stimulation: Research and Clinical Applications *by Peter Suedfeld*

Personal Construct Psychology: Psychotherapy and Personality *edited by Alvin W. Landfield and Larry M. Leitner*

Mothers, Grandmothers, and Daughters: Personality and Child Care in Three-Generation Families *by Bertram J. Cohler and Henry U. Grunebaum*

Further Explorations in Personality *edited by A.I. Rabin, Joel Aronoff, Andrew M. Barclay, and Robert A. Zucker*

Hypnosis and Relaxation: Modern Verification of an Old Equation *by William E. Edmonston, Jr.*

Handbook of Clinical Behavior Therapy *edited by Samuel M. Turner, Karen S. Calhoun, and Henry E. Adams*

Handbook of Clinical Neuropsychology *edited by Susan B. Filskov and Thomas J. Boll*

The Course of Alcoholism: Four Years After Treatment *by J. Michael Polich, David J. Armor, and Harriet B. Braiker*

Handbook of Innovative Psychotherapies *edited by Raymond J. Corsini*

The Role of the Father in Child Development (Second Edition) *edited by Michael E. Lamb*

Behavioral Medicine: Clinical Applications *by Susan S. Pinkerton, Howard Hughes, and W.W. Wenrich*

Handbook for the Practice of Pediatric Psychology *edited by June M. Tuma*

Change Through Interaction: Social Psychological Processes of Counseling and Psychotherapy *by Stanley R. Strong and Charles D. Claiborn*

Drugs and Behavior (Second Edition) *by Fred Leavitt*

(*continued on back*)

This book is dedicated to our spouses, Jo and Rich,
for their love, support, and patience.

Library of Congress Cataloging-in-Publication Data:

Oster, Gerald D.
Understanding and treating depressed adolescents and their families / Gerald D. Oster, Janice E. Caro.
p. cm. — (Wiley series on personality processes)
"A Wiley-Interscience publication."
Includes bibliographical references.
ISBN 0-471-60897-1
1. Depression in adolescence. 2. Teenagers—Suicidal behavior. 3. Family assessment. I. Caro, Janice E. II. Title. III. Series.

RJ506.D4086 1990 89-37665
616.89'022—dc20 CIP

Printed in the United States of America

10 9 8 7 6 5 4 3 2 1

Series Preface

This series of books is addressed to behavioral scientists interested in the nature of human personality. Its scope should prove pertinent to personality theorists and researchers, as well as to clinicians concerned with applying an understanding of personality processes to the amelioration of emotional difficulties in living. To this end, the series provides a scholarly integration of theoretical formulations, empirical data, and practical recommendations.

Six major aspects of studying and learning about human personality can be designated: personality theory, personality structure and dynamics, personality development, personality assessment, personality change, and personality adjustment. In exploring these aspects of personality, the books in the series discuss a number of distinct but related subject areas: the nature and implications of various theories of personality; personality characteristics that account for consistencies and variations in human behavior; the emergence of personality processes in children and adolescents; the use of interviewing and testing procedures to evaluate individual differences in personality; efforts to modify personality styles through psychotherapy, counseling, behavior therapy, and other methods of influence; and patterns of abnormal personality functioning that impair individual competence.

IRVING B. WEINER

University of South Florida
Tampa, Florida

Foreword

The phenomenology and treatment of childhood depressive disorders has been the subject of much discussion and research, especially since the mid-1970s. The signs and symptoms of major depressive disorder, dysthymia, adjustment disorder with depressed mood, and bipolar disorders have been measured, catalogued, and compared in systematic empirical research. This has led to categorical classifications of mood disorders in children and adolescents as well as conceptualization of dimensional measures of depression. Developmental comparisons have been made and are the subject of many current studies.

Biological and family studies have elucidated factors associated with major depressive disorder. These factors are markers for vulnerability to mood disorders. Developmental differences have been described for sleep architecture variables and for age of onset of family affective disorders.

Epidemiological reports have documented the high rate of co-occurrence with mood disorders with such disorders as anxiety and conduct disorders. Suicidal ideation and acts, violence, and substance abuse are associated with youth depressive disorders. The longitudinal course of major depression in children and adolescents appears to exhibit chronic and recurrent manifestations of this disorder.

The importance of studies that identify factors associated with risk for childhood and adolescent mood disorders is most evident in the need to use this information to guide research and clinical practice in treatment regimens and prevention programs for youth mood disorders. To date, most treatment studies have focused on medication trials and assessment of short-term outcome. In fact, these studies have been so widely publicized that an impression may have been generated that psychopharmotherapy is the treatment of choice for youth mood disorders. This impression has not been validated. In fact, systematic studies are needed comparing various psychodynamic, cognitive, family, and biological interventions. The results of such research may lead to the development of differential therapeutics on dimensional symptoms or categorical constellations of mood disorders in children and adolescents.

At present, clinical observation and clinical testing make up the elements that guide the "clinical wisdom" of treatment of mood disorders in children and adolescents. This book represents a focused effort to integrate a family therapy model and clinical wisdom into a framework encompassing the varied treatments utilized by clinicians for youth mood disorders. Texts such as this stimulate new ideas and lead to the testing of old hypotheses. The effects may highlight new and creative approaches to decreasing the morbidity associated with youth mood disorders.

CYNTHIA R. PFEFFER

New York Hospital-Cornell Medical Center
White Plains, New York
October 1989

Preface

In recent years, considerable attention has been focused on understanding, assessing, and treating emotional disturbance in adolescents. This attention is understandable within the context of the startling increase in the occurrence of adolescent suicide and problems related to adolescent substance abuse. At present, adolescent suicide is the second major cause of death among our young people. Recent media reports of multiple suicides have also refocused this country's attention onto the alarming and tragic effects of adolescent depression. Families, local communities, school systems, and medical and mental health facilities have become greatly concerned about this issue, as have state and federal governments, who have created bills addressing suicide education and other means of preventing youth suicide. It has become quite clear that to be effective in decreasing the prevalence of adolescent depression and in reducing the incidence of adolescent suicide, interventions must be multifaceted.

Also, to understand fully the various aspects of adolescent depression, clinicians must gain an appreciation for the influences of the family on depression's etiology and maintenance. Because the normative phase of adolescence is a time of rapid physical growth, emotional change, confusion, and turmoil, the emotional status of the family as a whole during this phase, beyond the functioning of the individual adolescent, has only recently received attention. Adolescents are affected by and have an impact on the family unit. This growing awareness that adolescent depression is also an interpersonal phenomenon has led theorists, researchers, and clinicians to include the family context in examining the etiology and course of depression, as well as in implementing corrective strategies.

Paralleling this focus is the growing interest in general systems approaches to treatment interventions. Within this theoretical framework, it is maintained that both adjustment and maladjustment are strongly influenced by the individual's interaction with the social environment. By delineating these interactional patterns between adolescents and their families, a more comprehensive understanding and treatment of adolescent depression can be achieved. This approach also has the capacity to incorporate the ways in which both intra- and interpersonal vulnerabilities play important roles in the expression of adolescent psychopathology.

For many years, leading professionals have worked in isolation to effect change. Traditional intervention models seem to have reflected only one aspect of the problem. This, in turn, has contributed to a more limited scope in terms of decreasing the prevalence of the depressive disorder. Many adolescents are not prepared for the forms of therapy that have been used successfully with adult depressives, and the fact that adolescents' actions still operate within the family sphere makes it difficult to try to understand and intervene without involving all family members in the agreement to change.

Understanding and Treating Depressed Adolescents and Their Families attempts to bridge the gap between traditional individualistic approaches to overcoming depression in individuals and newer approaches to effective treatment, involving therapeutic family interventions for troubled adolescents. In this book, family models of treatment and intervention have been emphasized due to their advantageous solution-oriented approaches. This book also acknowledges the fact that families must continually evolve as socializing agents of the young, and when they become stuck in maladaptive patterns, they become the source for maintaining disturbed interactions. It is hoped that this book can provide practical guidelines for clinicians, as well as substantive information for addressing the needs of individual teenagers and their families.

This book is a culmination of our experiences as two clinicians who have worked in a variety of private and public inpatient and outpatient settings and as supervisors of beginning therapists. Through our clinical experiences, we've gained a great deal of appreciation for the difficult, yet rewarding moments in working with depressed adolescents and their families; through our supervisory experiences, we've learned how to provide support, structure, and practical guidelines to novice therapists in order for them to effectively plan and coordinate their therapeutic sessions when confronting distressed adolescents and their often resistant, angry, and exasperated families.

This book has been divided into four parts, with three chapters per part. These parts address the etiology, assessment, and treatment of depression in adolescents, in addition to a separate part on the topic of adolescent suicide. The first chapter of the first part (on etiology) provides an overview of the current thinking and research in depressive illness and how it manifests itself in adolescent populations. This is followed by a chapter focusing on the issues related to the etiology of adolescent depression within the context of the family. In this manner, adolescent depression is conceptualized, in part, as a manifestation of underlying family conflict. Issues addressed include (a) how the adolescent is chosen to become the symptomatic family member, (b) contributions of marital discord to the development of depressive symptoms in adolescents, (c) influences of multigenerational familial patterns, and (d) the presence of adolescent depression as an indicator of blocked emotional expression within parental affect. The final chapter within this part familiarizes the reader with the contributions that individual models of depression have served in crystallizing thoughts about adolescent disturbance. Specific areas that are delineated include psychoanalytic theory, behavioral manifestations, cognitive and cognitive-behavioral approaches, and the biological factors contributing to an individual adolescent's depression.

The second part of this book addresses how to accurately assess and evaluate depression in teenagers in order to intervene effectively. The first two chapters of this part (Chapters 4 and 5) offer practical strategies for dealing with thc initial meetings of families with adolescent members. Chapter 4 offers broad guidelines and tips for engaging families in the initial evaluative sessions, and Chapter 5 provides several specific clinical tools that have become extremely useful and popular to practitioners in order to broaden the scope of therapeutic sessions. Chapter 6 underscores the need for a more comprehensive understanding of adolescent issues and for multimodal approaches in diagnosing adolescent depression; it does so by reviewing guidelines for interviewing individuals, as well as by exposing the reader to some of the current structured and semistructured interview formats and diagnostic inventories for measuring depression in adolescent populations.

The third part of this book broadens the focus to include the occurrence of adolescent suicide. This part applies to crisis situations the book's format of discussing etiology, assessment, and treatment. The risk factors contributing to suicide are presented in Chapter 7, in addition to a description of the "suicidogenic" family. The subsequent chapter (Chapter 8) deals with both how to assess the nature of the suicidal risk and what signs to look for when determining whether hospitalization is warranted. Chapter 9 extends this description and offers several manageable strategies for empowering the family to monitor a crisis and to expand their internal and external support in order to circumvent the need for inpatient intervention.

The final part focuses on the treatment settings where the work is done. The three chapters address outpatient strategies, brief hospitalization, and residential treatment centers, providing a wide range of coverage regarding the various treatment alternatives. In each chapter, the reasons for family involvement are emphasized because such involvement is essential if effective and lasting treatment is to occur. Issues related to the advantages and disadvantages of treating depressed adolescents and their families on an outpatient versus an inpatient basis are explicated throughout this part.

The main purpose of this book is to introduce the need for expanding the treatment of depression into an interpersonal context and to provide practical tips and techniques for the mental health professional working with depressed adolescents and their families. We want this book to be a guide for practitioners who are seeking a broader view of treatment with disturbed adolescents and who are willing to incorporate the family of the adolescent into their treatment structure. By providing these tools, along with an abundance of clinical material and case examples interspersed throughout the text, we hope that the readers will be able to obtain a degree of comfort, to take what is being offered, and to be able to integrate it into their own interpersonal and therapeutic styles and their own unique situations.

GERALD D. OSTER
JANICE E. CARO

Olney, Maryland
Silver Spring, Maryland
October 1989

Contents

PART 1

Historical and Etiological Perspectives

CHAPTER 1

The Depressed Adolescent: An Overview

CASE 1

Carol W., age 16, presented herself to her outpatient therapist as tearful and tense. When asked to construct a picture of her present world, she portrayed without hesitation the assorted problems that brought her into therapy (i.e., depression, confusion, low self-esteem, thoughts of suicide, and family history of abuse). Afterward, with much relief, she acknowledged having many depressed thoughts and feelings. She viewed herself as having very low self-esteem, and as being overly dependent on others. She admitted to becoming confused in interpersonal relationships, and her attempts at obtaining accurate feedback from peers often left her feeling dissatisfied. She also discussed having suicidal thoughts and had on past occasions made self-destructive gestures to gain attention. She described her background as having been abusive. Her parents had divorced when she was very young. On visits to her noncustodial father, she indicated that he had verbally derogated her, and she believed that she had internalized these bad thoughts and feelings. She also spoke of her mother and older sister being physically abused in their respective marital relationships. As her current relationships with males were beginning to appear to be similarly abusive, she was feeling helpless and angry at herself. With this history and her current conflicts, she had many questions concerning her identity and was eager for therapeutic support in pursuing these worries and concerns.

CASE 2

John L., age 17, a highly creative and intelligent individual, was initially hospitalized for severe drug and alcohol abuse, as well as for expressing suicidal ideation. During a mental status interview, he was asked to draw a person. The exceedingly depressed and thoughtful picture he drew attested to his depth of misery. John stated that he had not lived at home for 2 years. Before being hospitalized, he was enrolled in a boarding school, but he was eventually expelled. His parents were in the process of a long and drawn-out divorce struggle. While living with them in

Europe, he had been hospitalized twice for drug overdoses and had begun outpatient treatment. A previous psychological evaluation had described him as experiencing a deep depression and harboring strong feelings of guilt, with underlying anger and rage. He had also expressed many concerns about his conflict-ridden family situation and about his sexual identity. During an assessment of his emotional status, conducted in order to discuss plans for his placement outside of the hospital, John indicated that he was frightened to leave the support and structure of the hospital milieu and that he appreciated the attention and the people available at the hospital.

Much controversy has surrounded the diagnosis of depression in childhood and adolescence because its symptoms are likely to be intermixed with or masked by a plethora of other behavioral phenomena (Cytryn, McKnew, & Bunney, 1980). Nevertheless, there now is considerable evidence, drawn from countless research and clinical findings, demonstrating that preadults do experience depression (Kovacs, 1989). This present consensus stems from a diversity of studies conducted during the 1980s, which show consistent evidence of depression existing among children and adolescents, regardless of the definition used for *depression* (for reviews, see Digdon & Gotlib, 1985; Puig-Antich, 1986). These studies seem to be just a tiny reflection of how actively depression in preadult populations is being treated by a variety of health and mental health professionals in a number of diverse settings, using an array of therapeutic approaches.

Although less than 10% of the adolescent population could actually be formally diagnosed as experiencing a major depression, many of the feelings that constitute the syndrome (e.g., dysphoric mood, poor appetite, somatic complaints) may exist, singularly or in combination, and in varying degrees of intensity, in many youths beset with emotional turmoils (Kaplan, Hong, & Weinhold, 1984; Weiner, 1980). In clinical samples, research has shown the incidence of adolescent depression to be more than 33% (Robins, Alessi, Cook, Poznanski, & Yanchyshyn, 1982). More surprising, perhaps, studies on normative populations of adolescents have shown symptoms of depression occurring at the rate of 34% (e.g., Reynolds, 1984). Also, reported instances of depression in adolescents have increased significantly in recent years, as have the tragically frequent occurrences of teenage suicide, thereby interrelating the two phenomena and further emphasizing the seriousness of the problem (McWhirter & Kigin, 1988).

Accompanying the symptoms of depression are (a) the context in which they occur, (b) the reactions they induce in others (most notably the family members), and (c) the resulting responses that are elicited from the depressed person (Emde, Harmon, & Good, 1986). For example, if the depressed adolescents' response to sad feelings is blocked by a lack of sensitivity, denial, withdrawal, or rejection from significant others, will the teenager then act out the conflicts in order to receive the desired attention?

Also to be considered is whether the adolescent's depression is related in any way to the dynamics within the family life cycle. For instance, are the parents struggling with life-style issues, such as the feelings surrounding an "empty nest," retirement, or a mid-life crisis, and are these then creating disequilibrium in the family, which the children are feeling and responding to? One powerful option that the teenager possesses to provide stability for the family is to show severe depressive or suicidal feelings so that the parents can clearly see that they are now and will be still needed (Haley, 1980). The function of the symptoms then becomes a way for the parents to remain unchanged in their roles and to continue to communicate about their child's incapacitating condition. Clinicians in positions of treatment then must address both the symptoms and the symptoms' functions in order to understand accurately and intervene effectively in the depressed states of the identified teenagers and the family systems in which they are being expressed.

THE VARIABLE NATURE OF DEPRESSION

For the practicing clinician, the term *depression* refers to changes in moods and behaviors that range from a mild degree of reactive sadness to intensely experienced feelings of dysphoria and possibly even suicidal thoughts (Klerman, Weissman, Rounsaville, & Chevron, 1984). Listed among its symptoms are feelings of worthlessness, marked restlessness, changes in appetite, diminished abilities in concentration and decision making, loss of interest in daily activities, and repeated thoughts of death. Within the *Diagnostic and Statistical Manual* (3rd ed., rev.—DSM-III-R) classification system, these symptoms must have been present for several weeks, along with a noticeable disturbance in social and personal functioning (American Psychiatric Association, 1987).

Because feelings of sadness and joylessness are within the realm of normal human experience (for instance, about 40% of the population report having had depressed feelings during any given year, Bradburn, 1977), the distinction between mood changes and affective disturbance is not always clear, but it has immense treatment implications. Diagnosis, especially among adolescents, is particularly difficult because of the transiency in their moods and the maladaptive behaviors that may be occurring in conjunction with the underlying mood disturbance. Additionally, when depression occurs as a secondary symptom to other psychiatric or medical problems, an accurate diagnosis becomes even more difficult (Robins & Guze, 1972).

It is relatively common for depressive syndromes to occur with other psychiatric conditions, such as anxiety states, drug use, and eating and personality disorders. When this happens, it is customary to have both conditions diagnosed

(Rutter, 1988). Among youths, the most prevalent comorbid conditions tend to be anxiety and conduct disorders, which not only make treatment difficult but also have important repercussions for long-term outcome (Kovacs, Paulauskas, Gatsonis, & Richards, 1988). In everyday practice, a readily apparent precipitating event also muddles the picture, as mood changes are readily attributable to the event (Klerman et al., 1984).

The concept of clinical depression and associated affective or mood disturbances encompasses an increase in the intensity and length of the everyday expression of emotions. Because the experience of sad feelings is familiar to everyone and appears to be a typical response to life stress, family members and friends are likely to minimize the severity of symptoms and less likely to attribute a clinically depressed emotional state to a teenager who is showing signs of apathy or restlessness. Parents may describe, for instance, their problematic adolescent in less than sympathetic terms, such as lazy or manipulative, thereby attributing the symptoms to character traits. Even troubled adolescents often misdiagnose their own problems, as they are likely to blame their unpleasant feelings on family members or significant others (e.g., teachers). The result usually takes the form of power struggles, while the real issues surrounding the youngster's self-worth remain neglected (Emery, Bedrosian, & Garber, 1983).

Although depressed feelings are considered to be a part of emotional development, the intensity and severity of depressed thoughts and moods are important elements in determining psychological health (Nichtern, 1982). For example, Kovacs and Beck (1977) have demonstrated that a majority of adolescents who have attempted suicide have previously ruminated about whether to live or die. Further, intense depression has been found to be the most prevalent characteristic of suicidal youth (Gibbs, 1981; Tishler & McKenry, 1983). Often, it takes an objective observer to provide evidence that the affective, behavioral, cognitive, and bodily changes have taken on an intensity and persistence to justify professional treatment of this condition. The difficulties in diagnosis arise when varying intensities and combinations of symptoms have developed.

Affective Disturbance

Within the clinical manifestations of depression, the disturbance in mood actually defines the syndrome (Klerman et al., 1984). Such statements as feeling "sad," "down," or "blue" are often heard. While at times these expressions are acknowledged as being exaggerations or merely extended periods of normal experiences of depression, some individuals ascribe their feelings and general mood as qualitatively different from what has been usual for them. At these more intense levels, the experience is often painful and distressing.

Anxiety is another generalized feeling that is experienced within periods of depression. More than 60% of depressed individuals report feeling anxious, although the differentiation among unpleasant bodily states may make this percentage spurious (Klerman et al., 1984). In studies with different samples of older children ($\geq$ 9 years old) and adolescents, it has been shown that anxiety and depression do co-occur at rates of 35% (Strauss, Last, Hersen, & Kazdin, 1988), 45% (Kolvin, Berney, & Bhate, 1984), and 81% (Bernstein & Garfinkel, 1986). Because feelings of depression are frequently accompanied by descriptions of inner distress and fears, along with observations of sweating or rapid pulse, a differential diagnosis of major depression alone becomes difficult to justify.

Other feelings, such as guilt, shame, anger, and hostility are also often associated with depression. Guilt is usually produced when an incongruence exists between personal conduct and one's internal moral or ethical standards, whereas shame is thought to be produced when one fails external criteria designed by family or cultural groups. Expressions of anger and hostility also seem to be divided by internality and externality. The groups of depressed individuals who rarely express aggressive feelings are thought to have turned their anger inward onto themselves. However, there are many individuals suffering from depression who readily inflict their rage onto family members and friends.

Behavioral Symptoms

Depressed individuals almost always display a variety of behavioral changes that are associated with their depressed state. Instances of increased restlessness or agitation, differences in facial expression, reductions in overall activity levels, slowed latency in responses and in speech, and crying are usually readily observable. In children, these externalized behavioral changes may take the form of somatic complaints, whereas in adolescents, associated features of negativistic or sometimes antisocial behavior may be evident. The diagnosis of depression in children and adolescents takes on significance when these behaviors are (a) changes from ordinary behavior, (b) last for a period of time, (c) interrupt daily functioning, and (d) cannot be ameliorated by the usual interventions of the parents, teachers, and peers (Kazdin, 1988).

Changes in Attitude

Feelings of worthlessness and the subsequent lowering of self-esteem are primary characteristics of persons during depressed experiences. Many depressed individuals typically view themselves as inadequate or incompetent and have falsely formed the belief that others view them in a similar manner. With the decline in self-esteem, feelings of helplessness and sometimes of hopelessness persist; these feelings maintain low rates of behavior, causing depressed individuals to accentuate their inadequate demeanor. Worries and basic fears are then produced as they begin to dread the future and anticipate continued failure. When this experience intensifies, thoughts of suicide and actual suicidal gestures are likely to occur. Death by suicide does occur in about 1% of depressed persons during the year of a depressive episode and in about 15% of cases where depression occurs frequently over the lifetime, so the clinician must explore these suicidal thoughts, along with the potential of impulsivity and intentionality, in a systematic and thorough interview (Klerman, 1982). This is especially poignant during the later teenage years; suicide has become the second leading cause of death for 15- to 24-year-olds (National Mental Health Association Information Center, 1986).

Cognitive Dysfunction

Depressed individuals often seem to be preoccupied with inner thoughts and tension. When confronted, they usually offer vague complaints of having difficulties in sustaining attention and concentration. Along with their psychomotor retardation, reduced efficiency in thoughts and speech are often characteristic of their lessened attentiveness to the environment. Distortions in perceptions and reasoning have also been found to exist during depressed episodes. These cognitive distortions often manifest themselves through narrowed thinking, in which the individuals become overly pessimistic about themselves, their world, and their future (Beck, 1976). This leads to a viscious cycle of self-defeating thoughts and lowered motivation.

Physiological and Bodily Changes

Approximately three quarters of depressed individuals experience disruptions in their eating patterns, while even a higher majority have difficulties sleeping (Klerman et al., 1984). Symptoms of appetite and subsequent weight loss, and early morning or frequent awakenings are characteristic occurrences during depressed states. A change in energy level is also prevalent, with reports of fatigue and lethargy common. Combined with this decreased energy is the appearance of reduced social contact and the absence of pleasurable experiences. Persons who become depressed often attribute this loss to having a nervous breakdown or being exhausted. Also reported during this time is a variety of somatic complaints, from generalized nausea to numerous specific pains.

SUBTYPES OF DEPRESSION

When attempting to delineate the presenting problems into a coherent diagnosis, it becomes important to distinguish between depression as a symptom (e.g., sad affect) from that which is part of a syndrome (i.e., a cluster of signs that are grouped together). Because no one individual would report all of the symptoms surrounding the syndrome of depression, there has been considerable attention to defining subgroups of this disorder in order to yield more accurate knowledge about its etiology, research, and treatment planning.

Over the years, there has been much controversy over how to subtype depression, whether by presumed etiology or by expressed symptoms, and these issues continue to be reexamined. Subtypes have taken the forms of psychotic–neurotic, endogenous–reactive, primary–secondary, and unipolar–bipolar dichotomies. Of these, the unipolar–bipolar distinction is the primary division in today's diagnostic systems. It mainly separates the depressions between those with and those without manic episodes (i.e., elated mood and frantic behavior). The term *unipolar* commonly defines the individual who has had one or more depressive episodes (or in some cases only mania). *Bipolar* characterizes the person who has suffered from both conditions (i.e., mania and depression), either separately or concurrently. Present clinical and research strategies attempt to define diagnostic subgroups in a precise manner. The focus emphasizes applying consistent criteria in formulating diagnoses that are not based on theoretical or therapeutic assumptions. The current approach also takes the position that the essential features of depression are similar in children, adolescents, and adults, although the manifestations may differ across age groupings and developmental levels. For instance, whereas young children may display separation anxiety or school refusal when they are depressed, adolescents typically show a reduction in activities or an increase in school problems. This standardized approach has been accepted largely due to success in applying unedited diagnostic criteria for adults in order to clarify diagnoses in children and adolescents. This application of criteria has been incorporated into the recent revisions of *Diagnostic and Statistical Manual of Mental Disorders* (3rd ed., DSM-III and the revised edition, DSM-III-R). In the DSM-III-R, modifications were made among the various disorders in order to clarify terms and subtype distinctions and to either add or delete some of the disorders. Few substantive changes were actually made in the section on affective disorders, now termed "Mood Disorders," in which depression is clarified.

Like its predecessor the DSM-III, the DSM-III-R has included various depressive symptoms within the other categories of depressive disorders. This categorization is especially relevant to children and adolescents when milder forms of depression may exist without the presence of either the entire range or the intensity of symptoms found in major depression. These symptoms may be interrupted by periods when a normal mood occurs or when additional symptoms emerge. In each category, the intensity, length of time, and precipitants of the various symptoms provide the basis for defining the disorder. For example, a diagnosis of dysthymia (formerly disthymic disorder) occurs when the depressed symptoms are less severe. Also, the symptoms may be chronic (defined as 1 year for children and adolescents), and a depressed mood may occur most of the time. In providing a diagnosis of adjustment disorder with depressed mood, the defining characteristic is a reaction to an identifiable psychosocial stressor, such as parents' divorce or relocation, where the symptoms have occurred in relation to this event (i.e., less than 3 months). There is also an assumption that the symptoms will remit after a period of time. A thorough review of the individual's history is needed to judge the symptom pattern and to credit the precipitating circumstances of the expressed symptoms. Another category of depression is separation anxiety disorder, especially pertinent to children and adolescents, in whom symptoms of depression may occur other than in major depression. Symptoms such as sadness, somatic complaints, withdrawal, and worry are visible as a result of fear of separating from an important attachment object (i.e., parents).

Another area of recent interest in differentiating depressive illness involves the expression of symptoms during the winter months. This phenomenon, termed Seasonal Affective Disorder (SAD), has been documented in both adult (Rosenthal et al., 1984) and child–adolescent populations (Rosenthal et al., 1986). The symptoms usually include fatigue, irritability, sleep changes, and depressed affect. This condition, it is hypothesized, appears to be triggered by a neuroendocrine dysregulation. It is probable that during this time, significant adults (e.g., family members and teachers) may react to the moodiness of the child in a negative manner and exacerbate the situation. Effective treatment for this condition has focused on increasing the amount of full-spectrum light to which the individual is exposed during the winter months (i.e., phototherapy). It is unclear whether this disorder is a variant of bipolar illness or a kind of unipolar depression, and it remains for future investigators to clarify and document the precise pattern of its etiology and symptomology.

THE NORMATIVE CRISIS OF ADOLESCENT DEVELOPMENT

The period of adolescence, from approximately 12 to 18 years of age, is a time of intense cognitive, emotional, and physiological change. Teenagers must overcome a considerable number of developmental hurdles, including bodily change, identity clarification, sexual maturity, and separation (such as leaving home). The development of sexual impulses also coincides with this need for separation and individuation (Blos, 1979). Teenagers also reexamine themselves and reevaluate and clarify their personal values during this stage of development (Konopka, 1983). Concomitantly, there are strong desires for group acceptance, resulting in vulnerability to peer pressure, initial exposure to alcohol and other drugs, and concerns about academic performance.

With the onset of puberty, an upsurge of instinctual life is presumed to cause internal emotional upheaval and to lead to increased vulnerability toward disturbance in the developing personality (Freud, 1917). Additionally, the awakening of sexuality leads the teenager to look away from the family for other love objects. This begins the severing of emotional ties that have existed since early childhood. In order to deal with this surge of instinctual behavior and the resulting anxiety, the teenager begins actively to employ defenses that can interfere with adaptive functioning. Blos (1979), in describing this period as a "second individuation process," views this time as risky for the development of a stable personality if problems persist. In adapting to maturation and seeking autonomy, the teenager is confronted with ambivalent feelings about a variety of issues that can elicit erratic behaviors. This can lead to extreme fluctuations of mood, inconsistency in relationships, and nonconformity.

While disengaging from the family may be an exciting prospect to the adolescent, it is also fraught with many doubts and uncertainties that further make this period particularly difficult. It is also a time, according to Erikson (1968), for a "coherent identity" to emerge in the middle of immense biological and social change. If left unresolved, a "diffusion" can occur, leaving the teenager fearful of intimacy, unable to plan for the future, helpless to engage personal resources into work or study, and/or increasingly hostile toward society's structure and expectations. When visible to others, these adolescent intraphysic conflicts may also be a signal that the entire family is stuck in its attempt to move along its developing path (Haley, 1980; Watzlawick, 1984). For successful completion of adolescence to occur, the family must act both to overcome its own resistances to the individuation process and to promote an environment of independence (Berkowitz, 1987).

FACTORS CONTRIBUTING TO ADOLESCENT DEPRESSION

Since the late 1960s, increasing geographic, economic, and emotional changes, as well as a number of other factors, have made adolescence particularly risky for teenagers and their families. Today's teenagers frequently confront fears about divorce within their own or a friend's family (Wattenberg, 1986). They also face changes in living conditions, such as overcrowded schools, which have led to impersonal atmospheres and estranged environments (Hollinger & Offer, 1981; Packard, 1983). Much attention in the research literature has focused on this aspect of alienation and the inability of teenagers to form close, meaningful relationships (Coles, 1983). In this manner, realistic feedback from peers and significant adults has been considered crucial for the teenager to cope successfully with the separation process (Bloom, 1980), and its breakdown plays an important role in adolescent suicide attempts (Crumley, 1983). Alienation also creates an attitude of mistrust within teenagers, making them susceptible to feelings of rejection (Kaplan, Robbins, & Martin, 1983).

Additional signs of depression in teenage populations have also increased substantially since the late 1960s. These have taken the form of a sudden decline in grades or a withdrawal from peers and extracurricular activities (Petzel & Riddle, 1981). Another especially vulnerable factor leading toward depression, and sometimes suicide ideation, is a lack of friends and social support (Hawton, 1982). Additionally, those teenagers who seem easily overwhelmed or enraged have been noted as experiencing chronic bouts of depression (Lewis, 1982). Among children and adolescents, use of alcohol and other drugs has dramatically increased and has become a major public health problem in this country (Statistical Bulletin, 1987). Drug use has been viewed as a method for teenagers to defend themselves against the uncomfortable feelings accompanying anxiety and depression. However, it is these very drugs that may disinhibit the urge to attempt suicide (Greuling & DeBlassie, 1980).

DIAGNOSING THE DEPRESSED ADOLESCENT

Until the late 1960s and early 1970s, the prevailing attitude in the mental health field was that depressive disturbance rarely presented itself before adulthood (Puig-Antich & Gittelman, 1982). Since then, many researchers have taken the position that "masked" forms of depressive equivalents existed in youths as evidenced by disturbances in conduct and somatization (Cytryn & McKnew, 1972). They contended that depression could exist in childhood, but it just manifests in different forms. This position held that an underlying form of the depressed state was evident through such behaviors as aggressiveness, phobias, running away, fire setting, hyperactivity, school avoidance, and so on. Critics of this position, however, argued that these behavioral manifestations that supposedly hid or masked the underlying depression characterized practically the entire range of various psychopathology (Gittelman-Klein, 1977; Kovacs & Beck, 1977).

Although this newer view of depression placed limits on the aspect of depressive equivalents, it did focus much attention to the subject of depression in childhood, and it forced clinicians and researchers to consider that depression was being overlooked in the diagnoses of other disorders (Carlson & Cantwell, 1979). The controversy surrounding this issue also emphasized that depression was expressed differently in different age groupings. In infancy, for instance, excessive crying, failure to thrive, severe withdrawal, and disruptions in sleep could all be associated with depressive features. For preschoolers, depressive symptoms are more likely to be displayed by temper tantrums, somatic complaints, brief durations of sadness, and loss of interest in activities; whereas the school-aged child is likely to express behavioral disruptions, excess activity, more prolonged episodes of sad feelings, intense separation anxiety, school phobia, and at times suicidal ideation. During adolescence, the experience of depression may appear similar to that of adults, including fatigue, interpersonal isolation, loss of interest in family and vocational aspirations, enhanced sensitivity to social rejection, antisocial behavior, sleep problems, and suicidal gestures (Peterson & Hamburg, 1986). This view has also sparked interest in plotting a course regarding the development of depressive symptoms and how biology and the environment interact along the life cycle to produce episodes of depression (Cicchetti & Schneider-Rosen, 1984).

During the 1980s, a strong position has been held that depressive conditions that meet adult criteria can and do present themselves in childhood and adolescence (Cantwell, 1983; Carlson & Garber, 1986). Further, the emphasis has been on showing that various disorders can coexist, rather than one hiding, overshadowing, or masking the other (Matson, 1986; McGee & Williams, 1986). Although these conclusions stem from the use of operational diagnostic criteria (e.g., the revisions of the DSM), the matter of accurate diagnosis remains unsettled (Shaffer, 1985). At present, researchers are attempting to operationalize a set of diagnostic criteria from a perspective of demonstrating similarities between adults and nonadults in their expressed symptoms (e.g., sadness, low self-esteem, loss of interest, vegetative signs) and adding those symptoms that may be specific to youth (e.g., school refusal, negativism, somatic complaints). The DSM-III-R has incorporated this trend, at least acknowledging that major depressive disorders can exist in early childhood (Rutter, 1988).

Another disagreement has existed as whether to include adolescents in descriptions of child or adult psychopathology (Carlson & Garber, 1986). Until very recently, adolescents were included in theoretical discussions and research protocols of childhood. However, research has demonstrated that appreciable changes do occur in the frequency and nature of depressive symptoms during the stage of adolescence (Gjerde, Block, & Block, 1988). For instance, following puberty, depressive episodes are more common (Rutter, 1986). Research has also shown that the cognitive features of depression and symptoms of appetite and hypoactivity are rated more frequently in postpubescent samples (e.g., Garber, 1984).

There has also been some distinction regarding gender differences across age groupings. In research on clinic and nonclinic samples of depressed children aged 6–12 years, no gender differences were prevalent, whereas beginning in adolescence, the rate was higher among females (e.g., Lefkowitz & Tesiny, 1985). Additionally, studies have shown a differing severity of depression between males and females starting in early adolescence and increasing over time (Kandel & Davies, 1982). On self-report depression inventories, clear differences have been shown between groups of children and adolescents in the expression of symptoms and in gender differentiation (Weiss & Weisz, 1988). Previous research findings have also supported the notion that externalizing, aggressive tendencies are found more frequently among groups of depressed adolescents than in similarly diagnosed children (Geller, Chestnut, Miller, Price, & Yates, 1985). In a similar manner, the DSM-III-R has proposed that depression in adolescents may be associated with negative or antisocial behavior, while somatic complaints are more likely observed in children (American Psychiatric Association, 1987).

On the other hand, investigations concerning the phenomenology and natural history of mood disorders have shown that adolescents appear more like adults. In this regard, clear evidence of clinical depressive episodes in adolescents has been demonstrated (Strober & Carlson, 1982). For example, the occurrence of bipolar disorder has been seen often in adolescent inpatient units. In contrast, mania is relatively rare in children (Rapoport & Ismond, 1984). During diagnostic workups, adolescents with endogenous–melancholic and mood-congruent psychotic symptoms have been identified. Also, the course of major depression and bipolar illness in adolescence has been similar to durations in adult populations.

Thus, adolescents must be considered at least adultlike in their manifestations of mood disturbance. Although there is justification for viewing depression in adolescents similarly to that in adults, this argument also lacks clarity, as many differences between these two populations have also been shown. More focus on this transitional stage between childhood and adulthood needs to be done to clarify these differences in classification schemes (Oster, Caro, Eagen, & Lillo, 1988).

REFERRALS AND TREATMENT

Adolescents rarely present themselves to mental health professionals for assessment and treatment. Rather, they are usually referred by their schools, pediatricians, or other agencies that have become involved with them or their families, due to the adolescents' conflicts with society's rules or guidelines (e.g., referral by the juvenile justice system or departments of social services). At other times, their families take the initiative when frustrations and stress become intolerable, and no one else seems to have adequate answers to their dilemmas. A clear picture is usually not presented by these referral sources, and in daily practice, it is difficult to focus exclusively on diagnostic categories or to view these categories as static or comprehensive. Depressive symptomatology may be associated with various conditions (e.g., actual or perceived problems concerning one's identity) and with differing needs to be treated, even though the identified teenager does not meet all the criteria for a certain disorder. Very few adolescents are seen in treatment specifically due to depressive symptomatology, such as poor self-regard or sleepless nights. Primary referrals of adolescents stem from school failure, drug abuse, sexual promiscuity, suicidal gestures, or disregard of authority figures. Rare is the teenager, family, or referral source who seeks treatment for underlying depression. It is not until multiple problems are being presented by the adolescent that the family or the community finds it necessary to take some kind of action.

Thus, a salient issue for persons in positions of referring adolescents for assessment and treatment is to identify whether the presenting problems warrant specialized treatment for depression. This is especially pertinent because many of the signs of depression—such as poor peer relations, lack of interest in homework, reduced performance, and disruptive behavior in the classroom—have also been implicated in other dysfunctional behavior. Yapko (1988) presents a list of commonly observed phenomena that have been given as signs of adolescent depression. These include (a) deterioration in school performance and/or increased risk-taking behaviors (behavioral dimension); (b) marked changes in weight or vague somatic complaints (physiological dimension); (c) negative self-evaluation and/or absence of future planning (cognitive dimension); (d) marked feelings of ambivalence and/or high or low (extreme) reactivity (affective dimension); (e) need for excessive approval and/or self-sacrificing martyrism patterns (relational dimension); and (f) recurring nightmares and/or destructive images (what Yapko terms the "symbolic" dimension).

Because the concept of depression and its treatment in adults have been the focus of considerable theorizing and research during the 1980s, there has been a corresponding sensitivity to analogous features and interventions in children and adolescents. Although with this increase in attention there exists the possibility of overemphasizing the disorder and misidentifying the main problem, the magnitude of the disorder cannot be underestimated. Effective plans of action must be implemented to ameliorate the symptoms that are impeding the growth and development of the teenagers and their families. In order to meet this need, health and mental health professionals must be aware of the theoretical assumptions and the current treatment strategies that are available.

CHAPTER 2

Family Models of Adolescent Depression

To really understand the multifaceted aspects of adolescent depression, we first must gain an appreciation for the influences of the family on the etiology and maintenance of adolescent depressive behavior. While we are well familiar with the normative phase of adolescence as a time of rapid physical growth, emotional change, confusion, and turmoil, the status of the family as a whole during this phase has only recently received attention. The adolescent does not live in a vacuum but rather is affected by and affects the family unit. Family systems theory maintains that both "adjustment and maladjustment are strongly influenced by the person's interaction with his [or her] social environment" (Teichman, 1986, p. 13). Adolescent depression does not develop in isolation from the individual's inner psyche but rather emerges and is reinforced within the context of disruptive and disturbed family patterns of relating. It is through delineating these interactional patterns that a more comprehensive undertaking of adolescent depression can be achieved.

NORMATIVE FAMILY PROCESSES

Before outlining disturbed family functioning at the stage of adolescence, it is important to describe normative family processes. To begin, we start from the premise that adolescence is a time of confusion, turmoil, and rapid change for the entire family. Adolescents stand between childhood and adulthood, just as parents of adolescents stand between taking full responsibility for their children and recognizing their offsprings' full autonomy as adults. For the adolescent, this stage means leaving the dependence allowed in childhood, reaching out to a larger social environment, taking increased responsibility for personal actions, and forming an identity as an individual. For the adolescent's parents, adolescence means coming to terms with their decreased influence on their child, recognizing their child's emerging independence, and reordering the amount of time spent in their roles as spouse, parent, and worker. Therefore, adolescence is the stage during which the adolescent's and the parent's needs for dependence and independence are acted out (Jenkins, 1981).

No manual for adolescents and parents tells them how to negotiate between the pull to remain children or the parents of children, and the desire for more independent functioning. Consequently, parents and adolescents must engage in constant struggling and compromising between continuing to reinforce childlike dependence and moving too quickly toward adultlike autonomy. Quinn, Newfield, and Protinsky (1985) maintain that "the families of adolescents are confronted with decisions about the allocation of rights, privileges, and responsibilities without the certainty of knowing the physical, emotional, and social competencies of their adolescent members," while adolescents "request, if not demand, to be treated as adults while they live in a social world of children" (p. 102). To the degree that communication remains open between adolescent and parent, and that the family structure allows for some flexibility, then even the normative storm of adolescent independence can be more successfully weathered.

Additionally, in reaction to their adolescents, parents often experience a rekindling of their own unresolved adolescent issues, which may heighten the need to keep their child dependent or accelerate moving their youngster toward a more autonomous position (Stierlin, 1975). A clinical example may help further explicate this dynamic:

> Lisa P. (age 13 years) was brought to an outpatient clinic by her parents, due to her noncompliance with household rules, especially as the noncompliance related to defying her curfew and staying out late at night with her boyfriend. What emerged in the first family session was a rift between mother and father concerning the seriousness of her behavior, with Mr. P. feeling more outraged than his wife. In taking a family history, Mrs. P. revealed that she had a conservative upbringing, never being allowed to date until she went away to college. She remembers feeling very left out in socializing with peers as her father refused to allow her to go out even with a group of kids, if there were to be boys among the group. On the surface, Mrs. P. did try to limit her daughter's activities, but a part of her was living vicariously through her daughter's active social life, and therefore her parenting strategies were not entirely focused on being effective.

In the reactivation of their own previous difficulties as adolescents, parents may be in danger of either consciously or unconsciously reinforcing their adolescent's inappropriate behavior or denying participation in more normative endeavors. In relating to their own children, families that can adequately negotiate the demands of adolescence are characterized by the recognition of the emotional pitfalls that remain from their own adolescence.

Even if parents are able to recognize and deal with the effects of their own adolescent experiences, another issue must be addressed. Specifically, the stage of adolescence also signals parents that the energy required in their roles as parents soon will be drastically reduced. The couple, after defining themselves largely within the context of a family, will emerge from their offspring's adolescence with fewer parental responsibilities and increased time to engage in other activities. The focus will shift from child care to couple care. The degree to which the couple has been able to maintain a caring and intimate relationship helps this transition to be much more successful, although it remains difficult even under normative circumstances.

Thus, the major family developmental issues of adolescence involves (a) establishing a balance between independence and dependence, (b) being cognizant of the potential impact of the parents' own adolescent issues, and (c) pursuing new role definitions. Given the importance of resolving these issues, the question arises, What characterizes those families that can adequately negotiate the issues of this phase? Specifically, what separates those families who are able to weather the storm of adolescence from those who are caught within the eye of the hurricane? The various models of family therapy (e.g., Bowenian, structural, strategic, solution-oriented) differ in their conceptualizations of normal family processes. Each model takes a different focal point in delineating the development and reinforcement of family interactional patterns, as well as in articulating avenues for change. Rather than limit ourselves to one model, we can gain a more multifaceted and in-depth view of the family interactional patterns that characterize effective functioning if we review each of the major models of family therapy and the respective understandings of each in terms of normative family processes.

Bowenian Theory

Within Bowenian theory, Fogarty (1976) has delineated 12 characteristics of a well-functioning family:

1. It has the kind of balance that can adapt and even welcome change.
2. Emotional problems are seen as existing in the unit, with components in each person. There is no such thing as an emotional problem in one person.
3. Connectedness is maintained across generations with all members of the family.
4. There is a minimum of fusion, and distance is not used to solve problems.
5. Each twosome in the family can deal with all problems that occur between them. Triangulating onto a third person who is used to arbitrate or judge or solve the dispute is discouraged.
6. Differences between people are not only tolerated but encouraged.
7. Each person can operate selectively using both thinking and emotional systems with other members of the family.

8. There is a keen awareness of what each person gets functionally from himself, and what he gets from others. These are the areas of identification and differentiation.
9. There is an awareness of the emptiness in each member of the family, and each person is allowed to have his own emptiness. There is no attempt made to fill it up.
10. The preservation of a positive emotional climate takes precedence over doing what "should" be done and what is "right."
11. Function in the family is determined by each member saying that this is a pretty good family to live in over time. If one or more members say there is a problem, there is a problem.
12. Members of the family can use others in the family as a source of feedback and learning, but not as an enemy. (p. 149)

Of central importance in a Bowenian model is the notion of differentiation and fusion, with the foregoing characteristics representing a delicate balance between the extreme positions (with fusion on the one extreme and disengagement on the other). With regard to adolescents, the degree to which the family can tolerate the adolescents' needs for independence, thus fostering appropriate differentiation, characterizes more normative functioning. Parents and adolescents must then show flexibility in adapting to changed expectations in their relationships without their sense of self feeling threatened or abandoned. If families are not able to sustain a sense of balance between giving their child the freedom to pursue independent activities while still providing a holding environment when necessary, they may react either by preventing differentiation through overinvolvement and enmeshment or by prematurely separating and cutting off involvement with their child (Weltner, 1985).

Structural Model

The structural model also involves the notion of closeness and distance, yet it broadens the Bowenian focus to move from concentrating on the relationships between individuals to the relationships between generations. Of primary importance in the structural model are the notions of *boundaries* (the rules of relating) and of a *power hierarchy* (the process of decision making) (Minuchin, 1974). Normative family functioning is based on the parental subsystem being united in dispensing the executive decisions (hierarchy), while still remaining open in receiving feedback and input from the child subsystem (boundaries). In other words, Minuchin (1974) states that for "proper family functioning the boundaries of subsystems must be clear. They must be defined well enough to allow subsystem members to carry out their functions without undue interference, but they must also allow contact between the members of the subsystem and others" (p. 54). Within this context, he maintains that boundaries within a family can be placed on a continuum; at one end are those families who exhibit diffuse boundaries, where there is a blurring of demarcation between the parents and the child subsystems (Minuchin, 1974). For example, an enmeshed boundary would be characterized by a mother who is estranged from her husband and therefore implicitly encourages her daughter to stay home from school to keep her company. In contrast, a disengaged boundary is one in which the boundaries are rigid, and fluid interchanges and communications between subsystems are severely limited. A disengaged boundary would be exemplified by an adolescent who acts out and must engage in serious behavior such as a suicidal gesture in order to get the family to notice the adolescent's difficulties. The degree to which the family can establish a position in the middle of these extremes contributes to the ability of the family to negotiate successfully life's stresses.

A major tenet of a structural model is that the family's pattern of adaptation is continually tested through the various crises presented by new developmental phases (Minuchin, 1974). For families with adolescent members, the challenge is to allow for flexibility within the system yet not totally surrender the parental hierarchy. Minuchin (1974) asserts that "the adolescent should be moved a little away from the sibling subsystem and given increased autonomy and responsibility appropriate to his [or her] age. The parental subsystem's transactions with him [or her] should change from parent–child to parents–young adult. The result will be a successful adaptation" (p. 64). The development of symptomatology in an adolescent member therefore emerges in those families who are not able to alter their previous ways of relating, their transactional patterns, and their organization in accommodating to the adolescent's needs for autonomy (Fishman, 1988).

Strategic Model

While the strategic model of family therapy also understands family functioning within notions of organization and appropriate hierarchy and boundaries, the model concentrates on the here and now and the expressed and covert communication among family members (Madanes, 1981). In concentrating on the present through demonstrated behaviors, the notion of normative family functioning is not directly addressed within the theory. By extrapolation, symptoms develop as structures that block movement to the next stage of life (e.g., early marriage, childbirth, and families with young and adolescent members) (Madanes, 1981). Families that are able to negotiate successfully these life changes do not develop symptomatic members. When symptoms do develop, the emphasis is on changing behaviors and communications, not on changing overall family organization and structure (Fish & Piercy, 1987).

The premise of the strategic model is that bad habits have been learned and that with slight alterations, these habits can be changed, allowing for the inherent process of normative family development to continue. For example, an older adolescent may become depressed, forcing her parents to take notice of her and deflecting them from coming to terms with ending the stage of active parenting. Using the strategic model, the behavior is viewed as metaphorical, and strategies are developed to change the parents' communications and actions, thus halting the daughter's interference through maintenance of the bad habit.

Solution-Focused Model

Solution-focused therapists (de Shazer, 1985), who support a modified form of the strategic model, maintain that the solutions for effective functioning are inherently within the family system. Within this context, each family has at its core the capacity not only to be functional but also to discover its own solutions to the presented problems. Therefore, normal family functioning is assumed to occur in all families, whether they present symptoms or not. Specifically, symptomatic families have misdirected their attention to magnify the problems, while asymptomatic families continue to accentuate positive functioning.

For families showing difficulties, the job of the therapist is to help the family focus on its inherent capacity to solve problems by limiting the attention and concentration on the presenting complaints (Molnar & deShazer, 1987). Therefore, apparently symptomatic families only need to be reminded of the inherent coping strategies that they have forgotten during the crisis period (O'Hanlon & Weiner-Davis, 1989). For instance, a parent of an acting-out teenager is asked for any examples of the youngster's compliance with parental directives, no matter how insignificant. These successful situations are then analyzed in detail in terms of the interactional patterns in order to refocus the attention on instances of normative functioning, as well as to assist the family in reinforcing positive behavior, thereby increasing the occurrences of compliant behavior. Within a solution-oriented context, normal family functioning is the rule with deviant behavior being only a momentary diversion caused by the family's concentration on problems. Consequently, the therapist remains focused on examples of positive interactions to promote and reinforce more normative family processes.

DISRUPTIVE FAMILY PROCESSES

The preceding theoretical models differ in terms of their perspectives of normative family processes considering these processes to be a product of the balance (a) of closeness and distance between individuals (Bowenian), (b) between and within generations (structural), (c) between present interactional patterns and present communication patterns (strategic), and (d) between solutions and problems (solution focused). Consequently, their notion of disruptive family processes also ranges from inappropriate boundaries and disturbed family organization, through dysfunctional modes of communication and behavior patterns, to misdirected attention. Although these models differ in the degree to which they concentrate either on underlying structures (Bowenian and structural) or on presenting problems (strategic and solution focused), they share some commonalities in terms of the basis of etiology and reinforcement of disturbed family patterns. Because it is really in their approach toward changing these patterns that their differences are most pronounced, it is possible to discuss generally their common notions about disturbed family functioning.

If normal family functioning is characterized by families that can maintain a balance between stability and flexibility (Koman & Stechler, 1985), then disruptive family processes must be a product of a disturbance in this balance. The family unit comprises individuals who are related and connected to each other. Further, the family as a whole relates to a larger social environment. Relationships among family members, as well as their relationships to the larger social sphere, necessitate a twofold process of maintaining certain structures while allowing some fluidity to incorporate change; for example, parents must maintain some parenting responsibilities while allowing an adolescent to experience more independence. Family systems theory describes these two processes as "homeostasis" (mechanisms for sustaining stability) and "morphogenesis" (mechanisms for change and adaptation) (Teichman, 1986). Specifically, Teichman (1986) defines *homeostasis* as "a self regulating process which maintains the stability in the [system] and protects it from deviations and changes" and *morphogenesis* as the "capability to absorb inputs from the environment and to change" (p. 11). Families experience both the desire for sameness (homeostasis) and the push for change (morphogenesis), both in their relationships with one another and in the family's interactions with the external world.

Even under normal circumstances, adapting to change can be difficult; in disturbed families, their allegiance to old patterns and structures further limits their adaptation to change, even when adaptation is required. In other words, symptomatic families attempt to maintain homeostasis at all costs. For example, a single mother may continue to respond to her adolescent daughter as if she were much younger in order to maintain her existing parental role. To allow her daughter more autonomy would be threatening because it would require that she look beyond her role as a mother and would face either her own loneliness in not having a mate or her own job dissatisfaction. Although the family system resides in an ever-changing world, most families do not experience a constant threat necessitating that significant changes occur. Instead, family homeostasis is most often challenged during different crises (death of a family member, illness of a family member, divorce) or when the family is faced with a new developmental stage that requires role expansion (e.g., the birth of a first child, the pubescent changes of an adolescent). Disturbed families are not able to make these adjustments and to be flexible in the face of these crises; therefore, their adherence to their old equilibrium exacts a tremendous price.

When a crisis that occurs threatens the family equilibrium, an inordinate amount of pressure is created to maintain old patterns of behavior. In dysfunctional families, equilibrium is obtained through the development of a symptomatic member (Jenkins, 1981). In the foregoing example with the single mother, the adolescent girl developed an eating disorder, necessitating constant care by her mother. The mother's role as a parent was reinforced because she had to work even harder to sustain her child's life by literally cajoling her to eat. Therefore, the more dependent relationship between mother and daughter was maintained, and equilibrium was restored. However, return to equilibrium cost the daughter her ability to proceed with the more normative process of adolescence, in terms of gaining increased autonomy from parental figures.

A second consequence of dysfunctional maintenance of equilibrium is that the symptom also covers the underlying difficulties (e.g., mother's fearfulness of being alone) and further complicates resolution of this issue because the focus is directed exclusively on the presenting symptoms of the daughter. The symptom, while maintaining the old patterns of interaction, also arrests the family's growth (Fishman, 1988). Additionally, as these inappropriate patterns are sustained, the family comes into increased conflict with the larger social environment, putting increased pressure and tension on the family. Specifically, the eating disorder may interrupt the daughter's ability to perform well in and possible even to attend school. Not only may the mother have to attend to her daughter's problems, but she may also have to deal with the conflict created with school officials. Therefore, in actuality, the new equilibrium may be a state of chronic disequilibrium as the daughter's difficulties bring about increased crises and stresses (Contes, 1967).

While at any stage of family development, a threat to the family's homeostasis necessitating some accommodation may exist, often the first sign of significant family difficulties occurs in families with adolescent members. Contes (1967) asserts that there are three basic reasons for this occurrence. First, the adolescent is "in a more precarious state of equilibrium" (p. 69). Specifically, the adolescent is a good candidate for the development of symptomatology because he or she is struggling with normal adolescent adjustment. In part, the development of symptoms can be an extreme extension of the adolescent's issues in combination with the family's conflicts.

Second, as has already been discussed, adolescence is a very difficult period for parents because it reawakens the history of their own unresolved adolescent issues. Therefore, in these families, the homeostasis can be threatened just by the child entering adolescence. During the period of adolescence, parents can find it more difficult to remain objective, and they are at an increased risk of not being able to separate their own past experiences from their child's present circumstances. The youngster's symptoms can develop not only in response to the threat to the family's equilibrium but also as a product of parental externalization of their own adolescent conflict onto the child.

Third, the maturation process of the adolescent member can also create some vulnerabilities for the family (Contes, 1967). For example, an adolescent daughter, in reaching puberty, may become attractive to her father, causing an awakening of taboo feelings which leads to stress (Contes, 1967). This tension may also be externalized onto the adolescent, who may respond to this projected anxiety through acting-out behaviors. In attending to the acting-out patterns, an equilibrium (although precarious) can be reestablished as pressure is taken off the meaning of the parental feelings and inner conflicts. In essence, these three basic dynamics in families with adolescent members increase the potential that "the adolescent acts as a kind of carrier of the germs of conflict in the family" (Ackerman, 1970, p. 209).

It is important to note that even if symptoms have developed prior to adolescence, the inherent turbulence of this stage may further exacerbate symptomatology. Specifically, an already strained family unit can be further stressed when a member reaches adolescence. For example:

Johnny P., a 16-year-old male, was brought to an outpatient clinic following his being arrested for stealing a car. Although Johnny had a long history of behavioral problems in school, such as disruptiveness and poor school performance, this was his first experience with lawbreaking behavior. Family history revealed that Mr. and Mrs. P.'s marriage has had chronic difficulties but that they had long ago made a decision to stay together for "the kids' sake." Because Johnny, at age 16, was the youngest, Mr. P. had begun to travel more on business, staying away 2–3 days a week because "the kids don't need me as much now."

Johnny's increased acting-out behaviors can be conceptualized as a homeostatis-maintaining strategy. In other words, by engaging in more serious behaviors, Johnny forces his father to remain involved with the family, thus averting the threat of separation of the family unit and allowing the parents to avoid dealing directly with their marital conflict because they can remain focused on the repercussions of Johnny's behaviors. Therefore, family disturbance is not only a product of the current stressor threatening the present equilibrium, but also an event occurring within the context of the family's historical functioning.

FAMILIES WITH DEPRESSED ADOLESCENTS

If we accept the premise that family disturbance is characterized by an inappropriate solution to disruptions in family equilibrium, and that families with adolescent members generally are more vulnerable to threats of homeostasis, then what specifically contributes to the development of a depressed adolescent within a family context? In other words, what differentiates families with depressed adolescents (e.g., in which an adolescent arrives at an emergency room with a suicide attempt, or an adolescent goes to an outpatient setting with both a depressed mood and decreased school performance) from those families who are able to cope with stress effectively? Differentiating family disturbance is a process of separating *degrees* of family functioning and not necessarily *styles* of functioning. Specifically, all families experience crises of homeostasis, but some families are more vulnerable to this stress and are more likely to disorganize and to develop a symptomatic family member. In general, there appear to be four major dynamics that contribute to the level of expressed pathology within families: (1) family history, from both a genetic–biochemical and an emotional stance; (2) previous family processing of past traumatic events; (3) quality of family boundaries and structures; and (4) ability of the family to express and to process emotions. Next, each one of these factors is reviewed within the context of how it relates to the development of depression in adolescent family members. Therefore, the major emphasis is on placing these factors within a family system's perspective.

FAMILY HISTORY. Recent advances in the areas of biochemical and genetic studies have given some evidence both that some individuals by their biological make-up (Covi, 1986) and some families by their genetic makeup (Andreasen, Rice, Endicott, Coryell, Grove, & Reich, 1987) may have a proclivity toward depression. In terms of a family-systems perspective, this apparent predisposition may make adolescents vulnerable to maintaining family homeostatis through depressive behavior. The manifestation of the depression by the adolescent is therefore an interaction of the constitutional predisposition (either genetic or biological or both) and the familial turmoil. Depressive behavior in an individual may not be exhibited until adolescence because the family's coping strategies may have been previously adequate, but with the stress created by the adolescent stage, they are no longer effective. Thus, the outward expression of the traits or chemical imbalance is stimulated during adolescence, generating a blossoming of the depressive behavior within the adolescent member.

PAST TRAUMAS. Difficulties in resolving past traumatic events (e.g., the loss of a parent, divorce, early physiological deprivation) may also contribute to the manifestation of depression in families with adolescent members. Lewis and Lewis (1981) assert that children who experience early loss may in fact experience some alteration in their biochemical makeup placing them at increased risk to manifest depression. Early loss of a parent may contribute to difficulties when the child reaches adolescence, in terms of successfully negotiating the tasks of separation and individuation from the remaining parent. Frequently, adolescence is the period in which prior traumas are reexperienced as the stage of adolescence itself mandates a reordering of the perspective of one's childhood in preparation for the movement to adulthood.

For example:

Sue K., an 18-year-old female, was finally brought into an outpatient clinic by her father for increasing depressed mood and difficulties in concentrating on her college studies. Sue had planned to complete her freshmen year of college at a nearby university, choosing to remain home with her father. However, she had recently applied to and been accepted to an out-of-state university in order to do some specialized study. Her depressive behavior began to unfold when she learned of her acceptance. Worrying about her ability to cope with being away from home, her father had begun to question the viability of her attending the university. Family history for loss was significant; Sue's mother died when Sue was 5 years old. Although her father had periodically dated, he had not sustained a meaningful relationship since his wife's death.

Sue's symptomatology can be viewed in the context of the family's difficulties in resolving a prior loss. Sue's plan to attend a distant school reawakened the prior separation that the family experienced, and thus her depression was functional in terms of forestalling both the father's and perhaps her own resolution of the normative developmental task of emerging into a more independent status. By remaining at home, Sue could maintain the family homeostasis, as the fear of future separations and losses (owing to the trauma of the mother's death) presented difficulties in terms of the family's making a more satisfactory accommodation.

Boundaries and Structures. There are, however, families who have experienced previous traumas without developing a symptomatic member. Perhaps the nature of both the organization (boundaries) and the structure of the family somewhat predisposes the family either to cope effectively or to experience problems. For example, in families with enmeshed boundaries (little differentiation between generations), family members are overinvolved with each other, leaving little room for the development of privacy and autonomy. These families are also characterized by an avoidance of external family relationships, as family loyalty is all-consuming. The underlying threat in these families is that any moves toward independence can cause a dissolution of the family structure. This is most common in families where the marital unit is estranged. In these circumstances, one parent is usually overinvolved with the children. The adolescent's normative move toward independence would leave parents more acutely aware of their conflict and perhaps lead to further estrangement (potential breakup of the family). Thus, the adolescent's development of symptoms maintains the myth of family unity. In these families, depressive symptoms are quite common because the adolescent, in part, may be mirroring the depression of a parent. Additionally, adolescents within these families are often isolated from peers and feel inadequate in their interactions with the external world because this has been discouraged by the family. Consequently, this loneliness, negative self-esteem, and isolation further contribute to the development of depressive symptomatology.

However, overly rigid and detached families also risk engendering a depressed adolescent member. These are the families that prematurely launch their adolescent into the adult world (Fishman, 1988). These youngsters have all the freedom but few of the skills to handle the independence. Fishman (1988) further asserts that these adolescents feel rejected as a result of their parents' ejection of them into the adult world. In these families, the youngster really craves nurturance and attention. Their precipitous push into the larger world is viewed as a manifestation of their worthlessness. This lowered sense of self-esteem and anger at their parents for the rejection may be turned inward (Fishman, 1988). In reviewing influences on suicidal behavior, Wodarski and Harris (1987) noted an increased propensity to engage in suicidal behavior if the youngster felt estranged from one or both parents. The adolescent's suicidal behavior can be viewed as functional in terms of keeping a very precariously associated group of people (the family unit) together.

Coping with Emotions. Both overly enmeshed families and detached families share one common trait—the difficulty in expressing and dealing with emotions and conflict. Therefore, difficulties in processing emotional states are superimposed on the vulnerabilities already discussed as contributing to the symptom development in families with adolescent members. These families are characterized by avoidance of conflict, mainly through denial. In fact, the role of the adolescent as a maintainer of homeostasis is essentially the vehicle by which the entire family can deny the stress and tension brought about by the demands for flexibility and change.

In further delineating the role of avoidance of conflict in these families, Sargent (1987) views the development of suicidal behavior in adolescents as a partial manifestation of the parents' inability to manage their own affective situation. In essence, the parents feel an overwhelming problem (e.g., lack of direction in career, difficulties in marriage); the adolescent takes on the problem through symptomatic behavior in order to save the parents from feeling overwhelmed. The child's problem causes further difficulties for the parents such as feelings of incompetence and irresponsibility. With the worsening of the symptomatology, in order for the adolescent to further save the parents, the parents become so overwhelmed that they then abdicate responsibility for the adolescent's problems. The adolescent feels abandoned and betrayed because his or her intentions were to assist the parents. The suicidal behavior then becomes a desperate attempt to solicit parental attention. Thus, the adolescent acts out the parental emotion in order to forestall the parents from feeling the pain of their own crisis.

CONCLUSIONS

Although each factor has been outlined separately, in reality, the process is interconnected and complicated. Our notions of etiology of adolescent depression within a family perspective are essential in terms of both uncovering processes within families and delineating paths of intervention and resolution. For the most part, extensive study of depressive behavior has been conducted within an intrapsychic dimension. Most family-oriented materials have not concentrated on the issue of depression in adolescence specifically. Within the adult context, recent publications (Clarkin, Haas, & Glick, 1988; Covi, 1986) have viewed the family's reaction to and reinforcement of the depressive behavior with an adult member. This chapter has aimed toward starting with the family and reviewing etiological factors from that context. However, there is merit in delineating the individual influences within the adolescent, which, in combination with familial pressures and tension, precipitate adolescent depressive symptomatology. It is exactly this notion that is explored in the following chapter.

CHAPTER 3

Individual Models of Adolescent Depression

Although there have been many attempts to develop individual etiological and conceptual models of depression, the main emphasis thus far has focused on adult depressive reactions (Erickson, 1987). Although the professional and scientific literatures have grown enormously in identifying psychological and biological risk factors of depression, the delineation of these factors and their causal relation to depressive episodes (whether they are the cause or the result of them) remains an arduous task (see Barnett & Gotlib, 1988, for a comprehensive review). Further, attempts to extend these models and risk factors to preadult populations have lagged in comparison (Kazdin, 1988). As discussed in Chapter 1, this largely has been due to the controversies surrounding the assumptions about whether children and adolescents actually experience full-blown depressive disorders. There also has been a strong bias that depression, like other emotional difficulties before adulthood, simply passes with time (Lefkowitz & Burton, 1978). However, growing evidence indicates that this thinking is no longer accurate and that theories on the etiology of depression must include characteristics and situational factors relevant to the preadult years (Kovacs, 1989).

The psychosocial models of depression have implicated many abnormalities as descriptors of the depressed state. These have included such aspects of the depressed experience as dysfunctional cognitions, distressed relationships, anaclitic personality types, and deficits in social skills (e.g., Abramson, Seligman, & Teasdale, 1978; Beck, 1976; Brown & Harris, 1978; Hirschfeld, Klerman, Chodoff, Korchin, & Barrett, 1976; Lewinsohn, 1974). Many of these symptoms may be visible while the individual is depressed and then disappear upon remission of the depression. Because they have been identified as at least co-occurring during the depressed episode, much theorizing has resulted in featuring these factors as the basis for a competing model of depression. These psychosocial models, based on psychoanalytic, behavioral, and cognitive schools of thought, have been highly influential in the advances made in understanding, assessing, diagnosing, and treating depressed individuals.

At the same time, considerable gains have been made in viewing the depressed state from a biological framework. From these models, diagnostic and treatment interventions have also emerged in order to overcome the negative consequences of depression. The integration of biology and psychosocial models of depression has attracted some speculation and continues to be of utmost interest in the development of the comprehensive understanding of mood disorders. It is in this vein that the elucidation of these models is presented in this chapter.

PSYCHOANALYTIC MODELS

The earliest writings on depression were originated primarily by psychoanalytic theorists and researchers (Abraham, 1912; Freud, 1917; Rado, 1928). In attempting to clarify the distinctions between the normal aspects of mourning and a clinical depression, they emphasized both the conscious and the unconscious reactions to loss as the primary component in the experience of severe depressive reactions. Despite the attention paid to the underlying features of depression and its manifestations in adults, little mention was given to its correlates in childhood. In fact, this theorizing held that children, including adolescents, were unlikely to be able to express similar emotions (Rie, 1966; Rochlin, 1959). This position was further supported by studies that questioned whether the high incidence of depressive symptoms in childhood was merely a by-product of normal development, as opposed to any kind of emotional disorder (Lapouse, 1966). The acceptance of this viewpoint was so strong that until the late 1960s, only scant attention was paid to the concept of childhood depression (Trad, 1987).

An exception to this exclusion was the work by Rene Spitz, who researched and described depressed features in children and coined the term "anaclitic depression" (Spitz, 1945, 1946). His classic studies supported the notion that maternal absence during the early years could produce intense symptoms of weepiness and withdrawal in babies before the first year of life, and in more extreme conditions, it could produce emotional retardation. In relating his findings to Freud's concept of melancholia, he too placed the etiological emphasis on loss (i.e., the absence of a consistent mother figure). *Anaclitic depression* defined the infant's affective response to a highly aversive environment event. Spitz further observed that if the infant were returned to the mother within 3 months of the beginning of the depressive features, the child would recover; if not, a prolonged and possibly life-threatening condition could occur.

Bowlby (1973), another prominent theoretician, addressed the connections among affective state, grieving, and experiencing loss and separation from the mother. Bowlby subdivided into three stages the reaction of loss from the mother: (1) protest, (2) despair, and (3) detachment. *Protest* describes the child's frustrations and attempts to retrieve the love object through tantrums and anger. This phase assumes that the child believes that through his or her actions, the mother will return, and it focuses the anger on those individuals held responsible for the loss. In adolescents, this can be seen through intense rage directed toward others or sometimes toward themselves through suicidal gestures when absence or rejection from a loved one occurs (Pfeffer, 1986). The stage of *despair* occurs when the child becomes resigned to the absence and is left with feelings of sadness and hopelessness. It is at this stage that the child starts to lose interest in the environment and becomes apathetic and withdrawn. The final stage is *detachment*—the acceptance of the loss, the lessening of preoccupied thoughts, and the reduction of concomitant depressed feelings. It is at this time that new relationships may be sought and established.

During the stage of adolescence, many of these same actions, beliefs, and feelings are experienced as part of normal emotional development. However, clinical signs of depression in adolescents are usually viewed as stemming from earlier interruptions in development rather than from adolescence itself. For example, Anthony (1970) proposed that depression appears in reaction to earlier developmental problems. He categorized childhood depression into two types: pre-Oedipal and Oedipal. Pre-Oedipal depression includes a vulnerability to depression due to perceived threats of loss and separation that involve a history of these fears and occurrences. Adolescents who have experienced these losses are more inclined to overreact when confronted by the threat of breaking up a dating relationship. Oedipal depression occurs as a result of not being able to fulfill or complete tasks, resulting in feelings of worthlessness and leading to a poor self-concept. Adolescents who did not have the earlier opportunity to gain the necessary skills to master their environment would probably be prone to disappointment in their efforts and would give up easily in the pursuit of completing the task. Depression during adolescence could thus be viewed as a continuum with a varying range of symptoms and age of onset (Mishne, 1986).

From a classical analytic view, depression among adolescents is thought to be produced by a narcissistic breakdown, causing losses in self-esteem and feelings of helplessness and worthlessness (Jacobson, 1943). This can take the form of being predisposed to addictions or self-centered relationships, due to an intensely close relationship with an inconsistent parental figure who has been both overindulgent and critical. Another form of depression is characterized by guilt and moral masochism. Anger that is naturally directed toward the parent is internalized, while ideals about the family are fractured and guilt emerges over these hostile feelings. The resulting feelings in either form can, in extreme cases, lead to suicidal thoughts and gestures. Berkovitz (1981), another theoretician, has focused attention on late adolescence as a critical period for dealing with these stronger feelings of powerlessness. Separation and individuation normally result in a sense of mastery and competency, but for the adolescent who has not been successful in separating and individuating, a profound feeling of failure may lead to overwhelming eruptions in behavior. To reduce the intensity of these feelings and urges, the adolescent may turn to drugs as a method of self-medication, though this pathway may lead to a lowering of control over impulses because it diminishes normal ego functioning.

A summary of these psychoanalytic conceptualizations of depression focuses around five areas (Bemporad, 1978): (1) disturbed current interpersonal relations, (2) early disappointments with significant others, (3) difficulties in adaptive functioning, (4) problems in regulating self-esteem, and (5) current failures as a result of inner conflict. It is for these reasons that depressed individuals need to be assisted in autonomy and relatedness. The specific features of these five areas (e.g., low self-esteem and helplessness) have been the focus of other models of depression and have produced considerable attention and research into understanding this disorder.

BEHAVIORAL ANTECEDENTS OF DEPRESSION

During the 1960s and 1970s, behavioral viewpoints of depression flourished (see Clarkin & Glazer, 1981). In general, these models emphasized the principles of learning theory (i.e., the impact that the environment had on the individual) and how the acquisition of interpersonal skills and their deficits were associated with various emotional disorders. The symptoms of depression were thought to be produced mainly by difficulties people had in interacting with their world.

Depression, from a behavioral perspective, was initially defined by Ferster (1965, 1973) as a low rate of operant behavior emitted by a person. This reduction in behavior resulted from a disruption in a person's ability to receive positive reinforcement from the environment. With behavior no longer being reinforced, general activity was thought to be reduced through an extinction process. This set in motion a cycle of lowered responses, leading to a lessening of rewards, which ultimately resulted in a depressed state (Becker, Heimberg, & Bellack, 1987).

For the adolescent, a reduction in the amount of available rewards might be a by-product of (a) losing a parent through death, separation, or divorce; (b) breaking off an interpersonal relationship; (c) exclusion from a sports team or other school-related organization (e.g., band, cheerleading, service clubs); or (d) general anxiety that limits participation in social events, such as teen dances. These occurrences lessen the quantity of response-contingent positive reinforcement that would ordinarily be available to the adolescent by removal of a main source of satisfaction or by the impedance of access to potential rewards. Because the reinforcing feedback is no longer available or is limited, the behaviors that were being maintained by these rewards become extinguished, and the resulting reduction of behaviors leads to even fewer reinforcement possibilities. The adolescent ultimately becomes more passive and emits even fewer behaviors that could result in reinforcements. Depression is the final outcome of this vicious cycle.

Ferster's model of depression initiated an intensive investigation by other applied behavioral scientists. Soon it was discovered that this model was inadequate in its explanation of how individuals differ in their unique responses to unpleasant life events. Accordingly, this model would propose that any disruption in an individual's reward system would lead to depression, and anyone who is confronted by aversive life situations would become depressed. Of course this is not the case, because not all people become depressed in the face of loss or failure. As researchers have demonstrated, the interrelationship between depression and stressful life occurrences is complicated and not well-understood (Hammen, Mayol, deMayo, & Marks, 1986).

Peter Lewinsohn and his colleagues attempted to extend Ferster's behavioral model of depression by emphasizing the role of interpersonal interactions (Lewinsohn, 1975; Lewinsohn & Arconad, 1981). Although, like Ferster, Lewinsohn placed great importance on the aspect of response-contingent positive reinforcement, he noted the critical difference between the quantity and the quality of reinforcements received in one's life through one's own behavior. Lewinsohn postulated that the relative amount of reinforcement received is a by-product not only of the number of activities that a person has found rewarding and the availability of those events occurring in the immediate environment, but also of the person's degree of skillfullness in obtaining a maximum of rewards and a minimum of punishment through interpersonal behavior. Thus, Lewinsohn advocated that depression results from a lack of socially relevant skills capable of obtaining rewards and that these deficits are an important antecedent condition in depressive disorders. Therefore, those individuals who would be more prone to depressive affect when confronted with disruption in their lives are those individuals less able to discover alternative resources that would lead to personal reinforcement.

A corresponding behavioral viewpoint that overlapped with Lewinsohn's position suggested that social-skill weaknesses are evident in depressed individuals. Social skill deficits include such characteristics as being uncomfortable in social interchanges, receiving few positive responses, and being especially sensitive to negative feedback. Lewinsohn's model contended that a lowering of response-contingent rewards, such as decreases of pleasurable experiences or increases of unpleasant situations, will result in dysphoria and self-blame—two key features of depression. If this were so, a person with few social skills would be at a higher risk for depressed experiences due to an already minimal degree of reinforcement. Lewinsohn also suggested that if the depression elicited sympathy and attention, it would be likely to maintain or escalate the level and the length of the depression.

Because of this emphasis, intervention programs have been established that have focused on the training of social skills and assertive behaviors. Social-skills training focuses on teaching positive skills, rather than on eliminating negative behaviors, with the belief that the increasing use of more rewarding competence-based skills will displace the older patterns of maladaptive behaviors (Goldsmith & McFall, 1975). Social-skills training should therefore be effective in reducing depression by increasing appropriate behaviors and thereby increasing response-contingent reinforcement (Harpin, Liberman, Marks, Stern, & Bohannon, 1982).

Deficits in social competencies have been found to be major obstacles in overcoming emotional disturbance in both inpatient and outpatient populations (Kazdin, Esvelt-Dawson, & Matson 1984; Youngren & Lewinsohn, 1980). This is particularly salient for adolescents, whose major developmental tasks during their teenage years (e.g., self-sufficiency, resisting peer pressure, forming interpersonal relationships, developing self-concepts) are highly dependent on learning rewarding communication patterns and enhancing their interpersonal repertoire. A further indication for adolescents to develop appropriate social skills stems from observations that the communication patterns of adolescents are often viewed negatively by adults, which can ultimately lead to feelings of alienation and lowered self-esteem. When implemented in adolescent settings, the formal training of social-skill behaviors has demonstrated successful reductions in aggression and interpersonal conflicts. Concomitant with this reduction of ineffective behaviors are findings that have shown decreases in levels of depression (Becker, Heimberg, & Bellack, 1987).

Since these early investigations and theoretical models, later behavioral-oriented researchers have maintained the existence of a relationship between behavior and mood. These researchers have hypothesized that depression is reduced when individuals learn more efficient behaviors for interacting with significant others by reducing stress and conflict in their lives. Brady (1984), for example, suggests that a lack of social skills leads to interpersonal anxiety, isolation, and lowered self-esteem, all contributors to feelings of depression. Subsequent research has substantiated these basic premises (e.g., Thase, Hersen, Bellack, Himmelhoch, Kornblith, & Greenwald, 1984).

Alternative behavioral models of depression have attempted to more fully integrate psychosocial factors. For instance, Rehm (1977) proposed a self-control model that highlights the depressed person's maladaptive or inadequate self-regulatory processes for handling stress. The key features of this model demonstrate how persons with poor methods of self-monitoring, self-evaluating, and self-reinforcing would be more likely to focus on negative events, to set rigidly high standards for themselves, and to permit themselves little reinforcement. Thus, behavioral models emphasizing reductions of activity and lack of rewards can be combined with the somewhat more recent cognitive and cognitive-behavioral concepts of depression (e.g., Beck, 1976; Seligman, 1975).

COGNITIVE MODELS

Cognitive and cognitive-behavioral models of depression overlap so often in their theoretical constructs and their intervention strategies that they are not easy to separate. Both address distorted reasoning and the absence of rewards as being associated with the depressed state, and both use such methods as rehearsal and increased activity in their therapeutic modalities. Theorists and practitioners in these traditions assume (a) that the ways in which individuals view the world and themselves ultimately determines how they will feel and act, and (b) that thoughts and disturbed feelings are interrelated. They suggest that one cannot feel upset without also having associated disturbance-creating thoughts (Burns, 1980; Ellis, 1985). For example, it is believed that a common misperception (e.g., "I must be a success in everything I do"), would produce feelings of anxiety or sadness when failure is confronted. Conversely, feelings such as these may initiate distorted or irrational thinking (e.g., "I'll never experience success again"). This type of thought–feeling connection can occur fairly regularly in teenagers who are beginning to take greater risks toward independent behaviors and who must confront routinely the possibility of failure (e.g., dating, final exams).

Beck (1967, 1976) has provided the most comprehensive elucidation of the cognitive view of depression. According to his model, depressed persons' thinking and preoccupation represent erroneous and exaggerated modes of personally scrutinizing the self and the surrounding events. Subsequently, they simultaneously become exceedingly sensitive to frustration (interpreting insignificant impediment as substantial), feel slighted by otherwise harmless statements made by others, and devalue themselves. The cognitions are oftentimes irrelevant and inappropriate to the actual event and reflect a consistent negative bias toward the self—a process that Beck has termed "selective abstraction." During periods of depression, the formation of reasons (or attributions) for failure are limited to causes that provoke a negative self-concept. In addition, persons who become depressed mobilize a negative view not only of the self, but also of the world and of the future, termed the "negative cognitive triad" (Beck, Rush, Shaw, & Emery, 1979). This reciprocal relationship between depression and cognition is believed to form the foundation of a downward spiral that serves to perpetuate the depression. Thus, depressed persons misperceive, mishear, and misconstrue events to match their prevailing negative focus.

Beck's viewpoint emphasizes that the various symptoms observed in the depressed individual can best be understood in terms of this cognitive shift. Individuals who become depressed often perceive and interpret their situation as being defeated, deprived, or deserted, and they view themselves as inadequate or defective in most aspects of their functioning. They are likely to make negative self-statements when confronted with unpleasant circumstances (i.e., seeing only themselves as being at fault). They also tend to generalize their faulty assumptions to other situations, and they see no hope that change might occur. These negative conclusions often maintain and exacerbate the other depressed symptoms.

Other areas of cognitive dysfunction in depression have been identified by Beck and his colleagues (Beck et al., 1979; Wright & Beck, 1983). They have been termed "logical systematic errors" and "dysfunctional attitudes" or "idiosyncratic schemata"), both of which attempt to explain why particular internal or external situations may increase negative thinking patterns. The basis for this distorted thinking and maladaptive behaviors is the depressed person's inability to plan and follow through on more constructive plans of action. Examples of errors in thinking include such falsehoods as arbitrarily inferring a setback negatively (e.g., "My boyfriend did not call; therefore he does not love me"); overgeneralizing from a single event (e.g., "Because one person does not like me, everyone hates me"); personalizing a bad event (e.g., "I am to blame for my parents' separation"); minimizing accomplishments (e.g., "I was lucky to win that match"); and dichotomous thinking (e.g., "If I cannot get my way, then I do not want anything"). According to the cognitive model, these distortions in perceptions and these faulty conclusions increase an individual's vulnerability to depression. These faulty cognitions are also more active and more easily influenced during episodes of depression, but they are not as apparent upon remission. The cognitive model does not imply a cause–effect relationship; rather, it views the distortions as being but one component of the depressive syndrome.

While cognitive interventions with samples of adult depressed outpatients have been well documented (see Jarrett & Rush, 1985), more recent attention has been devoted to adapting this model to depressed adolescents (Emery, Bedrosian, & Garber, 1983; Wilkes & Rush, 1988). In cognitive therapy, clinicians and their clients combine their efforts to identify and alter faulty thoughts and conclusions. The therapy tends to be time limited and active, with the focus on mastery and reevaluation of the client's belief system. Because of cognitive and emotional limitations, the clinician working with adolescents must be flexible in providing established therapeutic formats in order to meet the adolescents' needs. For example, although there are similarities between depressed adolescents and depressed adults in their use of all-or-none thinking, adolescents are also likely to have a more limited vocabulary. The therapist needs to respond sensitively to these differences by providing an increased range of alternative perceptions and explanations. Also, as other researchers have shown, younger adolescents may have difficulty with the idea of logical errors, may display fewer interpersonal skills, and may have problems with consequential thinking (Kendall, Pelligrini, & Urbain, 1981). Therefore, adapting cognitive–behavioral techniques to adolescent treatment requires action-oriented methods during the session, concrete tasks assigned between sessions, and a limited continuum of alternative responses that relate appropriately to their level of cognitive development.

A Learned-Helplessness Perspective

The concept of learned helplessness was initially described by Seligman and his colleagues (Overmier & Seligman, 1967; Seligman & Maier, 1967) after discovering that dogs, following exposure to uncontrollable (i.e., noncontingent) aversive events, later displayed severe deficits in their motivational, cognitive, and emotional areas of behavior. It appeared that the dogs had given up and endured the painful shocks without recourse. In generalizing these and subsequent findings to human depression, Seligman (1975) suggested that depressed individuals were impeded from mastering adaptive means of coping with painful circumstances and therefore learned to be helpless. The main focus of the hypothesis was that depressed persons failed to see relationships between their own responses and any rewards they receive in the environments. When this lack of contingency repeated itself, depressed persons formed the belief that nothing they could do would alter the circumstances. A period of passivity, emotional distress, and hopelessness ensued.

Since the inception of the original model, revisions had to be proposed in order to incorporate the burgeoning literature, which has applied the model to various populations and situations (Abramson et al., 1978). This reformulated model focused on the attributional states and attributional styles that contributed to helplessness, as mediators in the anticipation of future noncontingency. According to the reformulated learned-helplessness model of depression, vulnerability to depression stemmed from a habitual style of explaining the causes of life events (i.e., a pervasive attributional or explanatory style) (Peterson & Seligman, 1984). This attributional analysis suggested that when persons were confronted by what they believed to be noncontingent, negative events, they questioned their ability to remove themselves from that aversive situation. The personal etiology for failure would subsequently determine the novel situations and the time span in which the anticipation of future failure (and resulting deficits) would occur. Three pertinent attributional components were incorporated into the model: (1) *stability* (whether the shortcomings or deficits would be chronic or transient), (2) *globality* (whether the failure was situation specific or was likely to occur across many situations), and (3) *internality* (reasons for failure considered to be internal or external). Thus, the initiation of internal, stable, and global reasons to explain aversive events and, to a lesser degree, the attribution of positive results to external, specific, and unstable causes composes a depressogenic or self-deprecating attributional style (Seligman, Abramson, Semmel, & von Baeyer, 1979).

The current view of the helplessness (or hopelessness) model of depression acknowledges that the negative expectations and feelings of helplessness are a sufficient, but not a necessary cause of depression (Alloy, Abramson, Metalsky, & Hartlage, 1988). It is recognized that depression may be heterogeneous in its causality, and that other factors (e.g., genetic vulnerability, chemical depletion) may also be involved in its expression. Much research has emphasized viewing hopelessness depression as a depressive subtype with respect to cause, symptoms, course, and treatment to other subtypes of depression (Abramson, Alloy, & Metalsky, 1988; Alloy, Clements, & Kolden, 1985).

In the late 1980s, research into this area has begun to use this model both to predict how attributional styles could affect depressed responses in children who may be vulnerable to psychopathology (Hammen, Adrian, & Hiroto, 1988) and to generalize its usage at a group level (e.g., the family) (Munton & Antaki, 1988). Previously, the investigation of attributional style in childhood and adolescence was limited to correlational studies indicating some association between depressed mood and explanations (e.g., Kaslow, Rehm, & Siegel, 1984). Also cognitive deficits, analogous to those suffered by adult depressives, were found in children who were placed in uncontrollable circumstances, which further suggests the link between depression and helplessness (e.g., Dweck & Reppucci, 1973). This model is now recognized to offer a useful perspective for developmental psychopathologists interested in depression (Seligman & Peterson, 1986).

This model of depression also appears to be particularly applicable to the period of adolescence, a time of risk-taking and experimentation. Many adolescents are attempting to define their own identities through a series of success and/or failure experiences that have the potential for aversive outcomes, particularly when combined with faulty conclusions. This leaves them vulnerable to viewing themselves as unable to change conditions, because adolescents have usually had little experience with rejection and may be unfamiliar with the situational origin of the failure. Up to that time, they also may not have had much experience with possible negative life events (e.g., death or divorce) that may be out of their control. Additionally, their spurts of physical growth and functioning may leave them feeling that things are truly beyond their control and that they are vulnerable to unconditional success or failure.

The following case study clarifies the assumptions surrounding the cognitive models of depression and shows how the models can be applied to clinical situations with adolescents.

Case Study

At the time of evaluation, Jason R., a white, Catholic male, was 16 years of age, in the 11th grade, and residing with his parents and two brothers (ages 17 and 11). A referral for follow-up outpatient treatment was requested by the hospital where Jason had been an inpatient for 7 weeks, following an attempted suicide. According to Jason, he had experienced frequent depressive episodes during the past several years. He described himself as being alienated from his family and "defensive and hostile" toward his peers, although he constantly sought their friendship and support. He stated that he often reflected on his behavior and "wondered what was wrong" with himself and why other people were against him. He related that he also had thought of committing suicide during these times of despair.

While intoxicated on beer and marijuana at a party, he stole $5.00 from someone for no apparent reason. Upon being discovered, his peers became very angry at him, causing much personal distress. At that point, he described himself as being "tired of it" and consumed an overdose of pills obtained from his parents' medicine cabinet (Tylenol®, Contact®, thyroid medication, diet pills, and Valium®). A psychological report, completed during his inpatient stay, described Jason as suffering from a mixture of anxiety and depressive reaction, as a consequence of rejection.

During the introductory therapy session, information was gathered concerning Jason's reasoning during times when he felt rejected from friends or from possible dates. He offered several statements that supported the selectiveness of his bias toward self-evaluations. These included such statements as, "I am a boring conversationalist," "I am stupid," "I am ugly," "I am too short," "I am lazy,"—all considered highly emotion-laden, internal, characterological responses. After Jason had delineated all his reasons for failure, he was offered alternative reasons that were less harmful to his self-esteem. These included the possibilities of a prospective date leaving town, wanting to partake in another activity, having an obligation to study, dating another person, and even having to do her hair. He wrote all these reasons (a total of 20) on a piece of paper, to evaluate and rehearse between sessions. This practice continued throughout the next several sessions, generalizing to situations such as arguments with parents, rejection from friends, and fights with his brothers. During this process, he began to detail his thoughts surrounding the conflicts and was successfully able to offer alternative, less-personal reasons for the outcomes. Finally, Jason was able to incorporate this revised attributional or explanatory style into his own terms on an everyday basis.

Providing a broader attributional framework allowed Jason the opportunity to construct the multiple causality necessary to adapt to what he had previously considered a hostile environment. These increased possibilities lowered his defensive posture substantially, and he became much more successful in risk-taking behaviors without fearing the possibility of rejection or failure. During the sequence of therapeutic sessions (a total of 22), he was able to engage the therapist more frequently, and after much hesitancy, he was able to engage his parents more effectively in family sessions. Outside of therapy, he was able to concentrate on school work (making the honor roll), to successfully obtain and maintain a job in a clothing store, and to begin a meaningful relationship with a peer.

BIOLOGICAL FACTORS

Biochemical Explanations

There have been many biochemical agents implicated in the psychological expression of depression (see Usin, Asber, Bertilsson, & Sjoqvist, 1984). Much of the research data has demonstrated that depressed persons have imbalances of *neurotransmitters*, which are the natural biochemicals that allow communication within brain cells (see Zis & Goodwin, 1982). In general, individuals suffering from mood disorders display (a) a deficit of neurotransmitters, which may lead to depression; (b) an excess of them, which may lead to mania; or (c) an imbalance of them. Two biochemicals that have been researched extensively are serotonin and norepinephrine. An imbalance of serotonin may produce many of the common symptoms of depression such as increases in sleep problems, irritability, and anxiety. In a similar manner, when an improper amount of norepinephrine (which regulates alertness and arousal) is produced, fatigue and a depressed mood may occur.

Other bodily chemicals may also be out of balance when a person becomes depressed. One such chemical is cortisol, a hormone that is produced in response to extremes in cold temperature or emotion (e.g., anger or fear). On average, the level of cortisol in the bloodstream peaks early in the morning and decreases during the day. It appears, however, that during times of depression, the early morning increases never level off as the day progresses. A blood test has been developed (the dexamethasone suppression test) to demonstrate this increase in cortisol level in depressed individuals (Brown, Johnston, & Mayfield, 1979).

The research into neuroendocrine abnormalities has also been a source of study into the biochemical explanations for depression (cited in Kazdin, 1988). It is believed that many of the symptoms expressed during the depressed state, including interruptions in mood and physical functioning, suggest problems in the regulation of the hypothalamus. Additionally, other neurotransmitters (e.g., acetylcholine and serotonin) that have been shown to become imbalanced during mood disorders normally monitor the neuroendocrine agents that mediate pituitary and other hormonal activity.

Genetic Vulnerabilities

Discoveries in the 1970s and 1980s have focused attention on the genetic influences that contribute to depression. For instance, researchers have begun to pinpoint genetic markers that leave certain individuals susceptible to manic–depressive illness. Though a specific gene has not been found, the existence of genetic markers brings researchers closer to this conclusion.

The discovery of genetic markers provides credence to earlier research that reported familial links in depression. For example, close relatives of individuals suffering from a major depression are more likely to display symptoms than are individuals who are not related (Nurnberger & Gershon, 1982). Evidence also comes from twin studies (Gershon, Targum, Kessler, Mazure, & Bunney, 1977); if one identical twin has a depressive illness, there is a 70% chance that the other twin will also experience the symptoms. These correlations have also been demonstrated in studies investigating rates of depression among adopted children.

These findings showed that while adoptive families are at little risk in transmitting their illness, adoptive children are three times more likely to become depressed if their biological relatives suffered from depression.

This evidence from genetic studies has induced other researchers to investigate a variety of questions linking genetic markers to family histories, treatment response, and subtype classification. There has also been a research emphasis in exploring biological markers in those individuals who are at risk for depressive episodes. The strategy has been to detect these markers in individuals regardless of whether they are expressing any symptoms of depression. With this line of research being interrelated to other work, such as identifying the mode of genetic transmission, insights may be forthcoming that can explain both the transmission and the mechanism of action during times of depression.

CONCLUSIONS

Like most conditions that are not very well understood, there is a possibility that an individual inherits a susceptibility to depression, but that this tendency is expressed and maintained only during times of environmental stress. Another question that has yet to be answered is whether the biochemical imbalances causes the depression or whether the depressed state gives rise to these imbalances. Although it is promising, the research into biology and genetics still does not explain all the reasons why people become depressed. For example, side effects of some medications—for instance, reserpine—have been known to produce depression, while another medication (used primarily to treat tuberculosis) has been associated with euphoric states in some people.

There exists an increasing realization that depression is not merely a single entity, but a common pathway for several etiologies that can be divided into more specific subtypes (Strober, 1983). Yet, multiple issues still remain in describing its symptoms, course, and treatment in adolescents. In validating the diagnostic picture of depression in adolescents, much of the research focus must verify the existence of biological and genetic models that have been a landmark in the study of adult populations.

PART 2

Assessment and Evaluation

CHAPTER 4

Family Interview

PREPARING FOR THE INTERVIEW

The Referral

Family interviews are a challenge even for the experienced clinician. We are taught in our culture that privacy and family unity are important concepts. Family interviews demand that the clinician be sensitive to these issues while being assertive in gaining information about family patterns, about significant family events, and about the history of the presenting problems. Clinicians who are able to establish an atmosphere of warmth and caring, who are sensitive to the different developmental stages of the individual family members as well as the developmental stage of the family as a whole, and who have an understanding of normal and pathological family processes will be the most successful at uncovering the inner workings of a particular family.

No more crucial are these words of caring and caution for the interviewer than for families who present themselves with a depressed adolescent member. These families already feel that they are failures before they contact a mental health professional because they have been deficient in helping their youngster to overcome depression or even possible suicidal feelings. Because it is quite common for other members of the family to be experiencing depression simultaneously, these families may feel even more inadequate and incompetent. The clinician who is able from the very first contact with the family to communicate empathy, to be nonjudgmental, and to offer some hopefulness will maximize both the level of trust and the amount of disclosure in families with depressed adolescents.

Prior to seeing the family in the office, clinicians must be sensitive to the circumstances under which families either seek services or are referred for services. In general, a family decides to contact a clinician because stress has unbalanced the family's ability to maintain harmony effectively (McPherson, Brackelmanns, & Newman, 1977). Within the context of this book, we are interested in the adolescent who shows symptoms of depression; these symptoms serve as an initial inappropriate attempt to reestablish family equilibrium. For example, in order to protect the family from dealing with the stress of redefining the mother's role as primary caregiver, an adolescent may begin to stay home from school due to vague somatic complaints and may become increasingly unmotivated to complete school work. In this way, the adolescent gives the mother a problem (i.e., getting the youngster to go to school and cajoling him or her to be more self-motivated) and thus both the mother and the family are shielded from the anxiety and perhaps the pain of needing to change familial relationships. The question arises, if the adolescent were not symptomatic, would the mother have to begin facing her own issues of emptiness and possibly depression? One of the problems with this inappropriate solution is that it blocks the emotional development of both the adolescent and the family. It may also cause an overly close alliance between the mother and the adolescent, thereby possibly contributing to an even further breakdown in the marital relationship and the family's ability to negotiate adequately future life stages.

Families usually come to the attention of mental health professionals when these inappropriate solutions do not contribute to a reduction of stress and anxiety. The families seek treatment in order to reestablish a more effective balance and harmony among family members (McPherson et al., 1977). Although families may solicit services because they feel under stress, they are not consciously aware of the dysfunctional patterns that have been instituted as an initial step in combating this collective anxiety. Their experience is one of repeatedly failed attempts to assist their adolescent in feeling less depressed. Additionally, feelings of frustration, inadequacy, and anger are also prevalent. It is the clinician's job to assess these dysfunctional patterns without invalidating the family's experience so that a plan for more satisfactory family existence can be implemented.

The Family Representative

The clinician's role in uncovering these dysfunctional patterns begins at the time the family actually makes contact with a mental health professional. Although initial contact with mental health professionals can be made in a variety of ways (e.g., face to face in an emergency room, school guidance office, or primary physician's office or via phone contact to a mental health agency or private practitioner), the interviewing process usually is initiated by a family member requesting help through a telephone contact. Even at this early stage of family contact, it is important that the clinician be sensitive to a number of issues.

First, it is essential to clarify the role of the person making the initial contact. Specifically, the clinician should question the caller as to the nature of his or her relationship with the individual who is identified as presenting the problem. In working with families with depressed adolescents, this person is usually one of the parents and is most commonly the mother. When an adult who is not the legal guardian makes the initial contact, the clinician should question the caller as to (1) why the guardian has not made the call and (2) whether the guardian has been informed that this individual is making this contact concerning the adolescent. If the adolescent him- or herself is the first contact person, the clinician should be very concerned about the level of the need of the youngster. It is very unusual for an adolescent to ask directly for assistance from mental health professionals (Stierlin, Rucker-Embden, Wetzel, & Wirsching, 1980). When adolescents solicit services on their own, this usually indicates that they are either in such crisis that they need immediate help or that they feel scared about approaching the parents or guardians, which can be a crisis in itself. For the most part, unless the adolescent is in immediate danger, all attempts need to be made to contact their legal guardian. The clinician should work to gain the adolescent's cooperation in contacting the parents or guardians (e.g., giving the adolescent support in his or her fears while detailing the importance of parental permission); this effect generally proves beneficial in gaining both adolescent and parental approval. It is only through clarification of the contact person's role that a plan for conducting the actual family interview can be appropriately devised.

Steirlin et al. (1980) have denoted the initial contact person as the "representative of the whole family"; therefore, appropriately engaging the representative in even the initial phone contact is pivotal in terms of maximizing both the likelihood that the family will come for the appointment and the amount of pertinent information that the clinician can obtain once the face-to-face interview has started (p. 59). It is essential that the clinician work through the family representative in order to gain the cooperation of all family members in the interview process.

Prior to inviting family members to an actual interview, the clinician must make an initial assessment as to the level of intervention that is needed, given the caller's description of presenting problems. For example, a mother who calls saying that her daughter (a) has refused to get out of bed for the past 3 days even though there are no physical complaints, (b) is tearful, and (c) reports decreased appetite should take her daughter immediately either to a scheduled appointment in the outpatient office that day or to the nearest emergency room for evaluation. Emergent interviews should also be conducted with an adolescent who (a) admits to recent drug usage involving serious substances; (b) displays acute psychotic or depressive symptoms, significant agitation, confused thinking or disorientation; and (c) engages in any talk of suicide or violence. Additionally, if an adolescent (a) solicits help for him- or herself and is a self-described runaway, (b) is in an agitated state, (c) admits to severe depressive or suicidal symptoms, or (d) reveals personal drug use, then all attempts should be made to secure the help of nearby adults so that the adolescent can be assisted to the hospital. If no adult is present, the adolescent should be given clear directions to allow the clinician to call an ambulance to assist him or her to get to the emergency room, or the clinician must clearly outline the steps the adolescent needs to take. Remember to ask the adolescent for his or her phone number and address before telling him about the plans, as many adolescents panic when they hear about the hospital and may refuse to give you their location. The best guideline is to try and find some adult on the scene who can be of assistance; however, if this is not possible, you may have to make some decisions regardless of the adolescent's refusals to cooperate. It is better to have a living and angry adolescent than a dead one.

The type of intervention selected by the clinician at the stage of telephone contact must be based on the information provided by the caller, in conjunction with the clinician's assessment of the level of severity of articulated symptoms. Although it is important that the clinician act prudently and cautiously when unsure of the exact nature or the severity of symptoms, the clinician should err on the side of implementing a more intensive and immediate strategy until a comprehensive and complete assessment can be initiated. This is especially true when we are concerning ourselves with adolescent depression, as adolescence is a time of such volatility and impulsivity that even accidental behavior can have serious repercussions.

Negotiating the Family Interview

Given that the clinician makes the determination that immediate intervention is not necessary, the next stage of the initial phone contact is to elaborate briefly on problem areas and to obtain an agreement to bring family members to a scheduled face-to-face interview. It is important to define and understand the problem areas, not only to decide on the appropriate level of intervention, but also to come to an initial understanding of the structure of the family in order to determine important family or nonfamily members to invite to the interview. As a rule of thumb, it is often helpful to have all the people who live together come at least to the first interview. At times, however, it is also helpful to have family members who live outside the home attend the first interview. For example, a grandmother who lives next door and whom the adolescent sees on a daily basis may be of assistance in clarifying the presenting problems. Additionally, in a divorced-yet-shared-custody situation, both parents are important sources of information. The clinician needs, however, to strike a balance between gaining important information in the first interview and potentially alienating important family members. In the divorced-but-shared-custody situation, the clinician may decide to meet with the referring parent in the first interview and then, once an initial alliance has been attained, ask for the other parent to join the family or to be seen separately in a second interview.

It is important to note that most family representatives call with complaints or concerns about an identified family member such as the depressed adolescent. Callers may be confused and resistant when the clinician asks them to bring the whole family to the appointment. Therefore, it is the clinician's responsibility to create an initial atmosphere of trust and safety and to offer the contact person a rationale for having the entire family attend the first appointment. The clinician must keep in mind that family functioning has broken down and that services are being solicited due to the extreme nature of experienced stress, anxiety, and inadequacy. The family, however, is not usually conscious that the identified patient is just a symptom of this family dysfunction. Also, it is usually not helpful for the clinician to describe over the phone the role of the symptomatic family member to the family representative, as this can be very threatening, and the representative may perceive that the clinician is blaming the parents. To avoid this perception, the clinician must embed the rationale for seeing the entire family within the formulation that the family representative has put forth regarding experienced difficulties. The following is a brief example of an initial phone contact between a mother and a clinician that exemplifies this strategy.

MOTHER: I am calling at the suggestion of Dr. Jessup, our family pediatrician, who has expressed to me some concern over our daughter, Sue. My husband and I have also been worried about Sue. She has grown increasingly more withdrawn, she doesn't like to go out with friends, her schoolwork has deteriorated, and I can't get her to take an interest in anything.

THERAPIST: How long has Sue been having these problems?

MOTHER: Well, she has been acting more and more depressed since my mother died. It has been hard on all of us, as we were all so close. My husband has also had to start traveling a lot, and I have had to cope with a lot more responsibility for the running of the household. We are really worried about her. I was wondering whether I can make an appointment for Sue to come see you sometime?

THERAPIST: I need to get a little more information from you, but first let me tell you how I usually work things. In the first interview, I would like to see your whole family. Are there any other children in the household besides Sue?

MOTHER: Yes, she has an older and a younger sister. But I don't think we can all come. As I explained to you, my husband travels so much, and the other girls are fine, so I don't really want to involve them in this. I would be able, however, to bring Sue and myself to talk to you.

THERAPIST: I hear your concerns about Sue, and you really did the right thing by calling. In order for me to assist Sue, though, I need to get a picture of the whole family so that I can see how Sue reacts to the family and how the family reacts to Sue. Would you be able to bring the family in for the first interview and then after I have a chance to meet with the family, we can see where to go from there?

This kind of structuring for the family representative usually is sufficient to secure the whole family's attendance at the first interview.

Occasionally, however, family members are resistant to coming to the initial interview. The family representative may be functioning as the family gatekeeper in terms of keeping salient family members from attending or may have a vested interest in keeping primary focus on the symptomatic adolescent. This is especially common in families with depressed adolescents, as these families are often characterized by difficulties in communication and alienation of some members from the family unit. The clinician needs to be aware of the possibility that the family representatives may be stating that certain family members will not come when in fact the representatives do not want them to come. In families characterized by marital difficulties, the statement "Father won't come" may be more accurately translated as "I'm so angry at him." Again, it is important for the clinician to strike a balance between alienating the contact person by insisting that the interview has to involve everyone and allowing the gatekeeper to decide the manner in which the interview is conducted. In general, a friendly yet assertive position with resistant families is the most helpful.

In a situation in which the family representative seems to be accurately portraying a resistant family member, the clinician should try to get the contact person's understanding of the other parent's difficulties with regard to the initial appointment. Occasionally, it is helpful to offer to speak with the resistant family member before the interview. Often people are resistant to coming because they are unsure about the interview process. Detailing the nature of the interview to resistant individuals over the telephone may assist in maximizing cooperation. It is important to note that frequently family members who initially voice their opposition to the appointment end up attending the interview without any intervention on the part of the clinician. However, in those cases in which it is quite clear that a family member will not attend, the clinician may decide to proceed with the interview with only the cooperative family members. Once an initial alliance is formulated and the clinician has a greater understanding of the particular situation presented by the family, the clinician has greater flexibility to work through those family members who do attend to include the missing individual(s).

Once a commitment to coming to the interview has been obtained, some additional preparation is still required on the part of the clinician before the actual face-to-face interaction. The clinician's task is to think through a plan for engendering an atmosphere for the family that promotes a sense of empathy and trust, thereby increasing the likelihood that the family will feel comfortable in disclosing information. Although, in part, adolescent depressive behavior is viewed as a manifestation of dysfunctional family patterns, Bryant (1984) argues that it is important to maintain an "open stance" with regard to the family. Specifically, "if the therapist is framing family members as unconscious agents of family pathology, who are victimizing a child, some signs of this may leak through and be perceived," thus potentially decreasing disclosures and at worst setting up a more contentious family–therapist relationship (p. 104). deShazer

(1984) maintains that when the therapist attempts to rescue the adolescent out of the mire of family homeostasis, the therapist is more likely to perceive resistances in families.

Although it is hard for anyone to make difficult changes, accepting the family's request for services as a genuine statement of desiring change will allow for a greater level of comfort even in the very early stages of an interview. This point is very important, as families already feel inadequate and incompetent to the degree that they have been compelled to reach outside the family boundaries for assistance with their depressed adolescent, and they therefore are hypersensitive to even the most subtle references to responsibility and blame. It is important under these circumstances to accept the family positively in the interview and to see the family as capable of change. Consequently, the task for the therapist becomes to cooperate with the family to effect change. This more positive attitude on the part of the therapist contributes dramatically to uplifting the family mood, which actually does more to further the potential for engendering different styles of family interactions than does a more negative and pathological view of the family's functioning (Bryant, 1984).

BEGINNING THE INTERVIEW: GREETING THE FAMILY

Unless you yourself have been in a waiting room waiting to be greeted by a therapist, you have little appreciation for the anxiety that is generated in coming to see a therapist. This is especially true for depressed adolescents who already defend against feelings of inadequacy, transparency, and the shame of being discovered. For the majority of adolescents, coming to a therapist is not their idea, and with some few exceptions, they are really confused as to what exactly a therapist does. In their confusion, they can become even more fearful, defensive, angry, belligerent, depressed, and withdrawn. Additionally, parents who are coping with their own feelings and with their own fears of being exposed as incompetent must also contend with the adolescent's feelings. They also may be in the position of arguing the merits of coming to a therapist to their adolescent before they are even convinced of the values themselves. They must be potentially strong willed and insistent at a time when they are feeling frustrated and overwhelmed. These are the people who the clinician is about to face when he or she walks out to the waiting room. The process of making families feel comfortable and willing to disclose very painful information about their functioning is a real challenge even for the experienced clinician, as he or she must communicate a respect for both the individual adolescent and the family as a whole.

The greeting stage (Haley, 1976) becomes very important in setting the emotional climate for the interview. This is a time for the clinician (a) to welcome the family, (b) to get to know everyone's name and position within the family,

(c) to share social amenities, and (d) to transmit a sense of caring and concern for the family. It is one of the times during the interview when the family feels most uncomfortable and vulnerable. As clinicians, we have been through hundreds of similar interviews, but we must remember that this may be the first time that this family has been involved in a formal interview process. Therefore, the clinician must take an active role in establishing contact with each family member and in providing some overview of the structure of the interview process. Specifically, it is helpful to articulate the course of events for the interview and some preliminary expectations. Within this context, it is beneficial to start the process by articulating to the family a synopsis of the information gathered over the phone. Even though this information may be known by everyone, it allows both the clinician and the family to fix on a starting point for the interview. It is through this initial commonality that the interview process can actually begin.

LEVELS OF FAMILY ASSESSMENT

Notions of the Problem

For the most part, families solicit an interview due to their concerns about a particular family member; therefore, clarifying the family's view of the problem is the initial step in family interviewing. It communicates your acceptance of them because you are willing to hear their story. Bryant (1984) contends that "a therapist who is genuinely interested in the problem presented, willing to listen to the family's theories about it, and at the family's service in bringing about desired change is using a powerful joining technique that tends to reduce the tension and set the stage for collaboration, cooperation and progress" (p. 106). Therefore, after pleasantries are exchanged, it is usually the family representative who begins to inform the clinician about the presenting problem. However, the family could have difficulties beginning; thus, the clinician may have to initiate the process by asking a family member to start. If the clinician must select a person to begin questioning, it is often helpful to select a parent. Beginning with the adolescent, especially a depressed adolescent, may be very difficult and may also set an uncomfortable tone for the interview because the adolescent may not consciously feel that there is a problem. The most important task for the clinician at this time is to be able to respect the family's formulations and to guide an exploration of the issues.

There are as many ways to investigate the presenting problems as there are theories of human behavior. Our questioning of the family is in part based on our own assumptions of behavior and dynamics in families, as we tend to ask the family to highlight certain areas and let others fall uninvestigated. Each school of family therapy is usually very specific on the direction of questioning regarding the presenting problems. Taken individually, they present one window into the functioning of a particular family. However, if we allow ourselves to combine the individual wisdom of these theoretical positions, we may be able to amass a more comprehensive view of the nature of the adolescent's depression within the family context. Gradually, we can move from (a) seeing the here-and-now expression of adolescent depressive behavior and of exceptions to that behavior to (b) viewing behaviors as metaphors for other familial problems and relationships to (c) conceptualizating these symptoms as emanating from dysfunctional interfamilial boundaries and structure. Thus, we progress along a continuum from specific behaviors to the underlying organization of family functioning. It is on all of these levels that an appraisal must be made in order to guide the family in discerning the mechanisms necessary for change.

The Manifested Problem

The problem is the first issue that the family is prepared to talk about because it is what makes the visit to the therapist legitimate (Caille, 1982). Often the clinician has a sense that the family's detailing of the problem has been well rehearsed and is the easiest point for the family to focus on in the first session. It is also the family's expectation that the clinician is interested and is most apt to ask about the problem. Avoiding or dismissing the symptoms or problems prematurely may seriously damage the initially tenuous relationship with the clinician because the family may feel ignored, put down, or misunderstood. However, considerable controversy exists in the family therapy literature as to the degree of concentration on problem behaviors because they are frequently viewed as just a symptom of more generalized family dysfunction. In elaborating on problem areas are we not reinforcing the family's scapegoating action? Caille (1982) suggests "there is no reason to consider the importance the family assigns to the symptom as a hindrance to the therapy program" because it gives "important information about the family's structure" (p. 33). Specifically, the family's conceptualization of the symptom itself can provide us with an important window into the world of the family functioning, organization, and structure. For example, in elaborating on the adolescent's depression, determining whether families view the problem's origin as biological, behavioral, or interpersonal gives added information concerning the role that the adolescent's depression plays in the family context.

In delineating the problem, it is important to gain an understanding of each family member's conceptualization of (a) etiology and present symptomatology, (b) common repetitive patterns of interactions, (c) previous attempts to solve the problem, and (d) projected similarities and differences in family functioning once the problem has been solved. Although the interviewer should scale down questioning to the appropriate developmental level for each family member, no individual—no matter how young—should be excluded from giving his or her opinion. Usually, the youngest member of the family is the most uninhibited and can offer the most spontaneous and unguarded response. For example, in questioning a family with a 6-year-old, the child responded to this question: "Who would people be worried about if Sue were feeling less depressed?" "Oh that would be my mommy—she is also very sad." The information this girl provided was invaluable in terms of allowing the therapist to root the adolescent's depression more clearly within the context of the family.

How the clinician approaches the family is as important as the content of the questions posed to the family. Specifically, interview probes should be a mixture of (a) asking direct questions to individual members concerning their thoughts and feelings, (b) using indirect approaches such as asking family members about how other members would respond to a question, and (c) suggesting hypotheses about a family member's behavior, to be commented on by another member. By asking one member to report on another member's thoughts and feelings, the clinician can circumvent the individual's defensive structure, which is often activated in direct questioning. Additionally, the clinician can gather information on two levels: (1) what the individual thinks and (2) what family members perceive that the individual thinks. Discrepancies may suggest difficulties in communication, empathy, or affective sharing among family members. This combined approach is usually referred to as "circular questioning" (Nelson, Fleuridas, & Rosenthal, 1986), and it offers an assessment of symptom understanding from a variety of perspectives. It is not just the family's explanation of the symptom that is important but how the family members related to the symptom among themselves. To uncover these processes, the clinician must move beyond the facts of the symptom to the feelings of the symptom and the interactions that the symptoms create within the family structure.

In identifying the problem areas, the clinician must assess a broad base of problem definition. Questions should center on (a) etiology and delineation of present symptomatology, (b) the crisis that precipitated the family's seeking of treatment at this time, and (c) comparisons with past behaviors. Some examples of specific questions within this frame include the following:

When were the problems first noticed?

Who was first to be concerned about the depression?

[turning to a sibling] How did your brother (sister's) symptoms affect you?

How has the depression affected the family? Specifically, what is different now than before you noticed that your adolescent was depressed?

Besides your adolescent, who do you think is the most upset about how things are going now?

While the goal of this stage in the assessment process is to understand the adolescent's depression within the family system, attention should also be paid to the degree of expressed symptomatology, as this supplies added information as to the depth of difficulties. Specifically, if the adolescent's depression is profound, or if suicidal ideation or gestures have been present, it is likely that dysfunctional patterns have been operative for some time. These extreme responses on the part of an adolescent are usually representative of families in which emotional expression has been consistently constrained and blocked, thereby preventing appropriate discharge and resolution of problem areas.

It is also important to assess the fluidity of the symptom. This is best uncovered through examination of the family's optimism versus pessimism that the problems eventually will be solved. Specifically, the clinician needs to determine whether the family can refocus from a problem to a solution orientation. If the transition can be made easily, the family demonstrates a capacity for accepting change (i.e., fluidity). Conversely, if the family resists the change in focus, a greater understanding of the importance of the symptom for the family's continued operation can be ascertained. The solution-oriented therapists (e.g., deShazer, 1985; deShazer, Berg, Lipchik, Nunnally, Molnar, Gingerich, & Weiner-Davis, 1986; Molnar & deShazer, 1987; Weiner-Davis, deShazer, & Gingerich, 1987) have developed an excellent group of questions for assessing the family's flexibility in entertaining a conceptualization of a future with the problems solved. Some examples of these questions (adapted from Weiner-Davis, 1987) include the following:

What will be the first sign that things are starting to change?

When things have been difficult in the past, how have you solved your family problems?

What would people in the family be involved with if there were no longer a problem with your adolescent being depressed?

When are the times that your adolescent looks happy or is able to do regular adolescent things?

If you went to bed tonight and a miracle happened, how would things be different in the family tomorrow?

Not only is it through these kinds of questions that the fluidity of the family structure is ascertained in terms of the importance of the symptoms, but these questions also allow the clinician an opportunity to explore the family's own resources for healing. This is possible because within the family's conceptualization of the problem, the family's mechanisms for solving the problems often are delineated. Although these mechanisms may not be in the family's conscious awareness, they are available for the clinician to store and utilize when the assessment process is completed.

Problem as Metaphor

If the manifested problems are to be eradicated, the analysis of the problem areas must be multidimensional on the level of the quality, the intensity, and the fluidity of the symptoms presented. However, the development, reactivity, and reverberations of the symptoms within the family context must also be assessed. Within this context, the function of the symptom as affecting and being affected by the interactions among family members must be uncovered. Madanes (1986) states that "in the first interview it is necessary to discover the metaphor expressed by the presenting problem and by the interaction around the presenting problem" (p. 184). Haley (1976) contends that in listening to the family's presentation of the symptoms of the identified adolescent, the clinician should be aware that these statements of apparent facts may also be verbalizations concerning other relationships within the family. For example, a mother berating her daughter for being withdrawn, uncommunicative, and isolated from the family may also be giving the clinician some indirect messages about her relationship with her husband (Haley, 1976).

Within the strategic family framework (e.g., Haley, 1976, 1980, 1984; Madanes, 1981, 1984, 1985, 1986) the adolescent's depressive symptomatology is metaphorical for other dysfunctional family patterns, most commonly for difficulties within the marital unit. The adolescent becomes symptomatic to protect other family members from experiencing stress connected to the initial problems. Madanes (1986) outlines the following sequences from this behavior: (1) with increasing severity of the symptomatic behavior, parents are forced to focus on the adolescent; (2) this newfound helpfulness distracts the parents from their initial conflict, and thus the adolescent's symptomatic behavior is continuously reinforced; (3) the adolescent becomes increasingly symptomatic in order to continue helping the parents; and (4) the adolescent's depressive behavior is viewed as helpless, yet the adolescent is in a powerful position with regard to regulating family functioning. When listening to a detailed account of the adolescent's depression, the clinician therefore must place the symptoms within the family context that perpetuates the problem behaviors.

Determining the metaphorical relationships inherent in the adolescent's depression is not an easy task, as the symptoms' very presence exemplifies the great lengths the family has to resort to in order to deny and avoid the underlying problem areas. Asking directly about potential metaphorical connections is often threatening and at times even impossible because the necessary dynamics are not often within the family's consciousness. Therefore, the clinician must use the presenting symptoms themselves as a mechanism for uncovering the more complicated interactions.

Haley (1976) suggests making general comments to the family when a family member's verbalizations about the problem behaviors seen also to define issues related to other individuals within the family. For example, in discussing Sue's isolated and withdrawn stance, the comment can be made, "You know, it seems that some families are made up of two groups—those who are approachers and those who are avoiders." This comment broadens the behaviors to possibly include other members. Often in reacting to these kind of statements, family members offer further direct and subtle information concerning metaphorical relationships. In this instance, in agreeing with this statement, Sue's mother nods her head and glances at her husband, thereby giving a clue to the clinician that Sue's mother does not feel supported in her efforts or is unsatisfied with her husband's lack of involvement. Assessing families within this framework involves questions regarding family members' relationships both to the symptomatic behavior and to each other in regard to the symptomatic behavior. For example,

> What happens between yourself and your husband when your son or daughter is most depressed?
>
> Who grows closer to whom? Who seems left out when you notice that your adolescent is in a crisis?
>
> Who handles stress most like your son or daughter?

It is important to note that the clinician must listen to the family's responses on two levels: (1) accepting these statements at face value, and (2) accepting them as indirect messages about other relationships within the family context.

Papp and Imber-Black (1989) discuss listening for an organizing theme presented by the family in order to help understand the role of the symptom. For example, a depressed adolescent daughter may be expressing her hopelessness, which may exemplify the nature of the marital relationship. Parents may feel stuck in a marriage that is characterized by the adolescent's sense of helplessness, anhedonia, and depression. In order to be of assistance in promoting change, clinicians at the interview stage should listen to common themes, especially those that offer help and a more positive frame for the symptoms. Specifically, a theme of helplessness may be reframed to offer the family steps toward independence.

PROBLEM ORGANIZATION AND STRUCTURE

Assessing the structure and organization of the family goes beyond the notion of the problem as metaphorical and it begins to uncover the family's dysfunctional patterns that may have contributed to the etiology of the depression within the adolescent. In moving from (a) defining the problem areas, to (b) viewing the problem as a metaphor, to (c) delineating the family structures and organization, the clinician not only listens to verbalized comments but also directly observes behavior. Clinicians cannot easily ask a family to define its structure and organization; thus, the clinician must be able to uncover subtle signs and indicators of family functioning. Within this context, these observations are generated by remaining on the periphery of the family subsystem as well as momentarily entering the system in order to probe and provoke (Fishman, 1988). Specifically, the clinician notes the family members' relationship and reactivity to themselves, as well as to an outsider. It is through this analysis that the family's particular style of organization and structure is more clearly defined.

Fishman (1983) defines organization as "rules that maintain its wholeness. Organization is ascertained [while] the family as a whole interacts with other subsystems" (p. 70). In relating to other systems, the family system reveals its organization. For example, family systems that are organized around fear and suspicion often interact with other systems in a distrustful and cautious manner, remaining more on the periphery than actually involving themselves with others unless they are forced to do so. When these families and their depressed adolescents are seen in the emergency room after their youngster has attempted suicide, they can be very suspicious of and opposed to hospitalization because it would require their more sustained involvement with the care providers. Within the initial assessment, the clinician should pay attention to the manner in which the family relates to her or him because the family members' relationships to the therapist may be a microcosm of their relatedness to the outside world.

For Fishman (1983), "*structure*, on the other hand, refers to the relationships [among] the components within the system, the internal workings. Structure is ascertained, in part, by intervening differentially with the different components" of the family (p. 70; italic emphasis added). The structural therapist's interview therefore involves observations of both the manner in which the family reacts to the interviewer and the manner in which the family members interact with each other. The interviewer is simultaneously outside the family system as well as a participant in assisting in the unfolding of the family dance.

Of central importance in the assessment of family structure are the notions of *boundaries* and *coalitions*. *Boundaries* refer to the degree to which there is access to, closeness among, and separateness between family members. In more normative families, there is a clear boundary between the marital unit and the children; however, the boundary is somewhat penetrable, allowing for communication and sharing between parental and child subsystems. In disengaged families, these boundaries are rigidly drawn and there is little interplay between subsystems. However, in enmeshed families, the boundaries are more ambiguous and undifferentiated. This often leads to inappropriate relationships between family members, usually referred to as "coalitions." The most common coalition involves a parent and a child sharing an inappropriate confidence. For instance, a female adolescent may be privy to her mother's marital problems. A depressed adolescent may be signaling that the boundaries within the family system are inappropriate and are blocking the adolescent's normative developmental course and growth.

Assessment of structure within a family often necessitates that the clinician has sharp skills of observation. Even as the family enters the room, the clinician should begin to make hypotheses concerning the family structure. The clinician should take note of how the family members seat themselves, who is quick to volunteer information, who is reticent, who generally interrupts whom and whose view of the symptom disqualifies or reinforces others' views.

The quality of the parental subsystem should be explored, and observations should be made concerning

1. On what issues do the parents agree?
2. On what issues do they disagree?
3. How are the parents' notions of the adolescent's depression similar or divergent?
4. Which child seems most aligned with which parent?
5. Do the parents support each other or undermine each others' authority?
6. Does there appear to be more warmth or hostility expressed between the couple during the interview?

Additionally, in terms of the child subsystem, observations should be made of the quality of the siblings' interactions. Competitive, unsupportive, or contentious relationships among siblings may be expressive of overall family dysfunction as well as metaphorical for the way the parents treat one another because children often mimic parental models of interaction. Similarly, the discord among the children may be expressive of the conflict and disagreements concerning the divergent conceptualizations of the symptom. It is interesting to observe which child reinforces or disqualifies which parent's position. Therefore, assessing the quality of demonstrated relationships among siblings may not only give the clinician a window into the metaphorical relationships, but also reveal issues of conflict, boundary confusion, and inappropriate alliances.

Awareness of the family structure and organization also emerges through direct observation of the environment created by family members in their interactions with each other and with the clinician within the interview room. In categorizing these areas that reveal underlying family relationships, Loarder, Burck, Kingston, and Bentovim (1982) describe levels of observation essential in assessing families. Three of these are especially pertinent to families with depressed adolescent members: evaluation of (1) the atmosphere, (2) communication, and (3) affective states that the family engenders within the interview.

Loarder et al. (1982) refer to the family atmosphere as including (a) the therapist's overall subjective reaction to the family (e.g., Is this a pleasant family to be with?), (b) the predominant affective mood that the family projects (e.g., Are family members depressed, isolated, apprehensive, or angry?), and (c) the emotional tone (e.g., Are they uncomfortable, ill at ease, and able to use humor in relating to each other?). The subjective reaction assesses the overall relationship between the family and the clinician and among individual family members. The clinician is both a part of the emotional environment and an observer. In other words, assessing the family atmosphere is based on the tenet that the family will construct a relationship with the clinician similar to the one it creates with others in their environment; therefore, the family brings into the interview a sample of its behavioral reactions to outsiders. Families with depressed adolescent members often create an atmosphere of constrained emotional expression. Additionally, there is often also a tremendous amount of blaming and a sense of hopelessness. Along with assessing the predominant atmosphere that the family projects, it is important to observe whether the atmosphere changes during the interview (e.g., Is a family initially bright and engaging but then later reticent and constrained when the adolescent's depression is addressed? Or are they initially revealing but later resistant when relationship issues are discussed?).

Loarder et al., (1982) maintain that making an assessment of the family's use or abuse of humor can be an important diagnostic instrument in determining the quality of the family atmosphere. The clinician needs to distinguish those families who use humor positively from those who ridicule family members under the guise of humor. Families with depressed adolescent members usually are so constrained in their affective expression that more positive displays of spontaneous humor are often absent. Therefore, families that are not able to laugh occasionally at themselves may further explicate for the clinician areas of difficulties and dysfunction. It is important to note that many of the familial interactions that contribute to the family atmosphere are subtle; thus, the clinician must listen with his or her third ear in order to be successful at conceptualizing the dominant emotional atmosphere maintained by the family.

The clinician also needs to make observations concerning the family's pattern of communication. Loarder et al. (1982) define communication as "directly observable verbal interchanges, paraverbal indicators (such as tone of voice), and nonverbal cues" (p. 153). The clinician must be sensitive to (a) the types of messages (both quality and quantity) that are passed among family members (e.g., Are they confusing or double binding messages? Are parents always making demands of their children with little acknowledgement of positive behaviors?), (b) the vocal intonation with which communications are delivered (e.g., Does the father only shout at the children?), and (c) if communications only include certain individuals to the exclusion of others (e.g., Do parents communicate directly to each other, or do they use the children to pass messages? Does one child know secret information that the others do not?).

An analysis must be made as to the degree of agreement between verbal messages and nonverbal behaviors (Loarder et al., 1982). For example, a mother who verbally tells her children to pay attention within the session but then engages in their distracting behaviors when her husband talks is not really communicating effectively and honestly. Yet these contrasting behaviors provide powerful information to the therapist concerning the degree to which the father is undermined. Or consider a family in which a parent verbally states that he does not want his daughter to kill herself, yet he expresses the statement without any emotion. The degree of congruence between the spoken and unspoken word and the emotion behind the words and the behaviors are especially important to observe in troubled families, because these families are frequently characterized by inconsistencies and double messages.

Assessing the emotional reactivity or lack of reactivity on the part of family members is another important component in assessing structure and organization of family functioning. Observations should be made regarding the level of the emotional interchanges among family members and the modes of communicating feelings (Loarder et al., 1982). Families often come to the attention of mental health professionals when there is an imbalance in the modulation of emotional experiences, both within and among family members. This is especially important in families that present depressed adolescent members because, by definition, these adolescents are having difficulties in adequately resolving their feelings of depression within the family context. In some families, the adolescent's depression can be in part metaphorical for a lack of affective sharing in the marital unit and also representative of the difficulties in expressing emotion within the family system as a whole. Within the interview setting, an adolescent who is more withholding in volunteering information can be in fact demonstrating the overall constraint and fear of emotions within the family.

The clinician needs to make an assessment as to the family's ability to deal with affective material from each of its members. Can family members communicate about their emotional experiences, or are symptoms used to avoid direct communication? The clinician should take notice of what happens within the family system when a family member openly cries or becomes angry in the interview. Additionally, it is important for the clinician to assess whether the family can communicate about negative feelings (e.g., anger, sadness, frustration, inadequacy) as well as positive emotions (e.g., love, happiness, pride) (Loarder et al., 1982). Assessment of affective communication is essential in terms of beginning to formulate an appropriate treatment strategy. For example, a family that has demonstrated little ability to communicate concerning emotional material would probably feel frustrated in a treatment modality that involves an uncovering process. This type of family may initially gain more success in a treatment program that aims at creating more overt behavioral change.

CONCLUSIONS

In making these observations of family atmosphere, of affective states, and of patterns of communication, the clinician begins to formulate an understanding of the family's strengths and its resources, as well as its areas of weakness and dysfunctions. These are the hypotheses and notions that must guide the clinician in mechanisms for joining and provoking the family subsystem within the initial assessment phase and that ultimately must assist the clinician in developing cogent plans for intervention. Assessment must come from clinician as observer as well as clinician as occasional participant in the family dance (Fishman, 1983, 1988). For example, within this context, the clinician can momentarily support the father's position in order to uncover further dynamics of the marital relationship. In observing how the mother reacts, the clinician can further refine his or her notions of the family functioning. Additionally, the clinician can make an outrageous statement or question directed toward both parents to view more clearly the underlying tensions and unconscious processes. For example, in asking parents, "Is it against the rules of the house for family members to kill themselves?" the reactions to this question often elicit more covert and subtle patterns of relating with regard to the meaning of suicidal ideation and behavior within the family context. When the clinician can observe support, and provoke the family, a more multifaceted conceptualization of symptom function within the context of the family structure and organization can be obtained.

Although many clinicians prefer the more free-flowing and less structured interview process, it is important to be active in the interview to the degree that important areas are explored and investigated. Therefore, each clinician has some underlying structure and organization for conducting an interview with a family, and it is more or less a myth that interviews with families are open-ended and undefined. Clinicians, however, do vary as to which external mechanisms they use for organizing their interviews of the families. There are a number of interview devices, but the construction of the family genogram, family sculpting, and family drawings are the most commonly used tools to augment the traditional family interview. These techniques offer a further delineation of family functioning, and some of them (family sculpting and drawings) allow for a more clearly articulated pattern of the family dance without the family fearing exposure. In essence, these techniques represent the communication between the family's third voice and the clinician's third ear. These techniques are detailed in the following chapter.

CHAPTER 5

Clinical Tools for Conducting Family Evaluations

Clinicians need to have at their disposal countless tools to help them emphasize important areas of family conflict and organization during evaluative sessions. This is especially true when clinicians are confronted with difficult-to-treat clients or those who are relatively nonverbal in their interactions. Various creative and visual, primarily nonverbal, techniques have been developed in the context of evaluating and establishing relationships with families who would ordinarily provide only limited information and access to their thoughts, secrets, and functioning.

These popular methods, such as genograms, sculpting, and drawings have evolved rapidly as adjuncts to aid the clinician in structuring family interviews, as well as in enhancing the communication and the social repertoire of all family members. Regardless of the clinician's philosophical or treatment perspectives these devices have become invaluable additions to the armamentarium of all clinicians who find themselves in the position of trying to intervene and have a positive impact on a family structure. Not only do these methods enhance family interaction and expression, but they also provide pleasure and heighten feelings of mastery and accomplishment in their users. Sometimes it is even the actual process of introducing these novel methods into the family evaluation session that brings about the amelioration of psychological distress.

These methods (a) facilitate spontaneity, (b) provide a platform for probing explorations in a safe and neutral setting, and (c) offer all family members some alternative and more adaptable modes of expression that may not have been readily apparent to them. These clinical tools also help the clinician and family to see clearly the areas of conflict that may be too threatening to discuss verbally in the initial sessions of therapy. They also lend themselves to the process of initiating hypotheses regarding the salient areas of concern. They provide the clinician with beginning themes that, when viewed within the broader scope of the existing information, can answer many of the referral questions and start the various aspects of treatment intervention.

Through the use of graphic and dramatic presentations, families can bring their problematic issues out into the open, confront them, and learn to gain control over them. These methods open the door to revelations and issues that are sometimes not available through any other approach to information gathering. The use of nonverbal techniques for exploring emotion-laden issues is especially beneficial to families with depressed teenagers who may find it easier to express their feelings through shared products or experiences. They also offer a safe outlet for the destructive or angry adolescent who may otherwise feel overwhelmed by the tone of the interview and who is afraid of losing control. Of course, the adolescent and family who are already creative in their self-expression have the basis for further enlightening exploration through these techniques.

It is during the initial sessions with the family and adolescent that techniques such as genograms, sculpting, and drawings can have an enormous advantage to the practitioner, as the behavior and expression of feelings may be excessively rigid, fragmented, or unfocused. Each method provides its own unique structure and facilitates selective information. Each offers concrete tools for establishing rapport and for building a bridge across which change can occur. Each also sends a message to the family members that they are responsible for establishing themselves in the therapeutic relationship and that they can use methods such as these for enhancing the understanding of their problems.

The following sections detail the historical development and practical use of genograms, sculpting, and drawings during family evaluations. Their use is advocated as a structured avenue through which to obtain information from the family that, for whatever reason, is not otherwise forthcoming. Because of the novelty of these methods, families may also be less resistant to disclosing any disturbing information. It is difficult to imagine any family that could not benefit from the introduction of these methods into an evaluative or therapeutic session.

THE FAMILY GENOGRAM

Several innovators of family therapy have focused their attention on relieving the pressure on the nuclear family by emphasizing the parents' families of origin in order to resolve old business (Boszyormenyi-Nagy & Framo, 1965; Boszyormenyi-Nagy & Spark, 1973; Bowen, 1966, 1972). This intergenerational approach enhances the relationships of the first two generations and thereby eliminates the vicarious use of the children to work through unfinished tensions or indebtedness. A particularly instrumental, as well as practical, method to help the clinician gather and understand the structure and history among generations is the family genogram (McGoldrick & Gerson, 1985).

Representing the family in the therapeutic process by constructing a genogram is simple and provides a basis for discussions about how the present family functions (Barnard & Corrales, 1979). Common patterns or significant events are viewed by the family to determine how specific behavioral patterns are manifested in present and past relationships. Some examples may include (a) the various boundary issues among generations, (b) important events that have not been resolved (e.g., incomplete mourning), and (c) how dyads or triads within the family have been maintained. To help facilitate these discussions, the clinician may ask about differing perceptions of relationships within the various family structures. During this process, important rules that have been governing the specific relationships may be clarified. These can take the form of rigidly stereotyped roles of the husband or wife (e.g., one or the other is totally responsible for disciplining the children) or the differential status provided to each of the children (e.g., the oldest male is given the most freedom).

During the process of developing the genogram in the evaluative session, the advocates of this method conceptualize four interpretive categories that represent present and past family organization and dynamics (McGoldrick & Gerson, 1985). These include

1. *Family Structure*, wherein the actual construction of the family genogram (or family tree) is completed, revealing such aspects as biological, marital, and adopted relationships; sibling position; and concrete markers of births, deaths, and divorces.
2. *Life-Cycle Fit*, which incorporates how the family has negotiated the significant events of their lives, including courtship, marriage, and birth of children and how the family has coped with each member's developmental stage (i.e., infancy, latency, adolescence).
3. *Pattern Repetition Across Generation*, which assesses the similarities across generational boundaries (e.g., positive family history for physical or mental illness, divorce rate, quality of same-sex and opposite-sex family relationships).
4. *Life Events and Family Functioning*, which includes information gathering on the influence of salient life events (e.g., births, deaths, relocation) and the anniversaries of those incidents on family functioning.

In focusing on these events defined by the foregoing categories, the evaluator can both gain access to the meaningful historical aspects of the family and solicit the family's perception of how these events have influenced the formation of the present family. This is precisely the context in which the adolescent's problems are occurring.

A particularly poignant use of the family genogram is to create a nonthreatening and maturationally appropriate atmosphere for children in the family to articulate and deal with some of the crucial intrapsychic, interpersonal, and behavioral consequences of family fragmentation that have occurred through death, divorce, or remarriage (Davis, Geikie, & Schamess, 1988). This method implicitly recognizes that some, if not all, members of the family have a strong need to understand both cognitively and emotionally what has happened to them, both as individuals and as part of a larger group (i.e., the core family). By instructing each family member to create a version of his or her family, a structure is provided to explore the present family situations and express heretofore unanswered questions without being overwhelmed by feelings of remorse or shame.

In both concrete and symbolic terms, the use of genograms in interviewing families who are going through restructuring helps the family members to visualize better the more complicated aspects of family relationships that they might otherwise not be able to conceptualize. The progressive elaboration of each member's genogram keeps the discussion of emotion-laden topics one step removed from actual family interaction, making the disclosures relatively safer and more emotionally comfortable. In establishing this format for the family, a gradual sharing of family information is likely to occur as each member responds to material presented by other family members. By focusing on one family member's genogram at a time, the examiner can increase or decrease the amount of time spent drawing or discussing the particular genogram, depending on the level of anxiety that is created. These imposed constraints both allow for an appreciation of the process of disclosing personal fears and concerns and facilitate the resolution of any turmoil concerning trust and self-revelation. The fantasies about the evolving family realignment can then be obtained more easily through the process of sharing the roots and progressions of the family organization.

The clinician may want to include the entire family in the development of a joint genogram in order to facilitate participating in activities together, or the clinician may have each family member construct his or her own personal view of important family relationships and events, to promote individual uniqueness. An alternative method is to have a few of the family members as observers to offer additional insights into the family of origin. For example, the clinician might ask one spouse to discuss the other's family instead of to participate in the actual genogram construction; in that way, the participating spouse may discuss issues that might otherwise be withheld in the construction, due to being too emotionally involved.

Regardless of its manner of implementation, the directions for constructing the genogram are relatively straightforward. The individual members or the family unit is instructed to represent each of the family members using squares and circles, symbolizing males and females respectively. First, the members of a single generation are drawn across the middle of the page. Firstborns are usually placed farthest to the left, with the remaining children placed in order of birth toward the right side of the page. Next, mothers and fathers of each participant are drawn, positioned above the existing generations. Then, vertical lines are extended upward about ½ inch from each symbolized person; later, these lines are connected by horizontal lines to symbolize the marriages within each generational segment.

From the middle generation, a line is then drawn vertically downward for each child of those marriages. At the end of each of these lines, a circle or square can be drawn, depending on the gender of the child. It is helpful at this point to place the name of each person inside (or beneath) the symbols, with their respective birthdates and locations of birth. If death has occurred, an *X* is placed over the symbol, with an accompanying date and reason, if those are known. If three or four generations are constructed, deaths are seen more frequently, but in any case, this visual representation becomes important in viewing lines of transmission, especially in families where genetically transmitted diseases are of concern. It also emphasizes the sense of belonging and begins a healing process through which extended families of origin are explored (Barnard & Corrales, 1979).

To facilitate this exploration process, the clinician may begin by directing the family to the significant events that have occurred through the generations. For instance, the focus of discussion can revolve around the births in the family and specifying the reasons surrounding the spacing between siblings. During this time, critical events such as stillbirths or miscarriages can be mentioned because they carry with them lingering and powerful effects on the history of the family. Other points of departure for discussion may include such family stressors as (a) relocations and the decisions surrounding the moves, (b) job changes and why they occurred, (c) major illness and its impact, or (d) lingering physical or mental health problems and how they may have affected the family functioning. Finally, daily decision-making events that importantly influence the family may also need to be discussed. These might include (a) decisions around babysitting or daycare, (b) the importance of religion in the family, (c) the decision for parents to return to school, or (d) the general expectations of each family member.

After the completion of the genogram, the clinician again emphasizes the rationale for its usage. Additional insights may be introduced at this time by any of the family members. After this structure has been exhausted and the many questions pursued, another more global question may be asked to stimulate intergenerational connectedness. The question, "What similarities do you see in these past generational relationships and your current marital relationships that we have not touched upon?" also allows for a summary of the session or sessions and aids the family in identifying goals and plans for future problem-solving strategies based on their newly discovered insights (Barnard & Corrales, 1979, p. 60).

As a method to obtain extended and significant information from the family during the interview process, the construction of the genogram adds much to the tools of the clinician. It is usually an enjoyable exercise for the family members and adds to the broader picture of the family, especially when it includes important others who may not have legal or kinship ties. When the genogram is used for a basis of discussion centering on matters of relational ties and events, it becomes an even more important instrument for understanding key dynamics within the family structure.

Case Example

The Burns family was involved in an emotionally draining marital separation when initially entering therapy. Both children, ages 15 and 12 years, were remaining with the mother, with visits to the father on alternating weekends and at intervals during the week. Although the separation was expected, the mother was very concerned about the ramifications it might have on the children. She made the early contacts with the therapist to focus on the adjustment problems of the children and on her own sense of loneliness and acceptance as a single person. The older child, Mitchell, appeared to be somewhat withdrawn, and he acknowledged much sadness about the sequence of the separation. He admitted to being shy but stated that he had begun to feel even more isolated from peers, and was having as much difficulty sleeping and eating as before the separation. The younger sibling, Mary, was more vocal, and was having more intense conflicts with the mother since the father had left the family. She was feeling partly responsible for the breakup and could not understand why the father had left. Although she was more engaging than her older brother, she also sensed that she was feeling more alienated from peers. She suggested that maybe she was being unduly hard on her mother but that she could no longer express her anger toward her father because she was fearful of seeing him even less often if she disobeyed him or disagreed with him.

In one of the initial sessions, the mother and children were asked to construct a genogram of their family. The directive was given not only to gather historical information, but also to emphasize to the children that they were still part of a family. This provided a strong message to them that they still belonged to a family unit even if their parents ultimately divorced. It also gave them a focus early in treatment that they could work together to find common ground and that there were other very important people in their lives on whom they could count for support. This message was not lost on the children as they involved themselves readily in the task and were able to more freely ask many questions about the family structure. By using this clinical tool early in the sessions, the family gained a better understanding of how the treatment could help them through their time of crisis.

The genogram that was constructed portrayed the mother's side of the family as beset by marital disharmony. Her parents and her siblings had all been through the experience of divorce. By providing this information in a nonverbal manner, it was easier for her then to talk about the broken relationships in her family by focusing on the genogram. In contrast to the mother's family, this was the first broken marriage in the father's family. Because this was the first broken marriage in the father's family, his divorce apparently had been creating much friction between him and his childhood family. In fact, his family seemed much more aligned with the mother, as she was highly interpersonally oriented. Also, they knew her well, as the couple had been married for 18 years. For the children, the experience of seeing all their extended relatives on a sheet of paper gave them a sense of comfort, knowing that they still had many people involved in their lives and that somehow they were still a part of a family unit.

FAMILY SCULPTURE

A much more action-oriented method for seeing family interrelationships as they have developed in the perceptions of each family member is termed "family sculpting" (Constantine, 1978; Duhl, Kantor, & Duhl, 1973). This technique, along with its variations, is among the best-known and widely used of the structured family therapy tools that involve image and metaphor. With its background based in psychodrama (Moreno, 1946), although with fewer words and more involvement with interactive patterns, sculpting provides the basis for exploring the main persons who give meaning to the lives of each family member and to his or her own interpersonal relationships in a highly visible manner. Through metaphorical idioms, sculpting allows each family member to express his or her personal view of the family structure and of how this structure is enacted on a daily basis. For instance, instructing the family to choose the member with the most or least authority and to enact this role through such actions as standing above or cowering below the others allows the family to create an emotion-laden portrait that can be used for considerable discussion within the remainder of the session.

Sculpting (or as some have termed it, "spatialization" provides a vehicle for the family to organize, define, and express what is often verbally inexpressible (Kantor & Lehr, 1975). For the clinician and the family, it is like being actors in improvisational theater with different family members giving immediate feedback. Subjective feelings about the family's living conditions can be answered from within the evocative format. For example, the family members who feel that they are walking on eggshells so as not to provoke anyone can share the tense atmosphere or emotionally draining experience. Each member of the family, regardless of age, can easily be cast in these roles that they know so well, but heretofore have been reluctant to express. With each sculpting experience, new insights are provided to the family members about themselves as individuals and about the context that they have created for themselves.

There is an endless variety of possible sculpting exercises to use in a family interview in order to break down resistances and to promote a foundation for future therapeutic intervention. These include several aspects of spatialization (e.g., linear, matrix, polar, and regional sculptures), in addition to several more elaborate forms of family sculpting (Constantine, 1986). In spatialization, the physical dimension of space is used simply to represent some portion of the family process. An example would be placing the family member who has been emotionally aloof physically apart from the remaining members. In these instances, it becomes important for the clinician to demarcate carefully the physical space through the use of chalk, string, or other materials, to clarify boundaries and clearly explain the analogies and metaphors. In performing these exercises, it is helpful to provide labels that represent specific positions or objects; these labels help both to reduce forgetfulness and confusion, and to place the individual family members without talking. Thus, labels help to eliminate arguments or attempts at negotiation. Sometimes it is also desirable to allow the family members to experiment with different positions and movements until everyone is satisfied that the context is correct.

As the family members are positioning themselves, it is helpful for the clinician to begin discussing the feelings that are being elicited. Various associated remarks may be produced, such as "It feels safe (or uncomfortable)," or the clinician may want to ascertain the different ways from "up top or down below." Repeating the directives from different family contexts can also be enlightening to the family that is facing future adjustments. For instance, the clinician may want to have the family resculpt their relationships as the family either would like to be or would see themselves once Johnny leaves home for college.

Linear Sculptures

A linear, or one-dimensional sculpture, usually takes the form of placing a marker (i.e., a line) that represents a family trait and having the members place themselves along the dimension to represent, for instance, how easily annoyed each member gets or how jealous each is. These traits are different for each family and usually emerge early in the initial interview. Other sculpting examples may highlight the differences between each family member's eagerness to please or his or her closeness in a shared family value. The advantages to showing a family its relevant concerns, in addition to related verbal discussions, is manyfold and makes the critical points of the session more impactive and emotionally involving. Its novelty also has the possibility of inviting fresh insights, and the overall picture can more easily be recalled in later sessions.

The process of inviting the family into forming a linear sculpture has its greatest use in exploring the family power structure. In using the "Power Line," one end of the line represents "being so powerful in this family that everything comes out just the way you want it to" with the opposite end implying "being so powerless in this family that nothing ever comes out the way you want it to" (Constantine, 1986, p. 220). Like other sculpture variations, this technique can be repeated several times, with each family member positioning the others. During this process, the least powerful member has the advantage of contributing his or her own impressions as emphatically as the most powerful member. The clinician can then explore during the remainder of the interview how each person feels about his or her position in relation to the dimension of power.

A particularly salient way to dramatize the emotional closeness within a family is to sculpt the family, using distance as the mediator. This resulting polar sculpture vividly demonstrates to the family how each member identifies with the other. For example, the clinician may want the family to represent how close each feels to an absent figure, such as a deceased relative. Another avenue to explore using this method is to represent different pressures within the family and position each member as to the approximate relationship to that particular everyday stressor (e.g., jobs, chores).

Two-Dimensional Sculptures

A modification of the linear technique, termed a "matrix sculpture," makes use of two dimensions that interact. Its main use is with more sophisticated families to emphasize more than one issue that has a causal relationship. Examples of these dimensions may be hopeful–pessimistic vs. achieving–failing.

In order to use effectively the physical space of the office, a clinician using sculpting as a therapeutic tool during an interview may designate certain areas of the room to represent certain developmental transmissions of the family or specific time periods. This "life space" method makes vivid the key moments in the family's organization that all or part have shared. For instance, a portrayal of a time before the children were born would demonstrate how the family evolved, as well as enhance the boundaries around the parents. From a historical perspective, it allows much detailed and emotional information to be brought forth that might have been overlooked through regular means of history taking.

Three-Dimensional Sculptures

Family sculpting is actually an elaborate form of spatialization (Constantine, 1986). In this three-dimensional representation, body movements and gestures are included with objects to create a global picture of the family dynamics. Typically, one member of the family performs the sculpting, with the clinician acting as facilitator. This allows for each member to express his or her own unique perspective of how the family functions on a daily basis. These techniques may vary in their focus, length, and specificity.

Whereas a comprehensive family sculpture may take up an entire session, minisculptures or abbreviated versions are normally used in the evaluation process. In very rapid sequences, family members can demonstrate effectively how they perceive themselves in relationship to each other. This array of sculptures can pinpoint quickly the conflicts, tensions, and alliances within a family. A structured approach to this task, developed by Kantor, involves using physical proximity to represent emotional closeness, vertical positioning to imply power, and bodily expression and gesture to identify other characteristics of the family. Other variations have used standardized postures or movements to symbolize the different positions in the family. Satir (1972) has incorporated four defended styles of communication (i.e., placating, distracting, blaming, computing) in her work with family sculpture, while Karpman (1968) has developed a family drama of persecutor, victim, rescuer, and audience. Another possible way for the clinician to introduce sculpting to the family in a less threatening manner is to use pieces of a broad game (e.g., chess) to represent the various members. A more systematic approach, the Kvebaek family sculpture technique, has been developed; it offers the use of small figurines and a 10"- by 10"-board (Cromwell, Fournier, & Kvebaek, 1980).

The use of sculpting within a family assessment, in addition to gaining a large amount of information in a very short time period, allows the clinician to refer to the resulting sculpture in a metaphorical way to provide valuable feedback to the family. An advantage to this approach is that it introduces the concept that the family members will be an integral part in the interpretation and understanding of their problems.

This contrasts with a summary that the clinician may provide, which can seem stilted and general and not directly applicable to the family's frame of reference. Also, by placing the family in a novel situation, the activity surrounding the sculpture often breaks through any intellectualization or resistance and is understandable on many levels by all age groups. The experience itself and the following feedback can often induce positive changes in the family structure as they face each other's reality in a friendly and supportive atmosphere.

Case Example

The Bridgewaters (fictitious name) were a blended family, with both parents bringing children into the present union. The family entered therapy shortly after their marriage. This was the mother's fourth marriage, the father's second. Brenda, age 14, was the mother's only daughter. She had a long history of emotional and behavioral problems associated with her mother's marriages. She was against the present marriage and was starting to act out her concerns through running away, poor school performance, and violent arguments in the home, where the incidents were becoming frequent and destructive. Not only were the parents concerned about Brenda, but they were also worried about the safety of the father's two sons, ages 4 and 2. Brenda's school had also given notice that they would soon be meeting to discuss whether to send her to a special school that would provide more structure and individual attention.

Because Brenda would immediately sabotage most attempts at family therapy sessions, it was decided that maybe her conflicts could be enacted through sculpting the situation as she viewed it. This gave her an opportunity to display openly her opinion of the family problems, as well as to give the parents and the therapist a reprieve from her outbursts. The therapist requested that the parents and Brenda (the boys were not involved in this session) demonstrate how each perceived how much power the others had in this new family. Brenda was amazed that both parents placed her in the central, more powerful position! In fact, when she was in charge of the sculpture, she placed herself in a corner tangentially aligned with her mother and cowering before the new stepfather. She had no idea that her behavior caused her to become the focus of attention. After this experience, Brenda became more willing to reveal her inner fears about becoming attached to this new parental figure and the equally upsetting thought of possibly being rejected by him again. The safe outlet of this and subsequent sculptures gave her an opportunity to express to her mother how much her mother meant to her and accorded Brenda a platform to explore with her mother and stepfather how the new family could become better aligned.

UTILIZING DRAWINGS IN FAMILY EVALUATIONS

The use of drawings has evolved rapidly as a clinical tool in the diagnosis and treatment of individuals and families (Oster & Gould, 1987). Because of their brevity, their nonthreatening nature, their ease of administration, and their vast interpretive product, drawings seem ideally suited to withdrawn and socially isolated youngsters; they also readily enhance the communication among family members who are stifled within their organizational context. Drawings can also become concrete markers of therapeutic goals and accomplishments and they have the ability to become vehicles for expression of fears or frustrations and wish fulfillments.

The use of drawings in family evaluative sessions can assist the clinician in exploring the complex dynamics between parents and children. Drawings offer the different family members the opportunity to portray pictorially their unique view of the family subunits (e.g., dyads and triads, dominant and passive members). By providing this alternative way of observing family interactions, the clinician can gain access to freer expression of emotion than more traditional methods of interviewing allow. When directives for drawing are presented to the family, they provide a neutral experience that is beyond the everyday experience of most family members. Several reasons why a clinician might want to choose this approach as an ancillary way to conduct an evaluation include (1) disrupting what seems to be maladaptive forms of family communication; (2) making therapeutic goals come to life in a concrete manner, in order to plan future intervention; (3) promoting specific familial relationships through joint drawing activities; and (4) exploring those relationships that may be inhibiting others in the family (Rubin, 1978).

It becomes easier to encourage participation of all family members when the focus of discussion is on a shared product (i.e., the drawings). This is especially relevant either to the identified patient, who may want to divert attention away from him- or herself or to reticent participants who may be reluctant to share personal information during an evaluative session. During both the execution of the drawing and the ensuing discussion, the clinician can gain many working hypotheses through observing the verbal and nonverbal forms of behavior and interactions. The form of the product, and each member's description or association can provide a wealth of information to generate points of entry into the family's preexisting strategies. For instance: Is one parent actually portraying or talking about his or her spouse when the drawing and discussion are supposedly focused on a child's problem?

The clinician directing the family portraits usually keeps a low profile by accepting all attempts in a supportive, nonjudgmental manner (Kwiatkowska, 1978). Although this sometimes differs in style or approach from family treatment, the main focus is to encourage spontaneous discussion and to facilitate discussion of the drawings with each family member. The clinician will sometimes become a role model to increase communication by asking certain leading questions about the drawings or about the process of their construction. These may include "What emotions were experienced during the drawing?" "Which family member worked hardest at the task?" "Were there similarities in the way that you worked on the drawing that also occur at home?" These key questions can also provide insight into family functioning and make the family members more aware of their own behavior.

The dynamics of a particular family are revealed through such aspects of the drawings as their content, quantity, placement, symbols, and process of construction (Rubin, 1978). Features of the family are observed by noticing the following: Who in the family takes the initiative in leading, and who follows? Who is resistant to participation? Who is assertive? And so on. For example, a depressed or isolated member of the family may prefer to work on a joint drawing alone or to construct his or her contribution off to one side. The usual scapegoat of the family will likely be blamed somehow if there is dissatisfaction with the picture. Alliances among the family members may typically be found working in close proximity to one another; or conflicts may appear when one member consistently crosses through the drawing of another.

When working with a problem-solving approach to family therapy, drawings can be used to disrupt the usual patterns of communication by directing the family away from the normal roles of participation; for instance, positioning an uninvolved father as the leader of a joint drawing. In this way, the clinician can aid the family to experiment in novel roles in a neutral setting to discover more functional methods of family equilibrium. Drawings can also maintain the balance once this change has been established (Landgarten, 1981).

Noted art therapists have established several formats to use when incorporating drawings into family evaluations. Because the possible family reactions and situations are multitudinous, the clinician using these approaches will probably need to modify them according to therapeutic style and setting. However, the entire sequence of drawing directives, or portions thereof, do provide a structured approach for planning family sessions and interacting with various family members.

Kwiatowska, a pioneer in introducing drawings into family evaluation segments, provides a structured format wherein the family is asked to complete six different drawings (Kwiatkowska, 1978):

1. Her method begins by instructing each family member to begin with a "free picture" of whatever comes to mind. This drawing directive usually allows the family member an opportunity to introduce or describe him- or herself or to disclose key features of a family problem.
2. The next, more directed drawing instructs members to portray their view of the entire family, including themselves. Typically, these drawings will produce differences in perceived family hierarchy (e.g., certain members portraying themselves or others as more important) or differences in family alignment (e.g., some members include only the nuclear family, while others choose to include close relatives).
3. The third requested drawing is an abstracted family portrait. This allows the evaluator to judge to what degree the family can see beyond the obvious. The clinician will usually introduce this aspect of the evaluation by directing each member to represent the family through shapes, lines, or colors. Striking examples can result as the family is introduced to something out of the ordinary.
4. The fourth and fifth drawings are completed through scribbles on the paper. The family is first asked to partake in arm exercises in which their sweeping motions are then transferred onto the paper. The resulting scribbles can then be made into pictures based on each member's own projections or associations.
5. After these drawings are completed, the family is then instructed to construct another scribble and to choose one to do together. This gives the evaluator the opportunity to observe the dynamics of the family decision-making process.
6. Another free drawing is chosen for the conclusion, to promote freedom of expression and relaxation from tension.

Another possible framework in which to engage families in evaluations involves only three major drawing tasks. Rubin (1978) begins by instructing each family member to complete a continuous-line scribble. When this is finished, the individuals are asked if they can see anything in the drawing and to elaborate on what is seen. Each member is then asked to title the scribble and to exchange it with other family members for comments. Another drawing directive is then introduced, in which all members are asked to portray the family in either a realistic or an abstract form. This drawing is again exchanged among all family members. In this more collaborative method of evaluation, the family is asked finally to construct a joint mural on a large sheet of paper taped to the wall. This again presents the evaluator with an excellent opportunity to observe family interactional patterns.

Although the foregoing formats are based on psychodynamic interpretation, another more recent approach to family evaluations is better understood through a family-systems perspective (Landgarten, 1981). The focus of this method is on how family members have an impact on one another. The emphasis on the entire family, as opposed to the identified patient, allows the clinician to observe how family coalitions are developed and maintained. Through a series of problem-solving drawing directives, healthy and unhealthy aspects of the family soon emerge.

Initially, Landgarten asks each member in the family to draw his or her initials as large as possible and to discover a picture in them, which is then elaborated upon. Each family member is then asked to title the picture and share the final product. The only other drawing permits the family to work together on a single piece of paper. In this drawing, none of the members is allowed to talk to one another so that the clinician can gather more material on nonverbal interactions and the family can freely enhance its expression of emotion. Each member is also asked to use different colored markers, to make identification and individual contributions easier. In this format, if there is a large family being evaluated, the members can be divided into teams to draw separate pictures or to draw a series of pictures with different members of the family. Much can then be observed through the composition of the different working segments of the family.

An additional model of utilizing drawings as a vehicle in family evaluations has been proposed by Sobel (1982). Her method attempts to integrate a strategic framework with specific drawing directives in order to elicit family hierarchies and alliances. Her work introduces Haley's (1963) concept of metaphor as the basis for family communication. Because art by its nature is metaphorical, the family can often represent its problems in a more accurate and less threatening way by using drawings instead of words or actions. The information obtained through the drawing tasks can then be used to establish goals and treatment plans for the family.

In this method, the evaluator, in attempting to produce metaphorical information, is likely to actively interpret a family member's drawing. For example, the evaluator may make a point that one drawing represents dominance and address that person with greater respect. Another approach is to determine the passive family member and encourage that member to become more active in his or her participation. Another way the evaluator is likely to intervene is through interactional sequences or disrupting of coalitions. For instance, the evaluator may choose to instruct the parents to complete a drawing without interruption from the children. A final example of this method allows the evaluator to aid a particular family member in expressing him- or herself. Sometimes, one of the family members is frustrated in his or her attempts to be heard and can be given ample time to communicate to the others by using this method. Some drawing directives that can be used within this framework include "Do a drawing to represent why you think you are here," or "Do a drawing to represent the problem." To help clarify the family's goals for treatment, directives are introduced, such as asking the members to construct individual drawings that represent how each would like to see the problems change. Another possible drawing directive to delineate family roles or alliances is to ask each member to "draw how you see the family" (Oster & Gould, 1987, p. 132).

Case Example

Karen W., age 15, was admitted into a long-term treatment setting after spending several months in the adolescent unit of a private psychiatric hospital. Her presenting problems on initial admission to the hospital included a pervasive depressed mood of approximately 3 years' duration, suicidal ideation, poor behavioral controls, and alcohol abuse. Her earlier history included chronic enuresis. Intellectual testing reported average to high-average functioning, with a pattern of variability consistent with a specific learning disability. Particular areas of cognitive difficulty included visual–spatial functions, sequential processing, and memory.

Karen was the only child of her adoptive parents. There was no documented history of physical or emotional problems by the birth mother. The adoptive mother, though, was the victim of early, intense, and continued physical and verbal abuse by her father. She was cautious about disclosing information to therapists, as she feared that she would be scapegoated for her daughter's problems. The adoptive father was the only child born in a first-generation European-American family. By his own admission, he suffered from expressive language problems and experienced intense anxiety in novel situations. When dealing with the emotional distress of the family, he would routinely withdraw into his work or hobbies and leave much of the turmoil between the mother and daughter.

During one early, very poignant session where the father was out of town on business and the mother came in for the regularly scheduled session, arrangements were made for the mother and daughter to complete an evaluation of their relationship through the use of drawing directives. At the time, the daughter had been constructing an emotional wall between herself and the mother, and it was believed that by introducing this novel experience, the two of them would be able at least to attempt to view each other in a different and perhaps more positive manner.

One of the first directives was for the mother and the daughter to draw a family

Figure 5.1 The mother's view of the family dynamics.

portrait. While the daughter's was somewhat nondescript, the mother found through this vehicle the opportunity to express much of her distress and frustration. By constructing the picture on page 78 (Figure 5.1) she was able to show both her daughter and the therapist her view of the family dynamics and the immediate problems.

The picture demonstrated to her and to Karen the lack of communication and isolation that each family member experienced. In trying to talk about it, the mother became tearful, but she was willing to pursue her concerns and wishes for the family to find a common ground. By making her concerns visible in a way that was less threatening, Karen was able to see that her mother wanted the same thing for the family that she so desired but was afraid to verbalize. This picture effectively broke the barrier that was being established between mother and daughter and strengthened their bond. Thereafter, they were able to share the experience with the father and to enhance their communication in a more effective manner.

CHAPTER 6

Assessing the Depressed Adolescent

Case 1

An 18-year-old girl was brought into a local mental health clinic by her father due to mood and physical changes that she was experiencing related to her imminent graduation and plans to leave for college. She had experienced both changes in her appetite and significant weight loss (25 pounds over a 3-month period), as well as sleep disturbances and lapses in concentration. She felt anxious, she had been irritable toward her father and brothers, and her schoolwork had declined significantly. She had been going to parties on weekends, but she would usually become intoxicated and would leave the party early. Her mother had died from a chronic illness several years previously, and her father was considering remarriage. She could not see herself leaving home at this time and becoming independent from her family. She experienced the burden of these conflicts and felt saddened and helpless because of them. She stated that she had started having suicidal thoughts and had made her family aware of them. This upset them tremendously, and they solicited professional help. After a family interview, she was seen alone, to assess the extent of her depression and the lethality of her suicidal thoughts.

Case 2

A 13-year-old boy was referred for psychotherapy by both the local fire department and his probation intake officer after he allegedly set fire to a cemetery. Although fearful and denying the accusation, he was able to admit that he was saddened by his parents' frequent arguments and recent talk of divorce. His preoccupation with this matter had negatively affected his athletic and academic performance. He had not talked to anyone about his feelings and admitted that he had stayed up many nights worrying about his parents and about his future. His relationships with others, he admitted, were becoming strained, and he felt alone. He seemed relieved to have someone to talk to about these matters. In order to understand fully the extent of his problems and to supply information to the referral source, psychological testing and a report were requested, specifying the degree of his emotional disturbance and treatment alternatives. As part of a comprehensive evaluation, he was given several self-report inventories to determine his areas of conflict.

Case 3

Clarence W., age 17, was referred for psychological testing after having entered an inpatient unit due to his disruptive behaviors at home, his school refusal, and his isolation from peers. When seen for an interview, he was overweight and emotionally constricted. He seemed hungry for attention, listened intently to the interviewer, and appeared to yearn for help and understanding. He readily admitted to having conflicts with his family, especially in his relationship to his father. He stated that he had been missing a lot of school due to a pattern of getting into arguments with his family, then retreating to his room for days at a time. The other family members, it seemed, felt helpless in their attempts to intervene on these occasions. He appeared to be experiencing great distress over his actions, and his attempts at breaking this cycle and his explanations for his conflicts seemed to depict a much younger child. He also related that he had few friends and rarely made attempts at dating. His interests were limited to solitary activities, although they were very sophisticated (computer programming and stock market trading). Psychological testing described him as shy, inhibited, and lacking in social skills. He appeared conflicted in terms of emotional dependency. This was seen especially in his continual battles between himself and his parents and in his inability to resolve this tension. As a result, he became immobilized and withdrawn from his primary responsibilities—mainly those at school. This further left him feeling anxious and alone, and it impaired any of his attempts at making effective interpersonal adjustments. He tended to internalize his anger and generally experienced sad feelings. To combat these feelings, he seemed to use projection, rationalization, and intellectualization as his primary defenses. Recommendations were made for family therapy and for social skills training.

As the preceding cases illustrate, referrals for assessing the degree and nature of adolescent disturbance are varied and unique. Adolescents are part of a larger context (e.g., family, peers, school, community), and it becomes important to review the context of the presenting problems, as well as the adolescents' abilities to cope with their present situations. Underlying these referrals is the need for additional information that will clarify diagnostic and treatment decisions. This is particularly true in educational and juvenile justice decisions where placement decisions are made based on the youth's disturbance, the family's ability to handle the presenting problems, and the youth's and family's capacity and willingness for therapeutic intervention. It then becomes imperative for the clinician, after a referral has been made, to clarify with the referral source(s) the reasons for the referral and the expectations for the treatment (Oster, Caro, Eagen, & Lillo, 1988). This clarification is crucial because it is often common in clinical practice to receive a referral with a vague presenting picture and to have little knowledge pertaining to the involvement of others. For instance, the 13-year-old boy in the preceding example, although referred by the fire department, did not mention his own prior altercations with the law or the court order indicating that he must be involved in treatment In this case, the parent also failed to mention these facts!

Another essential aspect to consider is whether the requested referral is for an evaluation or treatment or both. Many times, the clinician's assessment is just one segment of a broader evaluation that includes multiple tests, especially when there are physical complications. It is possible that the clinician may not see the adolescent again after the assessment has been completed, as the referral source may have already established a primary therapist when treatment is needed or desired. This is mainly true in psychiatric hospitals where, for instance, a psychiatrist may be ordering psychological tests or psychological histories to help clarify the diagnosis, as well as to perform the individual psychotherapy for the youngster. In the educational system, the referral may stem from the child's disruptive behavior in the classroom, but the primary reason for the referral is to abide by Public Law 94-142 in determining the level or degree of special educational services (Gabel, Oster, & Butnik, 1986).

In most cases, the requested referral is not an isolated event and most likely will have come after a long sequence of actions. It is necessary for the clinician to obtain details of all the precipitants, as well as to detail the other sources of conflict within the youth's contextual network. Discussions with these individuals are well worth the time involved, and they are valuable in coordinating efforts for treatment intervention. As the previous chapters detailed, this is especially pertinent when comprehensive family interviews have been completed so that the clinician can compare and interpret the results of the evaluation within the context of the adolescent's history and present living arrangements. Limiting the assessment process to individual interviews or psychological testing only provides a small sample of behavior. Adding these other components contributes significantly to a more integrated conceptualization of the adolescent's overall functioning.

The primary goal of the assessment process is to delineate clearly the strengths and weaknesses of the individual and of the context where the problem areas are being expressed in order to determine effective intervention strategies and to enhance increased behavioral and emotional functioning. The clinician must be skilled and comfortable in interviewing adolescents and must have a broad understanding of the developmental manifestations of the problems. This is especially important when confronting depressed teenagers who may generate negative and frustrating responses from clinicians by their sad moods, lack of interest, oppositionality, and sometimes open hostility (Gotlib & Colby, 1987). It becomes important for clinicians who are initially seeing depressed adolescents to examine closely their own personal reactions to avoid displays of impatience or irritability that may be similar to the usual adult reactions to depressive symptoms. Also, during the conducting of interviews, nonverbal aspects of behavior (e.g., quality and rate of speech, body movements, and posture) are equally important to the verbal content because depressed youngsters are extremely sensitive to perceived nuances of rejection or irritation.

It is also essential for the clinician to stay abreast of the many advances in diagnostic revisions, psychometric tests, and computerized assessments. During the past 10 to 15 years, in line with the renewed interest in describing childhood mood disorders, numerous questionnaires and interview formats have been developed that focus on depressed features of people prior to adulthood (Barkley, 1988; Edelbrock & Costello, 1988). These have included formalized interviews, such as (a) the Schedule for Affective Disorders and Schizophrenia for School-Aged Children, (Kiddie-SADS; Puig-Antich & Chambers, 1978) and the Diagnostic Interview Schedule for Children (DISC), developed by the National Institute of Mental Health (NIMH); (b) child behavior rating scales and checklists (e.g., the Personality Inventory for Children—Wirt, Lachar, Klinedinst, & Seat, 1977); and (c) family assessment methods that measure three levels of family influence (i.e., the individual, dyadic relationships, and the entire family) (Jacob & Tennenbaum, 1988). Clinicians involved in psychological assessment or in providing diagnoses also make judgments from various indicators on standardized tests, such as the Rorschach, the Thematic Appreciation Test (TAT), and assorted subscales of personality inventories (e.g., Minnesota Multiphasic Personality Inventory—Depression subscale, MMPI—D) that focus on depressive symptoms.

Although these instruments attempt to incorporate the many signs of depression, they cannot stand alone in identifying a specific disorder. Rather, multiple methods of measurement are required to provide accurate accounts of current functioning, as no individual form is likely to be totally correct or comprehensive (Achenbach, 1988). They must take into account the varying changes in an adolescent's biological, cognitive, social–emotional, and educational development, in addition to the multiple contexts of home, school, and clinical setting. It is incumbent on clinicians to become familiar with these devices in order to accurately diagnose and to treat the problems that are being presented to them.

The remainder of this chapter reviews the general procedures for eliciting relevant information from teenagers and provides a survey of the usual structured and semi-structured interviews used when collecting information about current functioning. In addition, a review of representative self-report instruments used to assess depressive symptoms from adolescents are offered.

GENERAL INTERVIEWING GUIDELINES[1]

Providing Rapport and Structure

Because adolescents are usually referred to mental health professionals due to someone else's distress over their behavior or mood, the adolescents' willingness to be interviewed varies widely. Also, whereas adults generally have had experience in a variety of interview formats, many adolescents have not had such exposure and may be puzzled in terms of what to expect or what is appropriate for them in this novel one-to-one situation. Thus, the clinician should be sensitive to the adolescent's informational needs and should provide enough information about the interview process to ensure a comfortable setting for the adolescent. In this way, the clinician can maximize the amount of information gained for diagnostic and treatment planning.

Also, to reduce the probable misconceptions and initial nervousness or resistance, the clinician must be very active in providing structure during the beginning moments of the interview. This is particularly true when confronting depressed individuals who are likely to be passive and lacking in spontaneity. If the clinician waits for the adolescent to lead, the unintended result may be to compound the adolescent's feelings of inadequacy and distress. Some methods for making the atmosphere less tense and more amenable include (1) being on time, which has the effect of reducing anxiety and overcoming the potential for any additional expressions of anger, (2) taking command of the introductions, leading the adolescent to the office and directing the adolescent to a chair, (3) exchanging social amenities (e.g., how to address each other), and (4) providing a brief description of the interview process, including approximately how long it will take and what is already known about the adolescent (Weins & Matarazzo, 1983). Adolescents, especially in clinical situations, are somewhat suspicious of the motives of the adults around them; thus, providing some education regarding expectations in a clear and straightforward manner has the advantage of de-escalating unnecessary anxiety and promoting a trusting and disclosing atmosphere.

Facing Hard-to-Reach Youngsters

Although the aforementioned methods are usually effective in allowing adolescents to begin exploring problem areas and reasons for their distress, on more than one occasion, the clinician is likely to be confronted with difficult moments in dealing with shy, withdrawn, or highly irritated individuals. For example, unduly

[1]Adapted from Diagnostic Interviewing of Adolescents, Oster et al., 1988, *Assessing Adolescents*.

reticent or depressed youngsters may be fearful of the interview process and may fail to elaborate on their problems even after the clinician has established a comfortable working format. In this situation, the clinician may have to be more directive in asking questions concerning daily functioning in order to increase the opportunity for these youths to be more spontaneous in providing personal information. As the give-and-take exchanges progress, the clinician can then begin to question in greater depth the thoughts and feelings being expressed.

When the clinician is confronted with angry and sometimes hostile adolescents, different strategies may be required. These are the youngsters who have often been brought to the interview under intense pressure and who have a history of being defensive and bitter in their interactions with adults. Their style of interacting is generally to project their anger onto external objects, and through their belligerence and their frequent destructive actions, they have alienated many a person before being brought into the clinical situation. Thus, they are likely to view the clinician and the interview as an extension of a threatening environment and initially offer very little of themselves in the way of compliance or self-disclosure.

Several strategies can assist the clinician in this potentially explosive or unproductive situation. Keeping an open mind to what these adolescents say instead of expecting the worst based on prior knowledge about their attitude may promote a more secure atmosphere. It is often the case that these youngsters are willing to talk openly in different environments other than the situations they have typically encountered. For instance, the anger that may be occurring at home or at school may not be expressed in a novel situation. Some adolescents may even try to create a split between what they think has been told to the clinician about their situation and what they could actually be like outside of their perceived aversive environment. Regardless, if clinicians expect hostility, they may unknowingly create a similar interpersonal context that increases the teenager's anxiety and creates a self-fulfilling prophecy. Finally, it is often the case that these adolescents have used their defensive or aggressive styles to protect themselves from perceived threats and to gain control over their emotions. They do so even though this is not their preferred way of interacting but is one that has developed out of problems they have experienced in dealing with their daily stressors. Clinicians who provide explanations to these adolescents that proper behavior is expected can undercut the adolescents' need to act out fears and can provide an opportunity to experience and rehearse more adaptive interpersonal behaviors.

Engaging Extreme Belligerence and Hostility

At times, even an open mind cannot overcome the resistance of an extremely angry adolescent. During these times when the adolescent is denying any and all problems and is refusing to offer much personal information, it becomes important to begin the interview by soliciting the adolescent's view of the concerns of the parents or other referral sources. For instance, a gentle prod, such as "Are your parents making this whole thing up?" may at least produce a beginning dialogue about what the adolescent considers unfair parental expectations. Once challenged in this manner, the resistance may dissipate to a point where other opinions are readily offered. This provides important information because one of the purposes of the interview is to gain the perspective of the adolescent and to make judgments regarding its appropriateness and basis in reality.

If all of these forthright approaches still fail to elicit the relevant information, alternative strategies may have to be implemented in order to facilitate the interview. One method is to use confrontational or provocative statements. For example, a subtle challenge to noncompliant adolescents is to ask them why they were so willing to come for the interview even though they have previously stated that they have always resisted their parents' or other adults' wishes. Their need for independence or to show their control of situations is so strong that a slight challenge (e.g., they must be curious about the interview, or they would never have come) may feed enough into their narcissism so that they would prefer to respond than to appear to be losing control. Although this is not the preferred way to engage an adolescent, it can be useful in the beginning stages of the interview. It is important to remember that the interview process is highly unusual for the adolescent. Therefore, the clinician who can be flexible in meeting the varied needs of the adolescent and who can interact with empathy and humor, as well as demonstrate some relatedness to the adolescent's inner and outer world, will have greater success in gathering the necessary information to provide an accurate diagnostic impression.

Collecting Meaningful Information

Once the interview process has been explained and rapport has been established with the adolescent, the emphasis turns to obtaining more specific information. It is during this phase of the interview that the clinician should focus on making an overall assessment of the adolescent's cognitive and emotional functioning. This can be accomplished through a more thorough investigation of the adolescent's perceptions and feelings about his or her intrapsychic and interpersonal difficulties and observations regarding those areas—that is, by conducting a formal mental status exam (e.g., the adolescent's speech, mood, thought processes and content, memory, judgment, and fund of general information) (Rosenthal & Akiskal, 1985; Siassi, 1984) or other structured interview format (see the subsequent section on structured and semistructured psychiatric interviews). Some beginning clinicians may feel awkward and stilted in soliciting information about such matters as orientation to person, place, and time; however, overlooking these subtle difficulties that the adolescent may be experiencing may lead to potential mistakes in diagnoses. Further, if the clinician appears uncomfortable in conducting these types of interviews, the adolescent may perceive the questioning as unimportant and may become distracted and increase his or her confusion or bitterness. It is best to be well rehearsed in these questions and to be able to interweave these specific questions into the context of an overall interview.

In this phase of an interview, the clinician must be flexible in coordinating efforts toward providing a balance between asking structured questions and eliciting spontaneity from the adolescent. Structure provides the opportunity to observe the adolescent's reaction to external demands and limits, whereas freedom permits the adolescent to demonstrate personal relatedness. Also during this time, the clinician begins to create a multitude of hypotheses regarding the adolescent's condition and explores specific areas to begin ruling out various disorders. While investigating the various clusters of symptoms, the clinician must remain sensitive to the adolescent's issues that do not necessarily fit clearly into diagnostic categories. The clinician who can demonstrate flexibility in this process between the structured and unstructured segments of the interview will be highly successful at gaining the needed material while not appearing repetitive. In addition, the clinician who can combine detailed observations with a flexible interview format will most likely sustain greater interest from the adolescent.

Defining Problem Areas

Blotcky (1984) has provided an effective interview format that includes seven essential areas of exploration. These include "1) individual concerns; 2) family relationships; 3) peer relationships; 4) school performance; 5) extracurricular activities; 6) pathognomonic indicators such as antisocial or bizarre behaviors; and 7) the ability to be self-reflective" (Blotcky, 1984, p. 76). It is also important for the clinician to explore the perceptions of the adolescent in several additional categories, including (a) major life events, (b) general coping style when confronted with stressors, (c) opinion of personal health and general functioning, (d) desire for change, and (e) future goals and outlook. With the adolescent's willingness to disclose information in these areas, the clinician can make maximum use of the diagnostic interview.

It becomes crucial in the detailing of information to determine whether the problems that the adolescent is discussing have been chronic or have been a more recent phenomenon. In this regard, it is best to assist the adolescent in comparing his or her present distress with previous levels of adjustment (Blotcky, 1984). For example, it may be helpful to structure the questioning by asking the adolescent to designate three strengths and three weaknesses and to see whether these have been long standing. Additional probes into possible recent traumas (e.g., death, divorce or separation, or relocation) may also increase the likelihood of gathering accurate diagnostic information. Other questions beginning with "Was there ever a time" also reflect whether the adolescent has lost some previously attained functioning.

Because adolescence is a time of great bodily change and focus, it is helpful during the interview process to spend some time reflecting on this growth with the adolescent. Gaining an understanding of the adolescent's perceptions of this experience may broaden any questioning that may have been overlooked if these concerns have not been directly addressed. A line of questioning into this area of personal health may include (a) investigating somatic complaints, (b) inquiring into sleeping and eating patterns, (c) asking about the experience of beginning puberty, and (d) exploring any extraordinary preoccupations (e.g., fears, recurring dreams).

Taking the time to explore the adolescent's previous significant life experiences and his or her ability to handle the related stress allows the clinician to gain a necessary understanding of premorbid functioning. It can also provide a clearer picture of why the current situation has reached a level of crisis for the family and why professional services have been solicited. Inquiries into problem-solving modalities used by the adolescent and the family also highlight their personal and combined resources and provide information related to their possible maladaptive means of coping with stressful situations. One such important area of concern, especially in planning intervention strategies, is whether mental health services have been used previously and if so, what was the reaction and the perceived benefit. If, for instance, previous attempts at individual therapy have failed, a possible recommendation of group or family therapies may be more beneficial.

Uncovering the adolescent's view of his or her family becomes imperative in providing an overall assessment. Areas to be addressed in this line of questioning include (a) How does the adolescent perceive his or her familial position? (b) Whom does he or she include in the family (e.g., is the separated father still in the picture)? (c) Who is responsible for daily chores, and are these distributed evenly among the family members? (d) Who has the decision-making power? (e) How do the family members address one another, and where do the areas of conflict lie? (f) Whom is the adolescent most worried about? and (g) Have there been recent or previous traumas? (Blotcky, 1984). Even though these are salient areas of exploration for the clinician, it is clear that adolescents may have trouble disclosing this information out of familial loyalty or fear of reprisal. Sometimes these family secrets are a pattern of the general pathology of the family's functioning (e.g., an alcohol- or drug-using family rarely admits to any difficulties) and the adolescent is protective of this style of dealing with the world. At other times, the family may have threatened the adolescent to not disclose any unnecessary information or else experience their anger and its consequences.

When this hesitancy is observed, it is best for the clinician to become encouraging, as well as more direct in questioning. For example, a request to "Tell me what it is like for you when your parents argue" may appear much less intrusive than "Do your parents argue frequently?" In attempting to help the adolescent elaborate on answers to questions, it is sometimes also useful to preface the line of questioning by stating "These are questions I ask everyone I see in a first interview." Finally, in order to ensure maximum disclosure on the part of the adolescent, a general comment about confidentiality is important, especially in regard to what, if anything, will be said to parents or referral sources.

Other areas of concern to explore during the interview process include peer contact, sexual involvement, school functioning, and overall activity level. A relevant understanding of the quality of friendships is pertinent in clarifying diagnostic questions. For example, the DSM-III-R distinguishes between those youngsters displaying disruptive conduct behaviors within the context of their peers (group type) from those who violate established guidelines on their own (solitary type). For the depressed youngster, this becomes especially crucial in forming therapeutic interventions. It is quite different to plan therapies for those who have never had the social skills to gain needed friends versus those adolescents who have forgone all interests, including previous friends. Specific questions that should be pursued may include "How long have you been friends?" "Can you tell me what you like about this friend?" and "Can you tell this friend your problems?" An adolescent's intimacy with others usually provides a better prognosis for the individual.

Likewise, appropriate sexual contact provides much insight into level of maturity, self-esteem, and adaptive functioning of the adolescent. Along with assurances of confidentiality, direct questioning (e.g., "Do you or have you ever had a boy- or girlfriend and for how long?" "Are you currently sexually active?" "Do you use any form of birth control?") is also indicated in order to gain a comprehensive picture.

In regard to school functioning, the clinician must gain a clear idea as to the adolescent's (a) consistency or deterioration in grades; (b) ability to concentrate in the classroom; (c) potential versus achievement motivation; (d) vocational interests; and (e) overall adjustment, including frequency of fights, suspensions, truancy, and general attitude toward school. It is likely that the clinician will want more specific school data, including previous psychological and educational evaluations, and will request that the adolescent and family sign a release of information form to forward directly to the school. In diagnosing depression, not only is it essential to gain an appreciation of sudden changes in behavior surrounding peer involvement and academic performance, but it is also necessary to gauge the level of activity and how this has increased or deteriorated. Again, direct questioning concerning the number of friends and the quality of intimacy, general interest patterns, school adjustment, expressions of boredom, and thoughts concerning future aspirations are all relevant in defining the depressed state.

Assessing Depth of Dysfunction

As part of the interview process, it becomes necessary for the clinician to explore in depth all the aspects of expressed symptoms in order to delineate clearly the criteria surrounding a diagnostic impression. In elaborating on the number of symptoms necessary to meet the criteria for major depression, for example, the clinician will need to know whether the adolescent has had recurrent thoughts of death, whether there has been a decreased ability in thinking and concentrating, whether the adolescent harbors excessive guilt or feelings of worthlessness, and so on. Many times, this type of information can be gathered in advance of the interview by administering self-report inventories that list various symptoms of depression, disruptive behaviors, substance abuse, and confused thinking. In determining the frequency of suicidal ideation and the potential risk of suicidal gestures, the clinician should explore such aspects of the adolescent's life as pervasive feelings of sadness, preoccupations with death, depressive tendencies, and previous suicides in the family (Pfeffer, 1986). Questions to ascertain this information may include (a) asking whether the adolescent has thought about or has made previous attempts at hurting him- or herself, (b) asking whether he or she has tried to or has wanted to commit suicide, (c) asking what would happen if the attempt were made, (d) asking about the precipitating events or thoughts that occurred before the attempt, (e) exploring the motivations behind the thoughts or actions, and (f) detailing the adolescent's other experiences with death. If the adolescent has thought about suicide, the clinician should pursue this line of questioning by asking whether a specific plan has been made. Many clinicians have suggested that this type of questioning is therapeutic in itself and gives the impression to the adolescent that the topic is not a taboo subject and can be discussed in depth (Gotlib & Colby, 1987).

Closing

In finalizing the interview with the adolescent, it is beneficial for the adolescent to be given the opportunity to ask general questions about the process. Most of these questions usually surround further issues of confidentiality and disclosure. For instance,"What other persons will be privy to the information?" and "How much of the information will be shared?" are typical responses. Adolescents will also likely be nervous about their performance and will want some feedback about their responses. Additionally, they will probably want to know what will happen to them next. Responding to the questions in the serious manner in which they were asked is usually the best policy, and answering them honestly and directly will increase the confidence level of the adolescent.

As a concluding remark to obtain even more information, the interviewer may want to solicit the adolescent's opinion about possible plans of action. It is not unlikely that an insightful youngster will have a good grasp of what is needed for him or her and the family in terms of better communication and what has worked in the past. For instance, "Let's say we are meeting a year from now, can you explain to me how you and your family solved the problems you are presently having?" may produce some much-needed optimism and the perspective that problems, no matter how difficult, can be managed successfully.

Clearly, for any clinician, more time is needed to integrate the results of the interview with other information that will be accumulated in the process of devising a treatment plan. In acknowledging that fact, it is helpful to conclude with the adolescent by mentioning that a lot of information has been shared and that future meetings will be planned to review all the data and to provide recommendations to him or her and to the family. It may also be helpful to establish the time when these meetings will occur in order to alleviate unnecessary worrying. It is also incumbent on the interviewer to clarify any further questions and causes of concern, as the adolescent would likely be quite nervous about the future meetings and plans for further treatment.

STRUCTURED AND SEMISTRUCTURED PSYCHIATRIC INTERVIEWS

Recently, there has been considerable attention directed toward conducting diagnostic interviews in a more structured and uniform fashion. Researchers and clinicians have begun to develop and standardize formal psychiatric interview procedures with child and adolescent populations due to their dissatisfaction with traditional diagnostic procedures (Edelbrock & Costello, 1988). Additionally, the greater emphasis on differentiating taxonomies of child and adolescent disorders and the greater precision of diagnostic criteria (e.g., DSM-III-R) have demanded more standardized assessment approaches.

There are several advantages to using more structured interviewing procedures as opposed to other methods of assessment (e.g., direct observation, psychological testing). Face-to-face interviews have been considered extremely useful in establishing rapport with the client, as well as in clarifying misunderstandings, resolving ambiguities, and documenting the context and prevalence of symptoms. Although there has been a recent proliferation of structured and semistructured interview assessment procedures, few have attained a level of standardization acceptable to be widely used, especially for clinical research. However, as both legal and economic pressures continue to exert increasing controls over mental health professionals, the use of more structured interview formats in terms of reducing variability among clinical approaches will become much more prevalent. Therefore, it is important that clinicians familiarize themselves with the most clinically cogent devices.

Although there are many commonalities among the measures, there are several differences in the manner in which they are administered and in the nature of the target areas to be assessed. Some interview procedures are semistructured in their format, providing only general, more flexible guidelines; others are highly structured in their specificity of order, wording, and recording of responses. Due to their greater latitude both in questioning and in pursuing responses, semistructured interviews are typically used by more clinically sophisticated interviewers. The use of the more highly structured interviews minimizes these ambiguities and can be used by laypersons who have been trained with the specific instrument. Also, while most of these interview schedules yield precise information regarding symptom expression, others provide quantitative scores in symptom areas or broader measures of psychopathology. Additionally, a few have been developed to provide psychiatric diagnoses.

With regard to adolescent populations, there are four main interview formats that represent the current state of the art in terms of attained psychometric properties: (1) the aforementioned Kiddie-SADS (Puig-Antich & Chambers, 1978), (2) the Interview Schedule for Children (Kovacs, 1982), (3) the aforementioned DISC (Costello et al., 1982), and (4) the Diagnostic Interview for Children and Adolescents (DICA) (Herjanic & Campbell, 1977; Herjanic & Reich, 1982). For the most part, these assessment devices are based largely on symptom cluster, which allows the clinician to question directly about the presence or absence of child and adolescent psychopathology. They all present lists of target behaviors, symptoms, and events, as well as guidelines for conducting the interviews and for recording the responses. Clinicians use the preceding techniques in order to question more thoroughly and in a more systematic fashion about the presenting symptoms. Additionally, these devices allow for some standardization with regard to research in the areas of child and adolescent pathology, as they reduce variability between interviews and interviewers.

Kiddie-SADS

The Kiddie-SADS (Puig-Antich & Chambers, 1978), a semistructured diagnostic interview for use with children and adolescents aged 6–17 years, was constructed from the Schedule for Affective Disorders and Schizophrenia (SADS) (Endicott & Spitzer, 1978) that is used for adults. The normal procedure involves interviewing both the parent and the adolescent and then attempting to resolve any discrepancies. The initial portion of the interview, approximately 20 minutes long, is designed to initiate rapport and to gather a historical record about the expressed symptoms. The final section is more elaborate and structured, taking approximately 30 to 40 minutes to specify symptoms. Each segment of the interview includes items to be rated (e.g., depressed mood) on a basis from 1 (not at all) to 6 (very extreme). Prompts are provided for specific questioning, and the interviewer is encouraged to ask questions until satisfied with an accurate rating of each response. At the end of the interview, there are 11 behavioral observational items to complete and questions to answer regarding the reliability and completeness of the interview. A global impression is then provided, indicating an overall level of functioning. Of the 49 core symptoms that the Kiddie-SADS covers, 23 allude to primary depression and 9 to clinical features of depression. Five additional scales related to depression have been adapted from the adult SADS. Diagnoses are derived from the interviewer's judgment of the responses.

The reliability of the Kiddie-SADS has been considered adequate. Because it was developed to select subjects for research in childhood depression, its use in characterizing depressed patients is excellent. However, this also limits its use in accurately differentiating other disorders. Its strength lies in its detailed questioning of symptoms in regard to onset, severity, duration, and related maladjustment. One must be a skilled interviewer in addition to being extensively trained in using the instrument to properly utilize it. Computer scoring has not been developed as yet, but efforts are being made in this direction.

DISC

In contrast to the Kiddie-SADS, the DISC is a highly structured diagnostic interview used with children and adolescents ages 6–18 years; it prespecifies the order, wording, and coding of items (Costello et al., 1982). Separate forms of the interview have been developed for parents (DISC-P) covering 302 items and for children (DISC-C) covering 264 items; the items pertain to the onset, duration, severity, and related impairments of various symptoms and behaviors. The ratings of each item, completed by either professional or lay individuals who have been specifically trained in using the instrument, range from 0 (no), through 1 (somewhat or sometimes), to 2 (yes). The administration time is approximately 40–60 minutes for children and 60–80 minutes for adults.

The interviews were constructed to assess the criteria that was established in the child and adolescent disorders specified in the DSM-III. After the data have been collected, diagnoses are computer generated, but interpretation usually requires broad clinical experience. Severity scores are also provided in 27 symptom areas that relate to specific diagnosis (e.g., overanxious disorder). Extensive reliability and validity studies have been conducted and have suggested promising results, although they seem less reliable than such assessment methods as direct observation, psychological testing, and behavioral ratings (Edelbrock & Costello, 1988). The DISC has been recommended mainly as a descriptive and epidemiological instrument. It appears best suited for the screening and identification of children and adolescents who are at risk of emotional disturbance and for best-estimates diagnoses during survey research.

SELF-REPORT INVENTORIES

Although the main tools for diagnosis in psychiatric research have been structured or semistructured interviews, they are expensive and time consuming. Additionally, especially in the case of children or younger adolescents, the parent(s) also should be present. When time is an issue or when the parents are not involved in the assessment, self-report paper-and-pencil inventories completed by the child or adolescent can provide substantive information (Costello & Angold, 1988).

One of the most widely used methods for obtaining descriptive information about adolescent distress is the self-report measure. This is especially true in the assessment of depression where the primary expression of symptoms is subjective feelings of sadness or perceptions of worthlessness (Kazdin, 1988). The fact that these inventories have been used in adult populations with frequency and success made their downward extension for use with children and adolescents inevitable. Several of the inventories are even direct modifications of the instruments used with adults (e.g., Center for Epidemiological Studies Depression Scale—modified for children—Weissman, Oruaschel, & Padian, 1980; Face Valid Depression Scale for Adolescents—Mezzich & Mezzich, 1979). In addition to these measures that are often recommended for use up to ages 17 or 18, measures used with adults (e.g., the Beck Depression Inventory: BDI) are still used frequently to assess adolescents (Strober, Green, & Carlson, 1981). Therefore, the numbers and types of available instruments for measuring symptoms of depressions in adolescents are extensive.

The inventories that have been developed for assessing depression in adolescents often differ in their goals, in their focus of expressed symptom (e.g., affective or cognitive), and in their empirical background. Additionally, the inventories were produced differently. Besides direct adaptation from the adult scales, others have relied on diagnostic criteria, on ability to discriminate population samples, or on clinical opinion of the items (Kazdin & Petti, 1982). Two such self-report measures merit special attention—the Children's Depression Inventory and the Reynolds Adolescent Depression Scale.

Children's Depression Inventory

Adapted originally from the BDI, the Children's Depression Inventory (CDI: Kovacs, 1983) includes 27 signs of depression that measure the domains of affect, behavior, and cognition in children and adolescents from ages 7 to 17 years. Each of the items provides three alternatives that ask the respondents to characterize their functioning within the past 2-week period. A score of 0, 1, or 2 is provided to the endorsed statement. The higher the number, the more severe the symptom. For example, a feeling of sadness can be marked from "once in a while" to "all the time."

The CDI has been one of the most frequently used research measures in investigations of childhood depression (Kazdin, 1988). High internal consistency (e.g., Cronbach's $\alpha > .80$) has been demonstrated, as well as moderate test–retest reliability. It has also been successful in distinguishing between clinic and nonclinic groups of children and has been shown to correspond to other factors commonly observed within the depressive syndrome (e.g., hopelessness, negative self-esteem) (Saylor, Finch, Spirito, & Bennett, 1984). Although scores on the CDI are relatively high among children who have been referred for mental health services, there has been some confusion as to whether the CDI identifies depression in particular or it identifies more global psychological dysfunction (Costello & Angold, 1988).

Reynolds Adolescent Depression Scale

The Reynolds Adolescent Depression Scale (RADS: Reynolds, 1987) was developed as a brief self-report measure to assess depressive symptomatology in adolescents ranging in age from 13 to 18 years, or in those individuals in junior or senior high school settings. Consisting of 30 items with a 4-point Likert-type response format, the RADS can be administered to individuals or to groups of individuals and can either be hand or machine scored. It takes approximately 5 to 10 minutes to complete. It attempts to elicit responses indicating the frequency of the various associated symptoms of depression. The responses are weighed on a 4-point basis; thus, a possible score can range from 30 to 120. A score at or above 77 signifies a symptom endorsement associated with clinical depression. The average score on the RADS standardization sample is 57 for boys and 63 for girls, showing substantial gender differences in self-reports of depressed symptoms.

Although the RADS is a relatively new instrument and must wait for further research and documentation of its psychometric properties and usefulness, the author does present high internal consistency and reliability ranging by grade from .909 to .939 and a split-half reliability coefficient of .91 (Reynolds, 1987). The measure has also been shown to correlate significantly with other commonly used self-report inventories, including the CDI and the BDI, ranging from .68 to .76. The emphasis on the use of this scale is that it is the first depression measure developed specifically for adolescents.

CONCLUSIONS

Comprehensive evaluations of depressed adolescents provide a wealth of informational data about their intrapsychic and interpersonal problems that is extremely helpful in generating appropriate treatment strategies. These evaluations also present the clinician with the opportunity to gauge the risk of suicidal behavior. Through family and individual interviews, self-report inventories, and more general data gained from formal psychological assessment (which profiles the adolescent's cognitive and emotional strengths and weaknesses and areas of conflict), an accurate assessment of the level of intervention can be made. This intervention may include (a) outpatient treatment, (b) hospitalization or residential treatment, (c) several types of therapies that could be most beneficial, and (d) a possible choice of medication that would be relevant. The following chapters consider the various treatment modalities for intervening with depressed adolescents and their families and follows them into the various settings where they are frequently seen in treatment.

PART 3

Adolescent Suicide

CHAPTER 7

Understanding Suicidal Behaviors in Adolescents

It has become almost commonplace to pick up a newspaper, magazine, or professional journal and find accounts of teenage suicides. The media have repeatedly featured stories and quoted statistics about how disenfranchised our youths are and about the alarming increases in suicides and suicide attempts among our young people. In a recent national survey of 11,000 teenagers, 25% of the males and 42% of the females admitted to having given serious thought to suicide at some time in the past (National Adolescent Student Health Survey, as reported in the *Washington Post* August 16, 1988).

Even the conceptualization of school guidance counselors is changing as they are being replaced in many jurisdictions with "Crisis Management Teams." The commercial airwaves have been saturated with advertisements of increased inpatient programs geared toward our troubled youth. The popularity of the movie *Ordinary People*, which depicted a depressed and suicidal adolescent, seemed to speak to a nation's concern about its teenagers. The professional community also has responded with an increase in attention to adolescent suicidal behavior through a proliferation of journal issues devoted to that topic (e.g., *Journal of the American Academy of Child and Adolescent Psychiatry*, November, 1988; *Seminars in Adolescent Medicine*, December, 1986) and textbooks on that theme (e.g., Lesse, 1988; Sudak, Ford, & Rushforth, 1984).

Why are adolescents who are at the threshold of adulthood and who face virtually limitless opportunities killing themselves in alarming numbers? As clinicians, how can we identify adolescents at risk and assist those already displaying symptomatology so that their momentary suicidal thoughts and behaviors do not have permanent and irreversible consequences? Adolescent suicidal gestures and behaviors are enormously complicated processes, and our interventions must take into account a myriad of factors. This chapter explores (a) definitions and common characteristics of suicidal adolescents, (b) the role of the "suicidogenic" family, (c) the assessment of suicide potential, and (d) the management and treatment of suicidal adolescents and their families.

DEFINITIONS OF SUICIDAL BEHAVIOR

Simply put, suicidal behavior in adolescents can encompass actions along a continuum from inflicting self-harm to total cessation of life itself. Most commonly, definitions of adolescent suicidal behavior involve the notion of intentionality, although the degree to which forethought and intentionality are necessary conditions to consider behavior of a suicidal nature is controversial. Death by suicide has become a major cause of death among teenagers ages 15–19 years (National Center for Health Statistics as quoted in Gispert, Wheeler, Marsh, & Davis, 1985). Homicides and accidents constitute the other leading causes of death for this age group.

The question has been raised repeatedly that perhaps some suicidal adolescents place themselves in dangerous situations (e.g., involvement in drug activities) in which they are frequently the victims of homicides. Similarly, teenagers who are reckless in their driving behaviors and who mix alcohol and other drugs with driving increase the likelihood that they will be involved in and perhaps not survive an accident. Additionally, the use of alcohol and other drugs has also been put forth as exemplary of suicidal behavior because repeated drug use can be life threatening, although in some cases it takes a more protracted course (Landau-Stanton & Stanton, 1985). With little value for their own lives, suicidal adolescents do not question the potential risks of such behaviors. It is therefore quite narrow in thinking to exclude these behaviors from being categorized as self-injurious just because there was no suicide note left or because an adolescent's actions do not incorporate the conscious or public expression of suicidal intent.

Enlarging what is considered suicidal behavior further complicates differentiating appropriate modes of assessment and intervention as the population under consideration potentially can become more heterogeneous. If every adolescent who experiences an accident, who is murdered, or who uses drugs is suspected of suicidal behavior, we may also conversely be guilty of overreporting the incidence of suicidal behavior. Perhaps it would be more efficacious to work toward identifying subtypes of suicidal adolescents. Attempts to differentiate characteristics of suicidal adolescents have usually surrounded classification along the lines of lethality of the actual gesture; however, it may also be advantageous to group adolescent behavior according to covert versus overt manifestation of both the suicide ideation and the potentially self-injurious actions (Molin, 1986).

Some controversy has surrounded the issue of whether adolescent suicidal behavior is in part an expected developmental phase, due to the turmoil-ridden characteristic of adolescence (Friedman, Corn, Aronoff, Hurt, & Clarkin, 1984a). Because a substantial portion of a random sample of adolescents in the country admit to having harbored suicidal feelings, the question arises as to whether this indicates that all normal adolescents may potentially manifest suicidal behaviors.

A differentiation should be made between adolescents who state that they have thought of such behavior compared to those youngsters who persistently think about or actively contemplate or engage in serious actions of a potentially self-harming nature. When more behavioral referents are used as criteria for both ideation and actions, there appears to be a difference between youngsters who answer affirmatively to a questionnaire versus adolescents who have engaged in a serious process of self-harm and annihilation. It is in the examination of adolescents who have initiated suicidal behavior that the distinguishing variables can be further clarified and identified.

In one of the most recent studies of descriptive characteristics of completed suicides in children and adolescents, Hoberman and Garfinkel (1988) analyzed the records of 229 youths from medical examiners' reports. They identified the following risk factors: (a) males tended to complete the suicide in a 4-to-1 ratio in relation to females, (b) females tended to have an increased likelihood that they had made a prior attempt, (c) older adolescents were more prone to complete suicide attempts than were younger adolescents, and (d) suicide tended to correlate with race as 94% of the suicide population were white (Hoberman & Garfinkel, 1988). Another important finding from the Hoberman and Garfinkel (1988) study was that 50% of the sample population, although not necessarily diagnosed prior to the suicidal behavior, met the criteria for emotional disturbance. Common nosological classifications manifested by the youngsters included (a) depression, (b) alcohol or other drug abuse, (c) conduct disorders, (d) schizophrenia, and (e) bipolar illness. Hoberman and Garfinkel (1988) are careful to point out that "these findings suggest a heterogeneity of personality characteristics that describe young persons who commit suicide. No single category defined more than 18% of the descendents. The most common descriptive categories were withdrawn, lonely and supersensitive" (p. 694). While the classification of different emotional difficulties may be more widespread, these results along with those of Friedman, Corn, Aronoff, Hurt, and Clarkin (1984a, 1984b) and of Shafii, Carrigan, Whittinghill, and Derrick (1985), support the notion that for a substantial portion of youngsters who engage in serious suicidal behaviors, there is strong evidence to suggest that the suicidal process is not a normal extension of the adolescent stage of development. In fact, Shafii maintains that in almost all cases, suicide is the result of "serious emotional disorders which, in most cases, were not recognized or treated" (Holden, 1986, p. 839). Thus, adolescents who demonstrate other emotional problems or who display character pathology are at an increased risk of using more self-injurious behaviors in their problem-solving strategies than those who are quite devoid of pathological symptoms.

In pursuing the relationships between psychological disturbance and suicidality, Apter, Bleich, Plutchik, Mendelson, and Tyano (1988) studied 140 youngsters admitted to an inpatient psychiatric unit. Their results were quite interesting in terms of differentiating levels of suicide ideation by diagnosis. Specifically, adolescents diagnosed as having conduct disorder admitted to comparatively increased levels of suicidality as compared with youngsters with major affective disorder and those diagnosed as schizophrenic. However, major affective disordered adolescents admitted to greater levels of depression in comparison to the conduct disordered and schizophrenic peers (Apter et al., 1988).

In discussing these findings, Apter et al., (1988) advocated that we need to broaden our conceptualization of suicidal behavior from actions that arise only out of depressed symptomatology to include symptom clusters that involve more impulsive, aggressive, and violent behavior. Additionally, we must also take into consideration that suicidal behaviors may not only be in response to the threat of loss or actual loss, but may also be related to "frustration and unrelieved aggressive tension, rather than depression. Many of these patients (conduct disordered) also show nonsuicidal self-mutilating behavior such as burning themselves with cigarettes, cutting their arms, or sticking themselves with needles. This, too, is for relief of frustrated aggression rather than a response to depression" (Apter et al., 1988, p. 698).

Similarly, in a study of 82 adolescents hospitalized for suicidal behavior, Gispert et al. (1985) found that the "overt expression of anger was significantly related to the seriousness of the suicide attempt" (p. 757). The value of these studies in terms of clinical practice suggests that it may not only be the depressed adolescents who are potentially at risk, but also that more chronically aggressive and rule-breaking adolescents should be considered at risk in terms of lethality. As more conduct-disordered adolescents tend to have more violent means of harm available, increasingly assessing the suicidal potential of these youngsters might result in partially decreasing the overall rate at which adolescents are successful at killing themselves.

With regard to more immediate risk factors, Hoberman and Garfinkel (1988) collected information on precipitants of the suicidal behavior within 3 days of the suicidal event. The population they investigated exhibited the following stressful events within 3 days of their suicide: (a) 19% of the sample had altercations with their families, (b) 16% demonstrated difficulties in school (with 76% having shown deteriorated school performance over the course of the year), (c) 11% experienced disappointments, (d) 10% became involved with the police, (e) 8% experienced either loss or the threat of impending loss, (f) 5% experienced a breakup of a relationship, and (g) 5% had difficulties at work (p. 692). While the foregoing list constitutes traumatic events, they are ones commonly experienced by a majority of adolescents. Hoberman and Garfinkel (1988) maintained that it is likely that stressful life events combine with inadequate mechanisms for dealing with this stress, due to the underlying presence of emotional disturbance that puts the youngster at greater potential risk for suicidal behaviors. Specifically, less underlying tolerance for stress combines with increased psychological tension, to increase the potential for lethal behaviors.

Another important risk factor identified in the studies by Hoberman and

Garfinkel (1988) and by Shafii et al. (1985) involved expression of suicidal ideation and previous suicidal gestures. The myth has long existed about suicidal comments that is analogous to the story about the boy who cried wolf; namely that some statements about suicidal intent need not be taken seriously. As previously mentioned, current research contends that serious contemplation of suicide is not a product of normative developmental crisis in adolescence but is suggestive of an underlying disturbance. Therefore, verbalization of suicidal intent or past gestures—no matter how feeble—are also not events to be minimized.

Specifically, Hoberman and Garfinkel (1988) reported that 62% of their suicidal sample had made a reference to suicide or to their death prior to committing suicide. Shafii et al. (1985), in conducting a psychological autopsy of 24 completed suicides, reported that 85% of their population had made an expression of a wish to die before engaging in a suicidal act and 40% had made a previous gesture. In fact, Shafii et al. (1985) concludes that it is more likely to be the exception for the adolescent to give no clues of distress rather than the rule. Specifically, "a close relationship exists between suicidal wishes, threats, attempts, and completed suicide. In our study frequently the talkers became the doers" (Shafii et al., 1985, p. 1064).

Pfeffer (1985) defined additional risk factors associated with suicidal behavior in adolescents. In reviewing a number of empirical investigations, Pfeffer concluded that in many of these studies, issues surrounding "loss" distinguished suicidal youngsters from their nonsuicidal peers. Specifically, she identified factors such as "separation from parents, hospitalization of a parent, birth of a sibling, divorce and remarriage of a parent, and death of a grandparent" (p. 220). It is also important to note that experiences of loss may not necessarily be as tangible as the death of a parent. Youngsters may live in a context where emotional loss in terms of loss of attention from a parent may just as significantly predispose the adolescent to being vulnerable to difficulties in adequately negotiating other subsequent interpersonal traumatic experiences. Often, if these early traumatic events are not appropriately worked through during childhood, the adolescent may not be able to sustain the anxiety surrounding a more current threat of loss, such as breaking up with a boyfriend, thereby precipitating a suicidal crisis. It is not the actual intensity of the precipitating event as much as the adolescent's interpretation of the event, given his or her history of loss of significant objects of love. It is in introducing the notion of loss that examining the adolescent's larger social environment becomes quite pressing in order to be more accurate in assessing and intervening in a suicidal crisis.

SUICIDOGENIC FAMILY

Although the preceding characteristics and definitions may define adolescent suicide behavior, they do not offer the full context in which the self-harming and sometimes self-annihilating process is embedded. As stated earlier, adolescents do not live in a vacuum, but because of their continued relatively dependent status, they are influenced by and feel the impact of the family environment in which they reside. Richman (1984), in detailing common characteristics of families that have experienced suicidal members, called these families "suicidogenic," denoting a typology of historical, relational, and current stress factors that contribute to the manifestation of suicidal ideations, gestures, and completed acts. By delineating family dynamics that potentially contribute to the adolescent's suicidal actions, those adolescents and families at risk might be more clearly elucidated such that intervention can be well timed prior to the initiation of serious or irreversible actions.

Some theoreticians (e.g., Aldridge, 1984; Everstine & Everstine, 1983; Landau-Stanton & Stanton, 1985; Richman, 1984) maintain that suicidal behavior is well rooted within the family context. Aldridge asserts that "suicidal behavior is not an individual phenomenon but a social phenomenon" (p. 311). He further suggests that it is not a form of communication but a "participation" in the communication process within a family (Aldridge, 1984). The entire family is involved in the suicidal process either by commission or omission. Suicidogenic families are characterized by (a) poor communication, (b) unresolved loss issues, (c) dysfunctional boundary systems, (d) difficulties in conflict resolution, and (e) a prevalence of emotional disturbance in family members. Nonetheless, these factors in and of themselves are not differentiating variables in terms of families where suicidal behaviors are manifested, as compared to alternative symptomatology. However, these characteristics, in addition to covert and more pathological expressions of anger or depression, and prior exposure to suicidal behavior in others, can all contribute to a suicidal crisis within the family.

While families in general are vulnerable during the period of adolescence due to its inherent turmoil, confusion, and conflict, this developmental stage is especially problematic for the suicidogenic family. The stage of adolescence is a metaphor for both previous and subsequent loss. This period also often engenders a reawakening of past disappointments and unresolved issues for both parents and teenagers. For example, early rejections are heightened within the developmental crisis of adolescence, as the adolescent's impulsivity and intensity of emotional involvement can exacerbate previously dormant issues. Current losses involve parents who must accept decreased responsibilities and influences over their adolescent, while the adolescent must bid farewell to more idealized concepts of parental nurturance and attention, whether those ideals have been realized or not.

Even under the best of circumstances, it is a time of increased risk of alienation and rejection, or on the other extreme, flight to enmeshment and overinvolvement. Additionally, while parents may look forward to even their own autonomy as their children move toward adulthood, the process is one that is very painful and extremely ungratifying because the adolescent's independence is usually gained through simultaneously vacillating between pushing for freedom and pulling for comfort and caregiving. It is the inability of parents and adolescents both to accept change and transition and to coordinate this dance of separation and connection that places families at risk of more serious problematic behaviors.

Aldridge (1984), and Aldridge and Dallos (1986) assert that suicidal behavior in adolescents can be related to threats of familial change and separation brought about by the crisis of the emerging independence of the adolescent member. Specifically, suicidal behavior "is a systematic move to keep a family together at a time of change and in a context of escalating conflict" (Aldridge & Dallos, 1986, p. 245). Families that are unable to more effectively change, and that in fact are threatened by transition, may collude unconsciously to create a deviant member in order superficially to maintain long-standing familial patterns of interacting. This may lead the adolescent to feel alienated and desperate, with only limited options for continued acceptance and support by the family. As a result of the family's restriction of the adolescent's development, the adolescent may engage in self-injurious behaviors as a mechanism for calling attention to the extreme constraints imposed by the family.

It is not only the turmoil, confusion, and threat of differentiation that leads to difficulties in families with adolescent members, but it is also the inability of the family to communicate adequately. These are families that have difficulty verbalizing emotions and supporting each other during periods of problems and crisis. Inappropriate alliances and confidences between dyads of family members may be present, with other members feeling alienated and shut out. Additionally, these family members have difficulties giving clear messages of their needs, for fear of rejection, and they often demand unrealistic expectations.

Kerfoot (1987) asserts that "in these situations communication appears to have broken down, there is less flexibility and openness and the adolescent may resort to actions rather than words in order to communicate distress" (p. 195). The suicidal gesture or act is the ultimate expression of both anger and hopelessness and is in response to alternative channels being blocked. With enmeshed families, the youngster's self-injurious behaviors may highlight the feelings of loss of a sense of identity and autonomy. On the other hand, in families that are disengaged, the extreme nature of the suicidal act exemplifies the severity of the alienation of family members because the youngster must use a very outrageous strategy in order for his or her plea to be heard.

While poor communication between family members is not in and of itself a defining characteristic of the suicidogenic family, it is an important ingredient in contributing to an adolescent's suicidal behavior. It is a defining characteristic, however, for families with unresolved issues around loss, where the adolescent's problematic behaviors are a metaphor for previous and current disruptions in familial relationships (Richman, 1984). Wodarski and Harris (1987) assert that it is not the concept of actual loss, such as the death of a parent, but the emotional experience of loss for the youngster; these losses can include parental divorce, separations, withdrawal, lack of involvement, or abandonment. The actual loss may even be embedded in a previous generation, with repercussions filtering down. The following case example illustrates this process:

Jane T., age 14 years, was brought to an outpatient mental health clinic by her father and mother, following Jane's expressing that she would be better off dead so as not to "bother anyone." Mrs. T.'s mother had committed suicide when Mrs. T. was very young. She grew up feeling responsible for her mother's death, and for that reason, she feared personal involvement, as everything she touched "was ruined." She got pregnant by Mr. T. with Jane while still in high school. Mr. T. "did the right thing and married her." Mrs. T. experienced a postpartum depression, as she was worried she was not "good enough to be a mother." She remained cautious and more withdrawn from Jane, worrying that if she became more involved, she would "ruin Jane's life as she must have done to her own mother's" yet also fearing that in being intimately connected to Jane, she would be setting herself up for another rejection and loss when Jane eventually left home. In response to his wife's depression, Mr. T. took over the majority of the nurturing and caregiving responsibilities. With her emergence into adolescence, Jane began to feel both guilty for being a burden to her mother, who was easily overtaxed, and angry that her mother had never really been there for her. Additionally, Jane's increasingly autonomous adolescent behaviors, such as spending time with peers, were interpreted by Mrs. T. as the beginning of Jane's abandoning the family; meanwhile, Mr. T. felt that Jane's activities relieved him of the extensive parenting responsibilities. Mr. and Mrs. T. were continually fighting over giving Jane freedoms. Caught in the middle of her parents' discord, Jane became more despondent, hopeless, and angry.

This case demonstrates the power of unresolved issues of loss for Mrs. T. and how it became manifested through her daughter's suicidal ideation. The fact that the crisis in this family occurred upon Jane's emergence into adolescence is not coincidental, but it underlies the precarious nature of the familial attachment relationships, which became further strained with the normative turmoil of adolescence. Without adequate resolution of prior losses, issues surrounding attachment and nurturance can become quite pressing, leading to behaviors reflective of the potential abandonment. The suicidal behavior is the ultimate demonstration to others of these feelings of rejection and loss. In the suicidal act, the adolescent is mimicking the familial pattern of perhaps more arbitrary and sustained cutoffs in relationships.

While unresolved loss is an important factor in families at risk for suicidal behavior, dysfunctional familial boundaries are also quite often superimposed on this loss (Pfeffer, 1988). These families are characterized by arbitrary and rigid boundaries either between the family and the external environment or between individual family members. The suicidal behavior can be a "cry for help" in a disengaged family from a member whose behavior demonstrates the severe alienation of the family. However, suicidal behavior can also be manifested in enmeshed families with few boundaries. In these families, boundaries between family subsystems are diffuse, with confidences and alliances across generational lines. This often places a burden on the adolescent member that can be so overwhelming that suicidal gestures may become manifested.

Kerfoot (1979), and Kreider and Motto (1974), in writing on familial influences on suicidal behavior in adolescents, put forth the theory that boundary diffusion in suicidogenic families often is manifested by the child taking on more of a "parentified" role. Specifically, "behaviors such as dependency, helplessness, etc., which are common to the child's role, are taken on by the parent and the child assumes the caretaking and nurturing behavior usually associated with the parental role" (Kerfoot, 1979, p. 337).

This role is tremendously burdensome for the child, as it inhibits a more normative developmental process from unfolding (Kerfoot, 1979). Kreider and Motto (1974) maintain that "unresolved dependency needs in the parent can lead to parent–child role reversal, but those needs can conflict with the child's own dependency needs, and this conflict may result in suicidal behavior in the adolescent" (p. 365). Both helplessness, in terms of being ill equipped to provide the parent with what he or she needs, as well as anger that the parent is not fulfilling the nurturing role, can contribute to intense turmoil on the part of the adolescent. Because the parent is already perceived as ineffective and fragile by the adolescent, this anger and confusion is often turned inward and acted out through self-injurious behaviors. The following case example illustrates this occurrence:

April, age 15 years, was admitted to an emergency room following the ingestion of 13 aspirin. April lived with her mother and younger sister (age 11). Her parents had divorced when April was 6, and she remembers being at her mother's side through the painful separation and eventual divorce. April's mother had reacted to the divorce by dedicating herself to raising the children because "she needed to be both mother and father." However, this made her quite isolated within the home. April and her mother had a very close relationship, with her mother stating, "She's better than having a best friend. I'm amazed at what she had been able to understand even at such a young age." While April had been a shy and reserved child, she had begun to befriend a coed group of adolescents during her 2nd year of high school. One of these youngsters became her boyfriend, and April began to spend more time with him, reducing her time with her family. Her boyfriend was putting pressure on her to be even more available to him and threatened that if she didn't, he may break up with her. The night before her suicide attempt, April and her mother had had a fight over the issues of her boyfriend, with her mother shouting, "You'll leave me just like your Dad, and then where will I be?" Distraught and angry over her mother's verbalizations, April made a suicide attempt the following day.

In this case example, an unresolved loss, as well as a role reversal, created an untenable position for April, who was caught between her own needs for autonomy and her being bound to a more caregiving role toward her mother. The process leading up to her suicidal gesture is delineated by Kreider and Motto (1974), who state that it is the "deprivation of nurturance" along with the restriction of the "range of behaviors available" that creates a heavy and emotional burden for the adolescent (p. 366). Consequently, the suicidal gesture comes out as both rage directed at the parent for placing the child in the parentified role and a sense of failure in the child's own ability to protect and nurture the parent.

Sargent (1987) asserts that the boundary diffusion is often manifested in a slightly more covert manner. Specifically, he views the suicidal behavior as an attempt by the youngster to distract a parent from his or her own depression and hopelessness. By taking on symptomatic behaviors, the adolescent hopes to assist the parent in becoming focused away from personal problems. However, the adolescent's suicidal behaviors usually result in increased feelings of inadequacy and a sense of failure on the part of the parent, which often leads to increased withdrawal; this creates a crisis for the adolescent. Specifically, in attempting to take care of parental pain, the adolescents are ultimately abandoned by their parents and are even blamed for being increased burdens. Out of this anger, frustration, and feelings of failure, more self-destructive actions result.

Recently, there has been some attention to further distinguishing subtypes of suicidogenic families with regard to diffuse or enmeshed boundaries, according to the lethality of the suicidal gesture. Senior (1988) suggests that adolescents displaying less lethal, and what typically are considered "gesture" behaviors, often are from more enmeshed families where the suicidal behavior is directed toward "self-punishment and punishment of the family" (p. 33). Specifically, the "primary intent is not separation through death, but rather engagement and attention seeking through suffering" (p. 35). Conversely, those adolescents who are involved in serious self-mutilating actions (and often more medically dangerous behaviors) tend to be from more disengaged families, in which the expressed wish of exclusion seems to be most prominent. Consequently, the aim of the behavior is in cooperating with this familial communication—namely, the "suicide intent is separation" (p. 36). Within this framework of subtypes of suicidal behavior, Senior (1988) views adolescents from disengaged families as being at more of an acute risk for successful suicides. Therefore, he asserts that in evaluating youngsters, the level of distance and isolation manifested between the adolescent and the family should be one of the markers of serious suicidal risk.

It is important to note that what is lacking in Senior's (1988) thesis is the notion that no matter what the underlying dynamics within the family, adolescents may die whether their suicidal behavior was initiated as a gesture or as an active attempt. Without clear medical knowledge, adolescents may engage in behaviors that they consider non-lethal, when in actuality they are quite dangerous. For example, aspirin (a common over-the-counter medication that is often widely available in the home situation) may be considered by the adolescent as less harmful than possible prescription medications that are also found in the family medicine chest. However, aspirin can be quite lethal; thus, it may be difficult to distinguish based on method or quantity those adolescents who want to die versus those who want to communicate desperation.

It appears that although there may be a tendency for youngsters in more disengaged families to use more lethal methods, clinicians should not be lulled into a false sense of security because adolescents who make gestures from more enmeshed families may in fact be in as much danger as those from disengaged families. Nevertheless, it does seem clear that families that are on either end of the diffusion–disengagement spectrum seem especially at risk in terms of the more self-destructive quality of their children's suicidal behaviors.

Suicidal behavior in families may also be a product of difficulties in expression, modulation, and resolution of conflict and aggression (Aldridge & Dallos, 1986; Everstine & Everstine, 1983; Richman, 1979). Suicidogenic families are often characterized by intense conflict of both a long-standing and an acute nature. Asarnow, Carlson, and Guthrie (1987), although dealing primarily with a child sample, concluded that the "strongest predictors of suicidal behavior in this sample were children's perceptions of their family environment. Children who thought of and attempted suicide tended to perceive their family environments as unsupportive and stressful, with poor control, high conflict, and a lack of cohesiveness" (p. 365).

The inability of a family to work through problem areas and to resolve issues creates a continued experience of intrafamilial strife and conflict. It is quite common for families with suicidal adolescents to describe a long history of such conflict. The intensity of the conflict is usually exacerbated by the emergence of adolescence because this is a stage during which issues of control become paramount. When children in these discordant families reach the stage of adolescence, any escalation in conflict can potentially tax the family's already fragile and inadequate coping strategies, thus contributing to more extreme behavior on the part of the adolescent. In a study of adolescent females who had attempted suicide, Rotherman-Borus and Trautman (1988) reported that 83% of their sample had had a fight with a family member prior to the initiation of their suicidal behavior. It is not the presence of acute conflict in these families that precipitates suicide attempts but the combination of a protracted history of conflictual relationships with an acute crisis of familial discord.

Not only is manifestation of suicidal behavior the product of conflict, but it can also be a consequence of latent aggression. Specifically, Richman and Rosenbaum (1970) maintain that comments regarding aggressive wishes are often verbalized between family members. Everstine and Everstine (1983) conceptualize suicidal behavior as a wish to kill others that is redirected toward the self. Within the family context, suicidal behavior can be both the directive of aggression from another family member to the adolescent, which the adolescent carries out by cooperating with the angry wish, and the internalization of the adolescent's anger toward others through self-injurious behaviors. Additionally, Aldridge (1984) comments that "suicidal behavior is likely to occur when there is increased stress accompanied by hostility and death wishes from the family and other significant external objects, when the other person is unable to retaliate and when external help is unavailable or withdrawn" (p. 313). The following is a case example that illustrates these dynamics:

Joe, age 17 years, had been becoming increasingly involved with alcohol and other drugs. He was brought in for an outpatient appointment by his parents after Joe began (in addition to his drug usage) to refuse to go to school and began to stay out all night. Three years previously, Joe's younger sister, Kate, had died of cancer after a long illness. Both Mr. and Mrs. S. had quickly returned to work following their daughter's death, as "What were we supposed to do—sit home and dwell on it?" Both Mr. and Mrs. S. became very active in their occupations, traveling quite a bit on business. Joe stated that they both stayed away from the home because the "spirit had gone out of the family." Looking for some closeness, Joe befriended drug-involved peers. He quickly became popular, as his parents frequent absences created an empty house for parties. Joe was heavily involved with drugs when his parents discovered the abuse and confronted him. In an argument about his drug use, Mr. S. yelled, "I can't understand it, one of my kids wanted so desperately to live but died, and you go out and try to kill yourself with drugs. Maybe the wrong kid died?"

While many additional issues are operating in this case, such as unresolved loss and a high level of alienation, the expression of Mr. S.'s anger is quite typical in families with suicidal members in which a covert (through direct communication of hostility) or overt (through withdrawal from the child) message is made. Given the intensity of the anger, it is not unusual that Joe's behaviors were of a self-destructive nature. His self-injurious actions epitomize both his feelings of guilt for disappointing his parents by not being the perfect child and his anger toward his parents; these feelings combined to generate the overt manifestation of self-aggression.

One of the very powerful factors of the manifestation of suicidal behavior in adolescents is the family's prior exposure to suicidal behavior. Family histories in which relatives have attempted or completed suicide give a strong message to surviving members—namely, that suicide is "an acceptable and possible solution when under stress" (Richman, 1984, p. 398). Kerfoot (1987) reports that "families of young people who make suicide attempts have often experienced similar behavior in the past from other family members" (p. 193). It has been suggested that such behavior may offer a precedent to adolescents, who then model their behavior on those around them. In other words, there is a relaxation of the taboo against suicide because it has been used previously by a family member. Even in families where there is no familial history of it, suicidal behavior is not clearly regarded as a taboo. This is often evident when interviewing families during the suicidal crisis of the adolescent. These families usually become uncomfortable when asked if "suicide is against the rules" and often cannot give the adolescent a strong message against suicidal behavior. Conversely, Richman (1984) maintains that it is usually quite easy for families with adolescent members who are acting out in other behavioral patterns to quickly agree to a "no suicide contract" (p. 398). Families that do not strengthen the taboo and that cannot engage in actions directed at safety and reinforcing limits of their adolescent's behavior are colluding with the adolescent's suicidal actions.

Molin (1986) maintains that more covert suicidal behaviors may also be allowed by the parents through ineffective or absent limit setting, thus reinforcing for the adolescent a lack of commitment to the taboo against inflicting self-harm. In defining "covert suicidal behavior," Molin (1986) considers "those forms of self-destructive behavior that involve a deliberate threat to life, but are not typically recognized as suicide attempts" (p. 178). "This may include drunk or reckless driving, accident-proneness, various styles of counterphobic behavior, and some forms of substance abuse" (p. 179). Within this context, the victim does not directly express suicidal intent, nor does the family acknowledge the seriousness of such behavior in terms of compromising the child's welfare. A common example of such families are parents who know that their child engages in speeding and reckless behaviors in the car yet do not take away driving privileges. In this instance, the message to the youngster is, "I know you are behaving in an unsafe manner, but I will not extend myself to ensure your safety through direct action." This omission on the part of the parent reinforces the adolescent's sense of abandonment which, in turn, can be internalized as a lack of commitment for his or her own safety. It is often the ignoring of such covert self-destructive behavior that may fuel further overt suicidal actions. Specifically, the adolescent must subsequently attempt to solicit parental attention for nurturance, limit setting, and structure through the overtly self-injurious behaviors (Molin, 1986).

There may also be more covert signs of a family history of self-destructive behaviors that are acted out by the adolescent in more direct suicidal behaviors. Thus, clinicians who work with families must be alert to more subtle and covert signs of self-injurious actions on the part of all family members that may be modeled by the adolescent. Specifically, Tishler and McKenry (1982), in studying the parents of 46 adolescent suicide attempters with matched control parents of nonattempters, reported that "both mothers and fathers of suicide attempters used significantly more alcohol than did mothers and fathers of nonattempters" (p. 407). It can be argued that the adolescent's suicidal behavior is modeled after the parental self-injurious actions of alcohol abuse. Within this context, the suicide attempt on the part of the adolescent could be (a) a combined process of demanding the parent's involvement with the adolescent through the suicidal crisis (and thereby trying to lure the parent away from the self-focused drinking behavior), (b) an expression of anger toward the parent for lack of involvement (which is internalized into self-destructive behaviors), and (c) the continued experience of loss of parental attention (which may be internalized by the adolescent as feelings of low self-worth). While parental alcohol abuse is usually of a long-standing nature, the suicidal crisis becomes manifested when an acute stressor is superimposed on these families. The particular stressor taxes the more pathological coping mechanisms of avoidance and denial in alcoholic families, which in turn can potentially lead toward the adolescent acutely acting out the parents' more protracted self-destructive behavior.

There are other categories of parental dysfunction that also contribute to the manifestation of adolescent suicidal behavior. Particularly, families in which a parent exhibits psychiatric symptomatology, especially depression and severe illness such as schizophrenia, are especially vulnerable to crisis with their adolescents. Tishler and McKenry (1982) also concluded that fathers of suicide attempters manifested increased levels of depression, lower self-esteem, and higher anxiety than fathers of nonattempters, while mothers of attempters manifested increased levels of anxiety (however, this finding was only significant when mothers of female attempters were considered). These parents are often so consumed with their own problems and are so overwhelmed that they have few resources on which to depend to give their children support; thus, the adolescent feels isolated and alone. Often, when the adolescent demands emotional guidance, those demands overtax the parents' coping strategies, which further reinforces the adolescent's issues of abandonment and rejection. Families in which significant pathology exists are often vulnerable to even low levels of external stress because their normative existence is often very chaotic and dysfunctional. These are the families in which the adolescent's suicidal behavior can frequently be most lethal.

There are many factors operative in terms of the genesis of the suicidogenic family. Unfortunately, none of the foregoing characteristics are absolute; however, the delineated family dynamics offer the clinician some basis for decision making in terms of assessment and management of the suicidal adolescent. Even if overt suicidal behavior is not displayed, the preceding articulated risk factors and intrafamilial organizational structure should be warning signs that a self-destructive process may be evident and that it is imperative that the evaluator be specific in questioning both the adolescent and the family in order to try to decrease the incidents of adolescent suicidal behavior. The following two chapters address assessment of the suicidal crisis and mechanisms for treatment of suicidal adolescents and their families.

CHAPTER 8

Assessment of Suicidal Adolescents

ASSESSMENT OF SUICIDAL POTENTIAL

Assessment of suicide potential is a very complicated and difficult process. As of yet, there is not a specific measure or interview structure that offers 100% accuracy at distinguishing those adolescents who have serious intent to engage in self-harming behaviors, versus those who do not present a risk for actually following through on self-destructive ideation. Differentiating between those overt or covert clinical symptoms that warrant emergent hospitalization or outpatient services can be an arduous task.

During an interview with the adolescent and the family, even the most well-seasoned clinician can attest to the difficult nature of grasping the underlying dynamics of the current stresses, the adolescent's available coping mechanisms and resources, the potential for a crisis to explode into a dangerous situation, and the availability of the parents to protect, to set limits, and to nurture the adolescent through the acute phase of his or her emotional turmoil. In order to make cogent and comprehensive evaluations of suicidal risk, the clinician must engage in both an individual assessment of the adolescent and an assessment of the ability of the family to be a safe holding environment during the suicidal crisis. Careful analysis of both present stressors and previous events must form the basis of any decision about admitting the adolescent to a hospital setting or allowing the adolescent to remain within the family and community environment.

In making an assessment of a potentially emergent situation with adolescents, the main task is to be able to decode the ongoing crisis (Morrison & Smith, 1975). This is especially pertinent when adolescents show suicidal ideation, intent, or actual gestures, as this behavior is usually a by-product of broader and deeper problems. Specifically, the clinician must evaluate the present emergent conditions, as well as the underlying factors that operate to create a crisis in which self-harm is threatened.

Usually, suicidal emergencies encompass two general categories. The first of these is the actual threat or demonstration of urgent behavioral symptoms by the adolescent, such as articulated suicidal ideation or attempts. The second category involves problems within the familial system within which the adolescent resides. That is, parental anxiety, family disorganization and helplessness can also contribute to a crisis situation with an adolescent. Specifically, what appears to be an adolescent in crisis may actually be a crisis for the parent or the adult primarily in charge of the care of the youth (Morrison & Smith, 1975). For example, adolescents may be brought to the emergency room following a suicidal attempt, or they may be brought due to a parent's lack of resources in coping with expressions of hopelessness and depression by their adolescent. Emergencies with adolescents involve both the inability of the adolescent to exert self-control, and the inability of the parents to introduce increased levels of support, guidance, and structure through the particular crisis.

In order to make an effective assessment, as well as to begin to formulate the appropriate level of services, the clinician's first goal must be to make an initial appraisal of the youth and the family. Subsequently, the clinician must assist in the reestablishment of the lines of communication among family members, in order to complete the assessment process as well as to begin to formulate possible interventions for the alleviation of the crisis. The clinician must assist the family in reintroducing or initiating the necessary controls in the environment, either by helping the parents more effectively structure the household, or, if necessary, by introducing the possibility of external structure (e.g., hospitalizing the youth). Through both direct interview and observation of the adolescent and the family during the crisis situation, as well as the clinician's existing knowledge of risk factors, the clinician must decide on the level of care needed.

ASSESSMENT OF THE INDIVIDUAL ADOLESCENT: CONCEPTION OF THE CRISIS AND OF SUICIDAL INTENT

Assessment of the individual adolescent should be made on two levels. Specifically, adolescents should be interviewed within the context of their families as well as alone. Frequently, it is most helpful to start an emergent interview with the whole family in order to observe mechanisms of communication, the degree of expressed concern with the suicidal ideation or gesture, and the adolescent's connectedness to the family. It is also important to observe the ability of the adolescent to be able to verbalize feelings within the family context. If a decision is made to have the youngster remain with the family, one has to have some evidence to indicate that if stressors again become overwhelming, the adolescent will be able to communicate these to the family prior to making a suicidal attempt. Prior to meeting with the adolescent alone, it is important to have directly observed the manner in which the family relates to one another, as well as the manner in which they relate to the present suicidal crisis. In addition to observing the family, the clinician should solicit information from family members regarding their views of family interactions. (Assessment of the family is covered in the next section of this chapter.) Additionally, strategies for interviewing adolescents and their families have been covered in prior chapters; thus, the following discussion is directed at uncovering information concerning the potential suicidal crisis, and it assumes that such interviewing skills as establishing rapport and questioning strategies are understood as part of the process even though not directly specified in the crisis interview.

Usually, when a youngster is brought to an outpatient setting or even to an emergency room, the clinician has some brief information regarding the specific nature of the crisis. It is this information that the clinician uses as a starting point in interviewing an adolescent in a crisis. In the individual interview, the task is (a) to determine the adolescent's conception of the crisis and her or his level of suicidal intent, (b) to assess the degree of underlying disturbance (hopelessness, depression, anger, impulsivity, and reality testing), and (c) to delineate the quality and quantity of the adolescent's internal resources and coping strategies. These factors must be uncovered in order to determine what constitutes an emergent condition.

Issues regarding the crisis situation should be discussed in a straightforward manner with the adolescent. The adolescent should be questioned very closely regarding precipitating factors that have contributed to the crisis. It is essential that the adolescent's perspective be taken very seriously. The interviewer should also not be tempted by the family to minimize the adolescent's difficulties but should remain open to listening to the adolescent's pain, even though on the surface, it may seem trivial. For example, adolescents can sometimes present crisis situations following the breakup of a relationship with an opposite-sex peer. While this event may seem rather innocuous, given the more normative tumultuous nature of teenage relationships, in a youngster with a history of unresolved loss, it can be very traumatic and devastating. While in part expressed suicidal ideation or attempts are a form of communication, listening to the adolescent not only allows for an assessment of the dangerousness of the situation but also provides a message to the adolescent that his or her feelings and concerns are important. Additionally, if the adolescent is able to feel some relief at "getting things off his or her chest," this may suggest some resources for talking and working through problem areas; the presence of these resources may indicate that the youngster could remain within the family during the crisis.

Interviewing for suicidal risk or intent is often a very anxiety-producing situation. It is, however, usually more uncomfortable for the clinician than for the adolescent, who in fact is often relieved that someone will talk openly and honestly about suicide. It is a commonly held myth, even among many mental health professionals, that asking about suicide intent gives a suggestion to the adolescent. For the most part, adolescents do not answer affirmatively unless they have been giving it serious thought. The degree to which clinicians are comfortable in interviewing for suicidal risk and approach questioning the adolescent in a clear and straightforward manner often relates to the degree of honest disclosure by the adolescent. Using euphemisms and more covert references to suicide and self-harming statements often communicates to the adolescent the clinician's discomfort in discussing suicide and reinforces the myth that suicidal thoughts should be kept secret.

Pfeffer (1984) recommends such questions as, "Did you ever feel that things were so upsetting that you wished you would die?" or "Have you been feeling so sad, angry, or upset that you thought of killing yourself" or "Did you ever want to commit suicide" (p. 178). Additionally, it is prudent to ask about any contemplated plans of carrying out suicidal ideation, initiated prior attempts, knowledge of family members and friends who have attempted suicide and their reactions, and any prior ideation. Also in this phase of the interview, it is important to be nonjudgmental concerning the adolescent's verbalizations, as the goal is to uncover as much information as possible, and any hint of criticism may also cause the youngster to become defensive, guarded, and withholding. The purpose of interviewing the adolescent is to determine the lethality and nature of the suicidal crisis in order to put into place necessary safeguards. Without the clinician attempting to create an atmosphere that promotes an open dialogue, the adolescent's suicidal intent may remain a dangerous secret.

With this information gathered, the clinician must then make some determination of the level of danger. While nothing is absolute, there are a number of general guidelines that can be followed to maximize the youngster's safety. First, all references, no matter how subtle, either to self-harm or to harming others should be taken seriously. As has already been discussed, a common myth is that at some time, everyone feels suicidal, and some statements need to be taken with a "grain of salt." With adolescents, this is a dangerous supposition, as suicidal statements or behavior are not a product of a particularly stressed normal youngster; instead, they usually indicate underlying problems. It is therefore more prudent to "consider any suicidal communication as a signal of potential danger and of underlying psychiatric disorder" (Pfeffer, 1984, p. 172).

It is better to err on the side of caution, and therefore any expression of self-harming statements; even those said in what appears to be jest should be taken seriously. Suicidal statements or gestures by adolescents should be interpreted to mean that the youngster is overwhelmed and does not have available the coping strategies necessary to deal with the acute level of stress. This cry should be answered by adults taking charge to ensure the adolescent's safety (this is discussed in subsequent sections).

Additionally, a more subtle form of self-harming behavior potentially can be hidden in the accident-prone youngster. If a child is repeatedly the victim of accidents, a closer evaluation should be initiated to determine whether this is not a product of an underlying process and perhaps an unconscious wish to do self-harm or self-annihilation.

When adolescents answer affirmatively to suicidal intent, further questioning is needed to assess (a) the amount of energy spent on suicidal thoughts and (b) whether any plans have been put into place to initiate a specific action. Adolescents with an articulated suicide plan must be taken very seriously, regardless of the interviewer's assessment of the viability of the plan. These youngsters not only feel hopeless about their situation, but also have engaged in deliberate thought as to how to be self-destructive. More covert signs of deliberate suicidal thought activity include the following: giving away prized possessions; showing a lack of interest in previously important activities; increasing resolution of personal issues with others, such as apologizing "out of the blue" for past behaviors or even existence; increasing social isolation; changing dramatically their predominant mood; and extensively questioning about an afterlife and other religious issues.

The clues emitted by adolescents can be quite subtle. For example, one adolescent male became quite obsessed with the threat of nuclear disaster and continuously argued the point with his parents that the nuclear threat was quite imminent, contributing to his sense that it was useless to be a part of this "horrible society." While his parents acknowledged some of the truth to the dangers of nuclear war, they often tried to cajole him out of his "morbid thoughts" without success. They became concerned when he refused to go to school and interact with peers "as nothing matters anyway." Even though realistically we all live under the potential threat of nuclear war, his obsession with this potential danger was immobilizing and appeared to be rationalizing processes for suicidal behavior. Therefore, it is not only an articulated plan that presents potential danger, but it is also the adolescent's general relationships with the environment in terms of degree of hopelessness about the future. Certainly, the combined presence of an articulated plan with overt hopelessness presents a very dangerous situation, often necessitating emergent hospitalization.

While the preceding scenario is relatively straightforward in terms of the need for intensive intervention, when no articulated plan exists, judgments must be made concerning the degree of present suicidal ideation and the current nature of the suicidal intent. Specifically, some youths have contemplated suicide, but when questioned as to whether they would follow through, they often comment "I just couldn't really do that." These are usually the adolescents with no specific plan of carrying out the suicidal ideation, and in some cases, their intent does not pose an immediate danger. However, to the degree that they have considered suicide, the nature of their inner turmoil should not be underestimated. For the most part, these youngsters often do well in outpatient services and do not require hospitalization.

On the other hand, the adolescents who are quite preoccupied with suicidal ideation and have an articulated plan present an increased risk and frequently require more intensive interventions, such as an inpatient setting. A simple yet helpful tool is to ask the adolescent, "On a scale from 0 (which is no suicidal intent) to 10 (which is very strong ideation and high chances of initiating an action), what number you would give yourself?" When the number is volunteered, it can give the clinician some frame of reference for the immediacy of the suicidal crisis from the adolescent's perspective. Questions subsequently need to be posed as to whether they have felt recently higher or lower on the scale, what factors would contribute to the number going up or down, and what was the worst they ever felt. For example if an adolescent reported feeling an 8, 9, or 10 in the past and had not followed through on any action, this may indicate that the adolescent has some adequate coping strategies even when in the heat of a crisis. It is also important to note that it is rare (if not nonexistent) for an adolescent to state that he or she is high on the scale without the situation being in fact an emergency one. Any high numbers should be regarded very seriously, as it is the adolescent's own admission of being or feeling out of control with regard to ensuring personal safety.

Additionally, when asked about suicidal ideation or intent, some adolescents admit that they have been feeling that way in the past, but they are not presently suicidal. These adolescents need to be questioned specifically concerning what led up to those feelings, how they dealt with those issues, and what differentiates their current crisis from their past experiences when they did feel suicidal. Once again, through these questions, the interviewer may learn both internal coping strategies available to the adolescent and past external support figures who may be reactivated in the present crisis, thereby perhaps avoiding hospitalization. Adolescents who remain more vague regarding how they stopped feeling suicidal may be of more concern. Within this context, adolescents may commonly report "I forgot about it," or "I don't know." Without information available to them on how they solved previous crises, they remain more vulnerable in the present crisis situation. Conversely, those adolescents who admit to current ideation present an increased risk. These youngsters' preoccupation and distress have compromised their coping skills, and they often need external structure and emotional guidance in order to reorganize their personal resources.

It is important to note that expressed suicidal ideation or intent is not a necessary condition for an acute crisis. Guarded and withholding adolescents may harbor suicidal ideation, yet they may be unable or unwilling to communicate this to the evaluator. For them, subtle possible indicators of suicidal ideation are depression, sad mood, emotional lability, a pervasive sense of hopelessness about the present and the future, obsession with death, persistent talk about an afterlife, questions about suicide, or fascination with morbid themes. While adolescence is often a time during which some of these issues are contemplated, continued preoccupation and/or verbalization of these topics are not common and thus should be considered seriously.

Depression and sad mood, however, are not a necessary condition for suicidal ideation or behavior. Adolescents who act out their anger and/or sadness by defying limits can also be in danger of causing harm to others as well as to themselves. In fact, as previously mentioned, adolescents with problems of behavior and conduct also frequently engage in serious self-harming behaviors. Consequently, threats or incidents of setting fires; of aggression directed toward parents, siblings, peer or animals; and of severe destruction of property are all indicators that the adolescent is out of control and needs a more intensively structured setting than can be provided at home. Behaviors such as running away from school and home, befriending adult strangers, alcohol or other drug involvement, and risk-taking behaviors (as for example skateboarding in the middle of traffic, jumping from high places, playing with knives and other sharp tools), all indicate that the adolescent has little value for his or her safety and potentially for the safety of others, thus necessitating immediate intervention.

Often, these conduct-disordered youngsters are even more vulnerable because they are not observed as being depressed and hopeless. Typically, those involved with these adolescents often react to their defiance and oppositional behaviors by reinforcing limits without investigating the inner emotional problems that are fueling their more negative behaviors. As already mentioned, conduct-disordered youngsters tend to be quite impulsive in their actions and to have a higher propensity for engaging in risk-taking behaviors. This combined impulsivity and dangerousness potentially can create a very lethal situation. Therefore, youngsters who present conduct-disordered behaviors should be questioned closely, and their ideation and actions should be considered within the potential for them to engage in self-injurious actions, either through denial of inherent risk or through lack of concern for safety issues.

Finally, adolescents who manifest severe disturbance of thinking processes (such as admitting to visual or auditory hallucinations, difficulties in following a thought through to completion, disorientation, paranoia, delusions, or blunted emotional expressions) also constitute a group of youngsters who necessitate emergent intervention. These behaviors represent the most serious of disturbances, as, by definition when these adolescents are in acute crisis, they have difficulties differentiating fantasy from reality. They may believe in a magical sense that they cannot actually die and may engage in behaviors in which they inflict self-harm without realizing the possible lethal consequences of their actions. Therefore, the clinician should be especially alerted to those adolescents who display both suicidal ideation and more psychotic processes, as these are adolescents whose ideational content can be quite destructive because they often lack any observing ego to differentiate their more delusional fantasy life from reality. It is the rare case in which these individuals are not immediately hospitalized due to this extreme level of potential dangerousness in pairing depressed emotion with distorted thinking.

There has been some inconsistent evidence regarding the contagion effect with regard to adolescent suicidal behavior (Range, Goggin, & Steede, 1988). While there is no clearly researched connection between knowledge of a suicidal act and subsequent behavior, this factor cannot be overlooked in assessing adolescents. Specifically, it is important to question adolescents concerning their knowledge of prior suicides within their family and their peers, or even any familiarity with such actions in the news media. Range et al. (1988) maintains that "people believe that a connection exists, whether it does or not. Unfortunately, this belief could turn out to be a self-fulfilling prophecy that is fatal for teens" (p. 340). Therefore, direct investigation should incorporate recent events, as well as issues surrounding anniversaries of deaths either by suicide or other causes. For example, one youngster attempted suicide on the anniversary of her father's death, as she maintained a delusion that her father's spirit visited earth each year on that day to take other souls to heaven. The importance of past historical events in the life of the adolescent must be considered in light of the present crisis.

Occasionally, an interview involves an adolescent who has had an actual prior suicidal attempt. While there has been some controversy in the literature regarding previous attempts and subsequent suicidal behavior, Shafii et al. (1985) maintains that both those who talk of suicide and those who have previous histories of suicidal behavior can be successful at inflicting serious self-harm and annihilation. Therefore, the adolescent with a history of suicidal attempts presents a very difficult and dangerous situation for the clinician who is making an assessment. Sometimes, with adolescents who have engaged in multiple attempts, clinicians get caught in the trap of becoming concerned that repeated hospitalizations reinforce the adolescent's suicidal behavior. While this may be true in part, it is usually better to confront these issues when the adolescent is a part of an inpatient setting than to challenge the adolescent when one has little ability to contain the suicidal behaviors. Perhaps shorter hospital stays and constructing the hospitalization to offer the adolescent less secondary gain may release the clinician from feeling in a quandary when faced with hospitalizing a repeat suicidal offender. It is also important to remember that adolescents with previous suicidal actions tend to be impulsive; this often makes differentiation of a more manipulative threat from serious intent an almost impossible task, as what starts out as a manipulative gesture may in fact result in deadly consequences. Adolescents with histories of multiple attempts often are quite seriously disturbed, and therefore it is usually more prudent to involve the structure of the hospital setting during crisis periods.

While it is also important to assess the level of lethality in an adolescent's past suicide attempts, one should not be lulled into a false sense of security concerning adolescents whose past behaviors seem more like "gestures." In a study of 82 adolescents, Gispert et al. (1985) concluded that "the medical lethality of the means used in the suicide attempts varied and did not correlate with the patient's perception of the risk of dying" (p. 756). As has already been mentioned, adolescents as a group may be unrealistic as to what are relatively more innocuous actions directed to be gestures and cries for help, versus those behaviors that seriously compromise the adolescents' welfare. Assessment of potential risk should more appropriately be made by questioning the expressed wish of the adolescent to die at the time of the attempt and on the fact that the adolescent was serious enough (whether it was a cry for help or not) to engage in a clear action directed at self-harm.

While the foregoing represent some guidelines for emergent situations, an additional important indicator is the clinician's own experience of the potential threat. Often, a good rule of thumb is that if you are constantly thinking about a particular adolescent in terms of making the correct decision when you opted for a less restrictive level of care (i.e., made the decision not to hospitalize the adolescent), then the chances are that that adolescent may have needed the hospital setting. In other words, adolescents who unsettle the experienced clinician frequently are unsettled and disorganized themselves. In working with suicidal adolescents, it is important to trust your own gut feelings and to be cautious, as the adolescents tend to be impulsive and emotionally labile. However, in terms of determining the actual potential for the emergence of a dangerous situation, it is not only your own assessment of the individual adolescent that is important, but it is also your view of the symptomatic adolescent within the context of the family that is important, particularly in terms of questions centering on the family's ability to protect the adolescent's safety and to provide emotional support. The preceding assessment allows for a comprehensive understanding of the crisis situation, thereby contributing to a more prudent process of decision making.

ASSESSMENT OF THE FAMILY

If the clinician accepts the notion that the adolescent's suicidal behavior is a form of communication (Aldridge, 1984), then the purpose of the family interview should be directed at uncovering the necessity, intensity, and meaning of the adolescent's communication. In discussing assessment of suicidogenic families, Richman (1984) delineates four conditions that must be addressed in terms of evaluating level of danger: (1) the individual adolescent's feelings of being overwhelmed and unable to cope; (2) the family and social network also feeling overwhelmed, with depleted emotional resources; (3) the presence of a crisis that is viewed by the individual and by the family as unsolvable; and (4) an acceptance, even if not overt, within the family that suicide is a possible solution (Richman, 1984, pp. 395–396). By assessing these four factors, an appraisal can be made concerning the ability of the adolescent and the family to create a safe environment, thereby avoiding hospitalization.

In addition to the individual interview with the adolescent, in which an assessment is made concerning both the level of crisis the adolescent is experiencing and the youngster's available resources or disabilities, the clinician must interview the family to discover their assessment of the adolescent's turmoil; this is often a good point of entry in the evaluation of the family environment. The family should be questioned as to (a) when they first noticed that the adolescent was having difficulties, (b) what steps were taken to deal with the presenting problems, and (c) how the child reacted to these attempts of support and guidance if or when they were instituted.

These questions are directed at deciphering the level of emotional communication and connection between the parents and the adolescent. Specifically, parents who first acknowledge a crisis with their adolescent after a suicidal attempt usually have been more distant from their adolescent. In fact, the adolescent's communication through suicidal behavior often involves the underlying message "I'm hurting. Is anyone out there listening?" Families that didn't acknowledge the emotional turmoil of the adolescent prior to an actual gesture or attempt present a less safe situation for managing suicidal ideation and behaviors on an outpatient basis. Simply put, when the adolescent's emotional pain is a secret from the family, the potential level of danger with regard to suicidal ideation or behaviors increases. Unless there is considerable attention and energy focused on the adolescent, it is likely that the family will revert back to more avoidant behaviors, thus creating a system that perpetuates suicidal behaviors in order to elicit help. Typically, adolescents within these families are hospitalized, both to protect the adolescents' safety and to use the intensity of the hospital situation to develop and reorganize patterns of communication.

While families that are disengaged from their adolescent's pain increase the potential threat of suicidal behavior, enmeshed families also need to be evaluated for their ability to listen to, communicate with, and support their youngster (Senior, 1988). These families have enlisted the help of the adolescent to maintain a more pathological homeostasis, especially when the threat of separation or loss is impending (Aldridge, 1984; Aldridge & Rossiter, 1984; Richman, 1984; Senior, 1988), or they are characterized by adolescents who have taken on the burden of being the support figure (parenting their parents) to parents under stress (Sargent, 1987). The potential danger involved in the adolescent's suicidal ideation or behavior is determined by the degree to which parents are unable to respond to the potentially compromising position of the adolescent as receptacle of family depression. For example, in a case mentioned in the previous chapter, April attempted suicide after her mother was unable to acknowledge the pain April felt about being pulled between her caregiving role with her mother following the parental divorce and her interest in pursuing more age-appropriate peer relationships. April's desperate communication was directed toward informing the adults in her life about her excruciating bind. When April's mother did not show any awareness of her contributions to April's dilemma and/or recognition of her child's pain, the crisis situation intensified. April consequently acted out her feelings of suffocation from the family dynamics through her suicidal behavior.

Even though the suicidal act often represents a breakdown of an appropriate level of intrafamilial communication, it does not always necessitate that an adolescent be removed from the family setting. Specifically, some families can use the crisis situation very quickly to adopt more adequate mechanisms for sharing information, for giving support and guidance, and for introducing appropriate setting of limits. These families usually are open to directives from the clinician, are not overtly critical or infantilizing of their adolescent, and appear to be genuinely responsive to their adolescent's verbalizations of pain.

Conversely, some families may be less able to be successfully managed on an outpatient basis, such as those that are less available to listen, that seem either overtly critical and hostile or overwhelmed and reluctant to get involved with their child (through support and/or through setting limits), or that are preoccupied with their own problems. For these families, the hospital often offers the parents some temporary relief in parenting their child such that they can separate their own difficulties from the problems presented by their child, thus allowing them to become more responsive to their adolescent's needs. In interviewing families, it is essential that the clinician listen very carefully to the awareness, desire, and ability of the parent in the present crisis situation to have empathy with regard to their adolescent's pain and to offer nurturance and comfort.

Even with parents who have the best of intentions, an important aspect of the assessment must be made concerning the level of the crisis situation. The clinician needs to make a determination of the demonstrated symptomatology and the ability of the family environment to provide a holding environment. Specifically, some adolescents manifest quite serious disturbances, such as an underlying psychotic process in addition to verbalized suicidal ideation. These individuals are often not able to remain at home, no matter how attuned the parents are to the adolescents' difficulties. Additionally, the quite acutely suicidal adolescent who manifests a clear and serious suicide plan frequently also presents too much of a risk to be at home. Consequently, it is essential that the level of expressed symptomatology not only be considered within the capabilities of the family environment to exercise control and support, but it must also be evaluated for the potential danger of the symptoms in their own right.

Crisis situations often also present themselves in reaction to parents feeling overwhelmed and depleted of necessary resources to assist their adolescent. In fact, relatively minor symptomatology can be quite devastating for disorganized families. It is important that the clinician listen very carefully to the parents' statements concerning their ability to summon the energy needed to protect their child's safety. A clinician who is told by parents that they feel inadequate in parenting through the crisis, unsafe with their adolescent, extermely angry and upset, or emotionally overwhelmed should think through carefully the viability of managing the adolescent within the home situation. If emotions are especially raw in family members, any further stress may escalate issues to crisis proportions. Thus, the first objective is to assess the ability of the family environment to manage the crisis effectively. For example:

Judy presented to an emergency room after her parents found a suicide note. No suicidal action had been undertaken as of yet, and Judy was vague concerning her plan for carrying out the threat of her letter. This was an extremely chaotic and disengaged family, and the mother verbalized that this was the "last straw"; she just "couldn't manage."

Sending this youngster in this particular situation immediately back into the family environment could potentially be dangerous. Both the family and the individual adolescent are in crisis, with few resources for exchanging support and comfort. Therefore, even though the relative threat of suicidal risk in this case may be more moderate (because no gesture has been yet made), the potential dangerousness of the situation to further deteriorate is quite high. It is important to define situations of increased risk by both the degree of emotional turmoil in the adolescent and the degree of exhaustion of the family system, in terms of generating appropriate coping and problem-solving behaviors (Richman, 1984).

Another important aspect of the family evaluation in terms of suicide potential is to assess the degree to which the family is rigid and relatively unavailable to change some inappropriate patterns of relating. Specifically, those families that perceive the crisis situation as unsolvable and hopeless place the adolescent at increased risk to engage in more extreme behaviors (Richman, 1984). These are often the families who come into the clinician's office full of anger, hurt, and resentment. They are guarded in the amount of information that is disclosed, and they often reject any hypotheses or reframing statements that are offered by the clinician concerning the suicidal behavior. Continually addressing blame onto specific family members is often also a major characteristic of these families. They remain fairly resistant to engage in alternative problem-solving behaviors even when so directed. These families are frequently most frustrating for the clinician, and it is important for the clinician to consider the level of frustration the family projects. For example, is this a family that is so binding and castrating to its members that suicide is viewed by the adolescent as a way out of the family turmoil and confusion? If this appears to be an operating dynamic, then it may be important for the family and the adolescent to be separated for a period of time in order for this collective frustration not to explode into self-injurious behaviors on the part of the adolescent.

Finally, it is important to assess the degree of either covert or overt acceptance within the family of the use of suicide as a solution (Richman, 1984). As has already been mentioned, families that do not maintain a clear taboo against use of suicide are at potentially greater risk to have a member verbalize suicidal ideation or to engage in suicidal behaviors when in a crisis situation. Discussing suicide with the family is as important as addressing this issue with the adolescent. Again, talking directly about the concept of suicide with family members is of the utmost importance, both to clarify their feelings about their adolescent's behavior and to determine the degree to which they are covertly supporting self-injurious actions.

While this type of discussion with family members may be uncomfortable, it often produces even more anxiety in suicidogenic families (Richman, 1984). Thus, with families that have been withholding, this discussion may give the clinician a window into the family processes that had been unreachable previously. The clinician should listen very carefully for ambivalence on the part of family members, especially parents, to reinforce the taboo both in verbalizations and in actions. For example, a parent who says, "of course suicide is against our family beliefs" but then argues with the clinician regarding removal of firearms from the house during the crisis is ambivalent (at best!) about ensuring that the taboo is reinforced.

While the aforementioned areas are important to investigate during the emergent interview, it may also be helpful in particularly stressed families for the clinician to ask about available resources outside the family before deciding on hospitalizing a youngster. For example, as previously discussed, if an adolescent's suicidal ideation is vague and in actuality more reflective of intrafamilial stress, the adolescent may be able to stay in the home of grandparents until the acute crisis is worked through. Occasionally in divorce situations, one parent can provide a cooling-off place while issues with the other parent are resolved. If hospitalization is being considered for the adolescent in crisis, it is often most prudent to meet the extended family members or friends who have offered to provide some relief to the situation, prior to making a final determination of the viability of an alternative living situation. However, in more mild cases, it is usually less disruptive to use these familial and community supports; nevertheless, caution should be exercised, and the clinician should be careful not to assume that these significant others can provide the containment and the safety a hospital would provide. The youngster should be hospitalized if an intensive holding environment is needed beyond the present capabilities of the family, extended family members, and larger available community resources.

The present chapter has dealt with important areas of assessment in uncovering self-destructive processes within the adolescent and the family. In order to be most helpful to these adolescents and their families, the clinician must use the information gathered to assist the family in breaking the cycle of the patterns of interactions that have both generated the suicidal crisis and sustained more isolation and desperation among family members. The following chapter centers on interventions used with the suicidogenic family such that these more disruptive and despairing mechanisms of interactions are replaced with more adaptive and growth-facilitating patterns of relating.

CHAPTER 9

Strategies for Dealing with the Suicidal Crisis

DECISION TO ADMIT

Being presented with a suicidal adolescent and her or his family (whether it is in an emergency setting, an outpatient practitioner's office, or a community mental health center) can provoke anxiety even in the most seasoned clinician. Within this context, clinicians often view as their primary task the decision whether to admit the youngster into a hospital environment or to maintain the adolescent within the family setting. The clinician's anxiety not only is a product of assessing the potential level of dangerousness and lethality of the adolescent, but also involves an internal struggle between using a hospital setting—and thereby seeming to usurp the power of the parental subsystem—and allowing the family to be responsible for the suicidal behavior—and thereby limiting the therapist's own control over the situation.

Many clinicians attempt to resist hospitalization almost at all costs, maintaining that to take the adolescent out of the crisis situation is to give in to the family pathology of scapegoating, as it clearly identifies the adolescent child as the dysfunctional member. These clinicians may feel that they have failed the family if they are unable to maintain the adolescent within the home setting. Conversely, other clinicians frequently use the hospital setting, as they define the suicidal crisis as a cry for help from the family, who, by the very nature of the manifestation of suicidal behavior among one of its members, is stating that it cannot cope effectively. At the extreme of this position are those who believe that separating the child from the family will assist in decreasing the suicidal behavior, as "it must be the family environment that is so toxic to this kid." Within this conceptualization is the notion that the family has failed.

Both of these positions (i.e., therapist as failure, family as failure) make a positive adjustment more problematic because the underlying notion is that of failure. Therefore, it is more helpful to view the initial session with a suicidal family as one of cooperating with the family to make a decision rather than one of solving the problem for them. The notion of working within a more positive framework is of the utmost importance, as these families are used to feelings of frustration, anger, and incompetence (Landau-Stanton & Stanton, 1985).

Within the context of cooperation, the responsibility to admit is equally shared between the clinician and the family, allowing for a pooling of resources. Specifically, the family brings its expertise on (a) the adolescent's and the family's history, (b) knowledge of the adolescent, and (c) knowledge of the adolescent's and the family's present functioning with regard to available resources and limitations. The clinician brings expertise concerning normative and pathological adolescent and family functioning, as well as knowledge about the parameters of emergent situations. Consequently, the suicidal crisis session becomes a forum whereby parents and therapist unite to determine the most appropriate level of care for the youngster. It is important to note that determination of the level of care is an evolving process throughout the crisis interview, during which the clinician must (a) listen to the family's verbalized and demonstrated level of distress, (b) observe interactions among family members, (c) offer the family some structure and guidelines, and (d) observe the family's reactions to the clinician's suggestions and interventions. If an atmosphere of cooperation can be established with the clinician, then the family often will demonstrate an increased capacity to cooperate with the needs of the distressed adolescent member.

THE CRISIS SESSION

The goal of the crisis session with the family is directed at both acceptance of the family and disorienting the family from its present ways of thinking, behaving, and feeling, which have engendered the current crisis atmosphere and have sustained the suicidal ideation or behavior (Brendler, Silver, Haber, & Sargent, 1989). Specifically, Brendler et al. (1989) maintain that the old patterns of behavior have jammed the normal processes of the family development and growth, preventing these processes from unfolding. The frustrations from this jam have produced a sense of desperation, hopelessness, and isolation—a lack of connectedness and interpersonal sharing. In suicidal families, this desperate state has erupted into the threat or the actual manifestation of violence directed by one family member toward her- or himself. Thus, the goal of disorientation is to release the jam and to allow for the more normative maturation process of all family members to continue (Brendler et al., 1989). The clinician works with the family (via acceptance) to uncover the amount of distress and to empower the parents to provide a safe environment for their adolescent, as well as to foster affective sharing and communication such that future crisis situations can be adequately resolved.

The following are the stages of the crisis interview:

1. Understanding the family crisis (from the family's perspective)
2. Expanding the frame (of conceptualization of the crisis)
3. Exploring pathways of safety and empowering the parents to provide them.

In order to further explicate the processes of the crisis work, a case example charts a path through these steps of working with a family that presented a suicidal crisis.

Mrs. D. called the admission/intake worker at a local private psychiatric hospital regarding her daughter, Melanie, who had verbalized suicidal intent that morning. After a brief interview with the mother, the intake worker confirmed that Melanie met the criteria to be admitted to the hospital. Never having been involved in therapy services before, Mrs. D. thought this was a drastic step and asked the intake worker for a referral to a private practitioner who could see her daughter that afternoon. Melanie had become increasingly hostile and depressed during the past month, fighting frequently with her mother over limits and household rules. On one occasion, the fight escalated to the point at which Melanie ran out of the house and was missing for several hours. Usually, an "A" or "B" student, Melanie recently had received notices that she was in danger of dropping to "C" & "D" grades in four of her seven classes.

Mrs. D. had separated from Mr. D. about 2 months prior to the present crisis, on a trial basis, due to her being "finally fed up with his drinking." Mr. D. had numerous health problems, which were exacerbated by his drinking behavior. Melanie had an older brother, Jim, who was away at college in a distant state. Melanie blamed her mother for the breakup and seemed preoccupied with her father's well-being. This was reinforced by her father, who continuously used Melanie as a confidant about his problems, hoping to solicit her help in having her mother take him back. Mrs. D. often became quite angry at Melanie when Melanie raised concerns over her father, which created a greater distance between Melanie and her mother. Initially, Melanie tried to establish an alliance with her father against her mother's rules, as evidenced on one occasion by her asking him if she could live with him. Mr. D. stated "that it wasn't a good idea and that Melanie was better off living with her mother." Feeling alienated by her mother and overwhelmed by her father's problems and angry over his recent rejection, even though "she had stood by him," Melanie stated to her mother in the heat of an argument that "I might as well slit my wrists because it isn't worth living in this hell." Mr. and Mrs. D. and Melanie all came to the initial interview.

Understanding the Family Crisis

The initial task of the crisis interview is to understand the nature of the family crisis from the viewpoint of the family. The suicidal symptomatology is the point of departure in beginning to work with the family. The clinician must not only explore the family's notion of the factors leading up to the manifestation of the suicidal ideation or behavior, but must also question the family as to how (a) the present suicidal ideation or actions, (b) the recent problematic behaviors, or (c) the precipitating events (such as the marital separation in the preceding case) have organized and had an impact on family relationships. In making the family feel accepted, the clinician begins the interview by allowing the family members to tell their story. Each person must be allowed to talk. The clinician's role should be one of facilitator, in terms of giving each person a chance to speak, as well as one of observer of familial interaction patterns.

While the clinician, in questioning the family, should use the family's language, the references to the suicidal ideation or behavior should be made directly. The clinician thereby models that talking about suicide directly and openly should be encouraged. This brings potentially dangerous secrets concerning such behavior into the interview. While assessing with the family the appropriate level of care needed, it is important also to initially sustain the crisis situation within the interview. In this initial stage, helping to calm emotions may contribute to important information being superficially glossed over. It is best for the family to demonstrate their conflictual, angry, and/or depressed emotions within the session rather than to allow a more distant treatment of the problem areas that may contribute to the continuation of a dangerous situation once the family leaves the clinician's office (Richman, 1984). Promoting the demonstration of the crisis within the office gives the clinician some appreciation for the level of stress present in the home situation. Additionally, by openly talking about the suicidal ideation or behavior, the clinician gives the family both the permission and the tools to confront crisis situations in the future in an open and honest manner. The goal at this stage of the interview is to gain the family's understanding of the problems, to take suicide out of the shroud of secrecy and/or denial, and to begin to create an atmosphere where more distant and isolated patterns of interacting can begin to be uncovered and changed. The following is an excerpt from the preceding case during this stage of the interview.

THERAPIST: When did you first notice that Melanie was feeling suicidal?

MRS. D.: Well, we got into this fight this morning, and she screamed at me that she wanted to slit her wrists. No one in my family has ever said such a horrible thing. Part of me really feels she just wanted to get my attention. I don't think she really meant it. She sometimes will do anything to get out of punishment.

THERAPIST: Melanie did you really want to kill yourself?

MELANIE: I am so sick of her stuff, she is constantly yelling at me, she wouldn't care if I did die. Then she could have one perfect child, Jim.

MR. D.: Melanie, you don't mean that. I think you just let things get to you.

MRS. D.: (turning to the therapist) I think [that] like most teenagers, Melanie is dramatic and wanted some attention. I don't think she had any intention of carrying out any actions. She just wanted to upset things.

THERAPIST: Yet, what presently concerns me, is even after some time has passed since this morning, Melanie is still talking about the possibility of dying and I am wondering whether this is just empty words or on some level that this reflects her seriousness, since in my work I often find that kids who talk about it have seriously thought about suicide.

This family is presenting a denying stance with regard to the seriousness of their daughter's verbalizations. The therapist's use of words such as "suicide," and "dying" are purposeful in order to raise the level of stress and crisis within the interview. If this family is able to acknowledge on some level that while the adolescent may be oppositional in many ways, her verbalized suicidal ideation also indicates that she feels overwhelmed, then perhaps some appropriate comfort and care can be given to her by the parents.

While it is often too easy to conclude that this family is cold and uncaring, families that present themselves in such a manner frequently feel very incompetent. It is out of this incompetence and underlying sense of failure that more defensive verbalizations and stances emerge. Therefore, even though the clinician may need to use rather strong language to raise the level of stress such that alternative patterns of relating can be explored and instituted, this must be done in a way that is respectful of the family. Careful attention must be paid to using pointed language without suggesting blame or criticism. Rather, a more matter-of-fact style with regard to discussing the suicidal intent with an acceptance of the value of each family member's perspective will be of the most benefit in maximizing the available information, as well as in fostering the family's cooperation during this stage of the crisis session.

Expanding the Frame

While families can initially appear rigid, inflexible, and ostensibly distant from their adolescent (as in the preceding case), in working with suicidal families, it is important to believe that at the core of these families is a dedication to and a caring for the youngster. The clinician's task is to allow this caring to emerge and to break through the barriers that isolate family members from each other (Brendler et al., 1989). Often, reframing the meaning of the adolescent's suicidal ideation or behavior can in and of itself open new avenues for the family in conceptualizing the behavior. In turn, this may give the family access to additional mechanisms of coping, thereby "dislodging the log jam in the river" (Brendler et al., 1989).

Landau-Stanton and Stanton (1985) enumerate three common positive reframes of the adolescent's suicidal behavior: (1) viewing the adolescent as incorporating the collective family grieving process over some current or past event; (2)

conceptualizing the suicidal behavior as being metaphorical or reflective of family distress (e.g., perhaps hiding mother's or father's depression); and (3) viewing the behavior as being directed toward helping others to avoid dealing with their own pain (e.g., such as deflecting attention from the marital discord) (Landau-Stanton & Stanton, 1985).

All three of these frames may be useful in the preceding case. For example, Melanie's suicidal intent may be describing the loss due to the breakup of the family (grieving). Second, Melanie's suicidal ideation mirrors the father's more subtle self-injurious actions through his drinking behaviors despite how it places him in a dangerous health state (reflecting family distress). Finally, her behaviors can be seen as protective of the parents as they can become so caught up in Melanie's problems that dealing with the end of the marriage is avoided (thereby deflecting attention from underlying issues). In order for reframing to have its desired impact, the stage must be well ordered, and the reframe must be well timed.

The following is an example of such a reframe in the context of the preceding case.

THERAPIST: We have talked for some time now about Melanie's suicidal feelings and the factors which have lead up to them. It seems like a very complicted process, with people feeling both angry and hurt. I am wondering that if things got really better with Melanie and she started to do well in school and go along with the house rules, who would the family worry about?

MRS. D.: Are you kidding, we would be worry free. I would be so happy if Melanie was O.K.

THERAPIST: I am going to press the family a little bit to think about my question. It seems that Melanie is a serious problem for you now, but each family often has some other worries even when things are going O.K.

MELANIE: (starts to cry) I have been worried that my father is going to die and no one can help him.

THERAPIST: (to Mrs. D.) Are you also worried that your husband may die?

MRS. D.: Well, the whole reason I left him was I couldn't stand waiting at night to see that he came home safely and didn't die in a car crash. I also couldn't stand him ignoring his doctors; I didn't want to be a widow and see him die right before my eyes. I was sick of taking responsibility for him and felt if he was going to kill himself, he might as well do it without my help. I can't wait in the wings to clean up the mess.

MR. D.: I think you are really exaggerating. It isn't as bad as you say.

MRS. D.: It is that bad, and I refuse to live in your hell.

THERAPIST: (turning to Mrs. D.) I know this may sound strange to you, but I wonder if in a way Melanie is suicidal to demonstrate to you and to the family how scared she is for her father's safety. One thing her suicidal statements did was to bring everyone to counseling today, and maybe she thought if the family came, Dad could get the help he needs. In some ways, she made a problem in herself to let the family know there were other serious problems.

MRS. D.: I'm not sure I understand. Lately, Melanie has been so self-centered I'm not sure she really thought of her Dad's welfare.

THERAPIST: Mrs. D., can you look at your daughter now? She is crying, and it really feels to me that in part, she is torn between wanting a relationship with you and yet feeling if she doesn't pay attention to Dad, he will die. In being caught between your separation, she became overwhelmed. In fact, I'm wondering if you felt like she does, so desperate and helpless, all those years you tried to get your husband to stop drinking. I'm also wondering what you could have used then from your family and friends for support. Maybe you could offer her some support from what you learned.

MRS. D.: Melanie, I wish if you had been feeling so scared about Dad that you could tell me instead of fighting with me. I know how horrible it is to watch people you love slowly hurting themselves. One part of what made me so angry at you when you talked about killing yourself was here I go once again with someone who doesn't care about what that means or about me. I couldn't bear to have another family member not care about themself or the family.

Within the context of this reframe, the emotional tone of the session dramatically changes. Melanie is no longer seen as defiant and manipulative, but instead is viewed as caring and overwhelmed—a position Mrs. D. is very familiar with, and thus mother and daughter are allowed to share their pain and concerns. Even Mr. D., who is rather isolated at this moment, is hearing the concerns about his welfare from family members. A well-conceptualized and well-timed reframe will cause a dramatic emotional shift in the session. This often allows for more flexibility and provides the family with much needed space to communicate and share feelings, especially within the conflictual parent–child dyad. As the shift occurs, the jammed areas of communication and interaction are slowly released. It is this opening of family functioning that sets the stage for the adolescent to feel released from the untenable position that previously led to the suicidal crisis.

While it is always preferable to work within a positive reframe context, sometimes the family is not ready to accept such notions as an altruistic act on the part of the youngster. These are often families who have lived in conflict and chaos for a long period of time. Estrangement and isolation among members is usually quite intensive and of a long-standing nature. A tremendous amount of anger has defied all strategies by the family to resolve or to work through their conflicts. Feelings of failure and incompetence are also quite elevated. In these cases, Landau-Stanton and Stanton (1985) have elaborated on the use of negative reframes (e.g., seeing the suicidal behavior of the adolescent as disobedient). The clinician, in utilizing a more negative reframe, must walk a fine line, because in ostensibly chastising the adolescent in order to join with the parent, the adolescent's feelings of despair, lack of nurturance, and anger are reinforced. Instead of focusing on a negative reframe, it seems prudent to pair negative with positive reframes (Landau-Stanton & Stanton, 1985).

An example using the preceding case would involve the following statement:

THERAPIST: I know that Melanie has been terribly disobedient lately. She has even violated some serious rules and has been very difficult to manage. She has made things worse and has created a lot of concern and anger. I think, however, that the meaning of her behavior is more complicated. On the one hand, she seems to have difficulties in following the rules and seems somewhat more defiant in comparison to other adolescents. However, I also think that she has a caring part of her within all the trouble she creates. I have a feeling, even though she probably will deny this, and this may seem quite outlandish to you both, that in some way her disobedience is in part purposeful, directed at keeping you both from feeling the pain of your recent separation or other worries. Specifically, if she makes you so angry about her defiance, you will be caught up in the struggles with her, leaving little time for your own concerns.

A number of components are important to enumerate at this time regarding how to develop reframes with families who are quite angry and feel "burned out" on their child. First, it is important to acknowledge their perception of the behavior, whether it be defiance, disobedience, or pure anger. Second, it is important to offer them only small shifts from their own thinking for them to consider. In other words, moving from their conceptualization of the child as disobedient to a polarized message by the clinician on the altruism of their youngster may be too great a leap and may likely result in their disbelieving the clinician's statements altogether. In the foregoing reframe, the family is offered both their own interpretation and the suggestion that additional processes may be operative. Their position is thereby accepted by the clinician, and an additional conceptualization is offered, to begin the process of disorientation.

Opening the family to alternative interpretations may happen rather quickly, or it can be a more time-consuming process. The ability of a family to accept a reframe is often inversely related to the entrenchment of the symptomatology. Specifically, those families whose adolescent's suicidal crises arise out of a period of acute intrafamilial stress, tend to be more flexible in their ability to view their child's behavior as serving different functions. In families who have experienced sustained conflict and turmoil, and who feel defeated in parenting their youngster, disorienting them from their current conceptualizations is often a more arduous process. For these more chronically distressed families, the clinician might have to spend the entire first session creating an atmosphere of acceptance for the family. This is especially true for those families who have had previous contact with a number of mental health professionals. The families who have felt that other treatments were failures, and who are mistrustful of the mental health profession in general will certainly not accept a reframe unless some level of trust is established with the present clinician. This trust can only come out of the clinician transmitting to the family a sense of respect and acceptance (Brendler et al., 1989). However, even though a considerable amount of time may be needed, the clinician and the family can still be faced with a youngster who may be potentially dangerous. Consequently, it is important simultaneously to explore parameters of safety with the family, such that the suicidal behavior can be contained during the process of joining and expanding the family's beliefs and coping strategies.

Exploring Pathways of Safety and Empowering Parents

Within the crisis session, the clinician must determine the adolescent's and family's safety. Specifically, the clinician and parents must explore alternatives for ensuring the adolescent's safety, such that the adolescent does not act on the suicidal ideation, or, if a gesture has been made, the adolescent refrains from any further self-injurious behaviors. The adolescent's safety is an issue for everyone involved. In order for there to be a containment of the suicidal crisis, both the adolescent and the family must be committed to safe behaviors. The components necessary for a safe environment include (a) a commitment on the part of the adolescent not to hurt him- or herself, (b) parental feelings of competence to handle the situation, and (c) open pathways of communication concerning suicidal feelings. An adolescent cannot be safe if the suicidal symptoms are holding the family hostage (Brendler et al., 1989). Thus, the goal of this stage of the crisis interview is to assist the family in determining their capacity for ensuring safety within the home environment.

Early in the crisis interview, in interviews either with the adolescent or with the parents, as well as within the family context, the overt manifestations of the suicidal ideation and behaviors are directly addressed. Questioning the adolescent and family presenting a suicidal crisis has been presented in the preceding chapter and is not reviewed here. Instead, it is from the point of the information already being obtained that the following strategies are used, in order to gauge the family's present ability to offer their adolescent a safe environment. Within this context, the clinician examines the impact of the level of both expressed and covert threats of danger on the adolescent and on the family, viewing this impact in terms of the possibility for changing this sense of danger into a manageable situation.

Exploring the parent's willingness to reaffirm the taboo against suicide is an important initial step in assessing the potential for the family to ensure a safe environment for the adolescent (Sargent, 1987). Simply, this means that the clinician asks the parents whether "suicide is against the rules in the family." Parents who are committed to safety not only will strongly agree with the therapist's statements but will also be quite willing to demonstrate behaviors (e.g., organize a safety watch, remove firearms from the house) to substantiate their verbalizations. Those parents who experience more difficulties in making a strong statement to their adolescent may be indicating their ambivalence with regard to the safety issue. In order for the adolescent's sense of threat or danger to be extinguished adequately, this ambivalence must be addressed.

In order to strengthen the taboo, the therapist often first sees the parents alone. This gives the parents the opportunity and the privacy to reflect on the issue. While it can be argued that the adolescent is probably aware of the parental ambivalence, privately meeting to discuss the strengthening of the taboo reinforces the parents' status in the family hierarchy and allows the clinician greater flexibility in exploring with the parents any underlying issues that may prevent their delivering a strong message to the adolescent.

The strategy of strengthening the taboo is presented here within the context of Melanie D.'s case.

THERAPIST: We have been talking for some time about Melanie's suicidal behaviors, and I am wondering whether in this family suicide is against the rules? In other words, have you told Melanie that it is against the rules to intentionally harm or kill herself.

MRS. D.: That's so ridiculous, I don't even want to talk about it. Of course, I never told her that, I didn't want to give her any ideas. Besides, I'm having difficulties even having her obey my simplest rules. Even if I tell her it is against the rules I'm not sure she will follow the rule.

THERAPIST: (turning to Mr. D.) Have you ever told Melanie that in this family killing yourself is not an option?

MR. D.: I really never thought that I had to. I guess I assumed that she knew, and anyway, what are you supposed to say, "If you kill yourself you'll be grounded"? We can say it, but how can we reinforce it? She does have that ability to hurt herself. We can't follow her around continuously. She does have to go to school.

Just within these short statements by the parents, both their feelings of incompetence in terms of being able to ensure Melanie's safety, as well as the father's ambivalence toward the issue of suicide is very much apparent. Neither parent has accepted the therapist's offer for them to begin to take charge of the behavior by reaffirming the taboo. Consequently, her father's self-abusive drinking behavior and his ambivalence both contribute to confusion with regard to safety issues. In

Melanie's case, during her acute crisis, her parents have admitted to defeat. Therefore, she is not afforded the external setting of limits, structure, and emotional support she needs to deal with her emotions and the intrafamilial conflict.

The situation with Melanie still presents a real potential for danger, and thus the therapist must gently press the family further on this issue.

THERAPIST: (addressing both parents) Well if we could devise some strategies for putting you in charge such that Melanie would be safe, would you both be willing to carry out the necessary steps and to strongly tell Melanie that suicide will not be tolerated under any conditions?

MR. D.: Of course.

MRS. D.: Absolutely, but how can we get her to comply?

THERAPIST: Well, first of all you need to face your daughter and tell her clearly that suicide is against the rules in the family—that killing yourself is not an option and that you both will help her and support her with whatever is necessary in working her problems out such that she doesn't feel so desperate. But you have to be honest and willing to back up your statements with clear behaviors because adolescents are very adept at seeing through empty promises. For example, it seems clear, Mr. D., that people are quite convinced that your drinking behavior is very dangerous for your welfare. It is going to be hard for you on the one hand to tell Melanie it is against the rules to harm herself, while you are engaging in potentially self-harming behaviors yourself. On the other hand, if you are willing to stick to a contract of getting professional help for your drinking, then the message to Melanie will be consistent and even that much more powerful.

There is the potential in this case, that Mr. D. will not make a commitment to get treatment for his alcoholism. His behavior is quite well entrenched, and he has defied even the threat and eventual breakup of the marriage, as well as his own compromised physical health. The question then arises that if Mr. D. cannot commit himself, can the environment be safe for Melanie? While it is most advantageous for both parents (if possible) to affirm the taboo, certainly the parent with primary custody must be able to clearly state the taboo and to follow up on behaviors reinforcing the rule. If Mr. D. agrees to treatment services, then when Melanie is brought back into the room, both parents will face her with a strong message. However, if he is unwilling to get assistance, perhaps he is willing to be in treatment with the family, and through subsequent family therapy sessions, work may be initiated that is directed toward his seeking of substance abuse evaluation and treatment.

THERAPIST: Melanie you have been in the waiting room for some time, and I have been talking to your parents. They would like to say something to you.

MRS. D.: Melanie, I have something important to tell you. I was quite upset by what happened this morning. I know it means that you were very upset. Things have not been going very well for all of us lately, and I'm sorry that you see things in such desperate terms. But suicide is not the answer to your problems, and I am not going to let you use that option. I am prepared to do whatever I have to in order to assure your safety. I would like it if we could go home and begin to deal with things openly and honestly, but if you don't think that is possible, and if you can't give me a commitment that you won't hurt yourself, then I will make sure you are safe until you can give me a commitment.

MELANIE: What does that mean, are you going to put me away?

MRS. D.: The doctor talked to your father and I about various options, with one of them being a hospital, and as much as it would be hard for me to have you be in a hospital, I want you to be safe while you are having all these problems.

MR. D.: You know, Melanie, that it is the last thing in the world either your mom or I want is to hurt you. But we have agreed to do whatever is necessary to safeguard your welfare. If you can give us a commitment you will be safe in word and actions, then the hospital won't be necessary. If you can give us a commitment, we will begin as a family to work on problems in therapy together. I know you have some concerns about me, and I also know that your mom and I often put you in the middle. We are willing to try some other ways, but we need your help in letting us know if you are safe so we can take the right actions.

The parents have now gained some new strength and have been empowered to deal with the crisis. Even if Melanie is not able to give them a serious commitment, it will be the parents' decision to hospitalize her. The frame for the hospitalization is that the parents have implemented the appropriate level of care to assure her safety. With some ambivalence on Melanie's part in terms of assuring her safety, some alternative strategies to hospitalization could be implemented if the family is serious about safeguarding their child's safety. For example, the family could be instructed and assisted with planning and carrying out a suicide watch (Landau-Stanton & Stanton, 1985). This simply involves that relatives and/or friends be enlisted to help the family provide continuous direct supervision of the suicidal adolescent. Shifts are even taken during the night in which a responsible adult maintains a watch while the child is sleeping. The adolescent is never left alone during the suicidal crisis. Additionally, the adolescent's regular activities are curtailed until the youngster can assure his or her safety both in statements and in actions.

The watch serves a number of purposes, including putting the parents back in charge, giving the adolescent a net of safety against impulsive behaviors, and having adults available on a 24-hour basis to discuss problem areas. In order for a safety watch to be implemented, both therapist and parents must have formed a working alliance. Mechanisms for reaching the therapist in an emergency must be clearly stipulated, as well as plans for bringing the youngster to the nearest emergency room should the situation quickly deteriorate. The process of empowering the parents has emerged to the point where the family is not held hostage by the suicidal symptoms, nor are they completely dependent on the therapist. The therapist subsequently becomes consultant to the parents, who are implementing the day-to-day strategies of protecting their adolescent.

With the parents' cooperation obtained, the task now is to solicit from the adolescent an appraisal of his or her ability to maintain personal safety. It is quite powerful if the adolescent is able to give parents a genuine commitment because it represents an opening of trust and communication between parents and child. In other words, the log jam is loosened as the adolescent and parents are willing to work together on problem areas instead of being isolated in their misery. It is important that the adolescent's commitment be real and honest. Any doubts on the part of the parents or the clinician should be fully evaluated before the adolescent leaves the session. The clinician should be wary of the adolescent who gives a commitment just so "we can get out of here." If the adolescent is flippant in responding, trusting him or her would be difficult. As this is often the first meeting with the adolescent, the clinician should use the expertise of the family to gauge the honesty of the adolescent's remarks.

THERAPIST: Melanie, now that we have a commitment from your parents to do everything in their power to ensure your safety, we now need to find out whether you can make a commitment to your own safety. The question is, can you make a commitment to not hurt yourself? And if you do have suicidal feelings, can you make a commitment to tell one of your parents before initiating any action?

MELANIE: I am not going to any hospital.

THERAPIST: Whether you go to a hospital or not is not your decision. The question your parents need answered in an honest way is whether you are willing to safeguard your own wellbeing. Can you make a commitment to being safe?

MELANIE: I will not hurt myself. Are you satisfied now?

THERAPIST: Melanie, I would like you to face your parents and give them your commitment.

MELANIE: I will be safe and not do anything dumb. I will also let you know if I feel like doing something before I do it.

THERAPIST: (turning to the parents). In your experiences with Melanie, when she gives you her word, can you trust it?

MRS. D.: Well, lately she has violated my trust on stuff like curfew and keeping up with her schoolwork, but she has never done anything like threaten to hurt herself before, so I am leaning to trust her.

THERAPIST: I am asking you both how sure you feel, knowing your daughter, that her word today can be trusted on such serious a matter.

MRS. D.: Well, Melanie didn't put up any fuss, in coming here today to talk to you. I genuinely think she wants the help. After going through what we did this morning, I am a little shaken. I thought about asking my mother to come spend a few days with us just so there is someone else in the house to help out. Also, Melanie likes my mother, and sometimes my mother is able to talk to her in a way that gets through.

MR. D.: I also think Melanie wants to try, she is a good kid underneath.

THERAPIST: It sounds as if you both agree that Melanie is genuinely giving you her commitment. It is important that for the next couple of days you keep an eye on her. An area that may cause her stress is being placed in the middle between the two of you, and consequently it will be important for you both to be wary of this. Also, I am pleased that Melanie and the family were able to work together in here and communicate. A signal you need to be aware of is that when these communication processes break down, there is increased risk for some acting-out behaviors, and Melanie already seems vulnerable to act in a very self-defeating style, as well as potentially self-injurious. A clue to disruptions in communicatin may be her becoming increasingly noncompliant with school and home rules. This should be a warning that things are deteriorating. Since Melanie has been having difficulties for the last month and she sounded very serious this morning, I think it would be a good idea to give the family and Melanie short periods of time to see how things are working. What I am suggesting is that we arrange a time to see each other tomorrow just to make sure everyone is holding up their end of the bargain.

In determining the next step at the end of the crisis session, it is important to evaluate a number of issues. First, the parental subsystem needs to be assessed for their present level of strength in tolerating the adolescent within the home environment. Some families are so overwhelmed that organizing a watch or gathering resources to help them manage the adolescent is quite outside their grasp. Additionally, parents who minimize the adolescent's concerns or ideation may be too distant from their adolescent to assist in ensuring the adolescent's safety. These situations may necessitate hospitalization.

Second, the adolescent's commitment to working with the parents must be determined. Impulsive, angry, and hostile youngsters, as well as those manifesting severe depressive and psychotic processes, may not be able to give a genuine commitment. Finally, the interactions between the family's resources and the adolescent's commitment becomes the final component in assessing the level of care needed. Within the context of the presented case, Melanie's parents were able to make a connection with Melanie within the interview, they were able to make a commitment to working on issues, and they were able to access supports (e.g., therapeutic services and Mrs. D.'s mother). Melanie was also able to share information within the therapy hour and was able to offer a serious commitment to her safety. At the end of the interview, there also was a greater sharing between parents and child.

Deciding on Follow-Up Services

If the adolescent is to be maintained within the home environment, deciding when to schedule a follow-up interview is the final—and essential—part of the crisis interview. In the preceding case, the therapist decided to see the family the following day. A number of factors entered into that decision. First, Melanie did have an articulated suicide plan of slitting her wrists, so suicide had been seriously considered by her. Second, the family in general was in an inordinate amount of stress due to the recent marital separation. Third, while Melanie was able to share some feelings within the session, she still was somewhat reticent. Yet despite these factors, the family was able to work together in the crisis interview and to make a commitment to safety such that the hospital did not seem necessary. Giving the family a 24-hour period to negotiate with themselves and to honor commitments allows them to have some autonomy and mastery while having in place supportive structures should the situation prove to continue to be overwhelming.

The therapist needs to gauge the appropriate amount of time between sessions in both considering the level of stress the family and adolescent are under, as well as reinforcing the family's available resources and coping strategies. While in most families, it is usually clear what level of care is needed at the end of the crisis interview, in those situations that are vague, it is best for therapists to trust their own gut reactions to the family. If experienced clinicians are anxious about allowing an adolescent to return home, they are probably picking up on the collective family anxiety. Before a determination of the level of care is possible, further work with the family may be needed, or the youngster may need to be hospitalized. It is helpful to be flexible with families and to develop plans that are sensible and that can be implemented easily by the family. Either being too restrictive (e.g., in sending almost every suicidal adolescent to the hospital) or too permissive (e.g., keeping dangerous adolescents at home) defeats the purpose of cooperating with the family to work through the suicidal crisis.

The goal of the crisis interview is to assess the level of dangerousness presented by the adolescent and the family and to work with the family to remediate the crisis in order for an atmosphere of safety to be reinstated within the home environment. The crisis session should be clearly focused on issues relating to safety and on making connections among family members such that the secrecy about and/or denial of suicide can be interrupted. Once a decision is made regarding the level of care needed (whether it is a hospital setting or outpatient services), the therapist should delineate the direction for further treatment and should assist the family in contacting appropriate referral and community resources if necessary. While the work of the crisis interview is to ensure protection of the adolescent and to begin to change former inadequate patterns of interactions within the suicidogenic family, it is the goal of either the hospital or the outpatient setting to reinforce the gains that are made and to continue to assist the family in adopting patterns of relating that reinforce growth of individual members and that enhance communication and collaboratively working to resolve emotional material.

PART 4

Therapeutic Interventions and Treatment Settings

CHAPTER 10

Outpatient Strategies

The most important issue in treating depressed adolescents and their families is to be respectful of both the family unit as a whole and the individuals within the family. Families come to treatment services with both their pain and their hope. No matter how disillusioned the family is; how intractable and chronic they feel their adolescent behaviors have become; or how incompetent, angry, and depressed they feel, they come to the therapist's office with both the hopeful expectations of change and the fear of change. Even at the first contact, acceptance, caring, and respect for the family are essential in helping these families to make the changes they desire yet are so overwhelmed by the idea of "rocking the boat." It is the clinician's job to create an atmosphere where simultaneously fears can be explored and emotional growth can be stimulated and honored.

SETTING THE STAGE FOR THERAPY

Sargent (1989) discusses the common similarities among families in which disturbance of mood of an adolescent member is present. The primary characteristic is a feeling by family members, especially by the parents, of being overwhelmed (Sargent, 1989). There is a sense of helplessness, as the family has not been able to talk, cajole, support, threaten, or punish the youngster out of his or her depression. Deciding to use an outsider to assist the family only further reinforces this sense of failure and incompetence. In working with these families, the clinician should be aware of the family's extreme sensitivity to and fear that their feelings of failure will be confirmed.

Change cannot occur within an atmosphere of failure and incompetence, because change processes need to release and gain access to the energy used to criticize, blame, and self-punish. Therefore, the clinician must transmit to the family, from the very beginning, a sense of trust in the ability of the family to work through problem areas. While it may initially be difficult for the family to share with the clinician this competence, it serves as the foundation for later work when the family members are ready to accept their own strengths and powers to heal their wounds. The clinician, however, must modulate the outward expression of this trust, given the family's point of entry. For example, families that are very disillusioned and exhausted may feel misunderstood by a clinician who quickly tries to convince the family that they are strong and powerful. The family may need time to vent their frustration and to review past difficult periods. With these families, acceptance and trust can be communicated when the clinician listens to the pain and learns about the family (Sargent, 1989). This allows for the notions of strength and undiscovered resources ultimately to be shared with the family at a time when they are ready to listen and in a language they can understand.

Families with depressed adolescent members also commonly feel anger, irritation, and helplessness that predominate the interactions among family members (Sargent, 1989). This can be manifested generally either by a tremendous amount of intrafamilial conflict or by an avoidance of interactions. Alternatively, there may be a selected family member who serves as the receptacle for all the negative feelings in the family. Quite often, this receptacle is the adolescent whose behaviors have incurred both the wrath and the feelings of helplessness of others. Criticism and blame of others are also common occurrences, either with the adolescent being blamed for the family's misery or with one parent blaming the other for failing to follow through on parental responsibility. These families are often locked into a negative world view that is constantly reinforced by the omnipresence of the depressive symptoms. Because the family continues to be helpless in the attempt to cure the depressive member, this failed attempt may have further fueled additional mood changes in others as they react to the entrenchment of the problem (Sargent, 1989).

Within families with depressed adolescents, Sargent (1989) comments that there is an erroneous link made between the behaviors and actions of an individual, the individual's self-concept, and the individual's feelings for other family members. The individual's actions in the family are viewed as communications regarding feelings about self and feelings for others. This pairing generates such parental self-statements as "If you really loved me, you wouldn't be so depressed" and "If I was a better mother (father), I wouldn't have a depressed child." The manifestation of the depression and the helplessness in effecting change then becomes a set of statements concerning the value of the family relationships. It is this belief in the causal relationships between depression and valuing that inhibits family growth. Therefore, work should be directed toward untangling the behavior from family members' self-concept and their feelings of personal worth with regard to the family unit. Actions need to be viewed as behaviors that can be solved and not as demonstrations of people's inadequacies or indictments of their valuing of others.

Setting the stage for therapy must involve helping family members to limit the personalization of the behaviors of others. Actions must be externalized, thereby allowing for them to be broken down into solvable problems that can generate solutions. In order to change the family's focus from blaming and criticizing (self and others) to concentrating on the actual actions and behaviors, the clinician should focus on asking families to describe how they have solved other problems and how they would conceptualize their lives if the depression went away.

Some families, however, are resistant to letting go of their myths about the motives of behaviors. This often is most prevalent in families in which there is (a) a lack either of forgiveness of others or of self-forgiveness, (b) an intense anger, or (c) a mood disturbance in a plurality of family members. These families cannot move forward because they fear letting go and being released from their misery. Within their pain, they are intricately tied to one another. Without this bond, they fear disengagement, abandonment, and loss.

In beginning work with these fearful families, the pain and misery must be reframed in a context that allows the family members to venture into uncharted waters—namely, conceptualizing the problem within a different framework. A helpful reframe for these type of families could be as follows: "Your suffering indicates to me how close the family is and how much everybody cares for each other. It is much harder to help family's change in which this sense of caring and intimacy is absent." This communicates the clinician's trust that the family will survive changes, that they are connected to each other, and that they are not hopeless. Reframes such as this one assist in limiting the fears of giving up the pain. When the fear is lessened, both the energy needed and the opportunity to externalize problem areas can be realized.

While the foregoing represents commonalities among families with a depressed adolescent and mechanisms for setting the stage for therapy, it is important to note that each family presents its own uniqueness, and the clinician must listen carefully to their individuality in order to collaborate with the family for change (Sargent, 1989). Being able to work with a family within such emotional turmoil involves both a delicate and empathic stance and an intrepid courage to talk directly and to confront difficult subjects. Specifically, the clinician must be sensitive to the family's pain without being consumed by it. The clinician must regard the family's sense of hope as a precious and fragile gift: Move in too quickly, and it will break; be too scared to use it, and the beauty of it can never be realized.

PRESCRIPTIVE FAMILY STRATEGIES

To describe outpatient strategies is, in essence, to simplify the process of needing to listen to and to tailor therapeutic interventions to the exact needs of the specific family present in the outpatient office. Prescriptive family strategies involve collaborating with the family in order to orient treatment to the individual problems, concerns, and conceptions of change that are shared by the family with the clinician. In this era of the educated consumer, therapists are beginning to recognize that families themselves should be involved in decisions about the type and the direction of treatment. Some families seek symptom relief, while others want to change relationships, and still others need therapy to be a forum in which expression and release of emotion can be obtained. Each of these categories is not mutually exclusive, and the course of outpatient treatment may involve sessions in which each area is addressed. However, in order to delineate outpatient strategies in working with family's with depressed adolescents, three different (although not mutually exclusive) categories of treatment focus are delineated, with a case example in each category: (1) families that need to strengthen the parental role, (2) families that need to restructure the parental hierarchy, and (3) families that need to share affectively. As each family's uniqueness must be respected, these common strategies can then be adapted in the specific work with individual families.

Families That Need to Strengthen the Parental Role

Families often begin treatment by concentrating on the symptoms of their depressed adolescent and in either overtly or covertly asking the therapist to address themselves toward relief of these symptoms. As has been mentioned in Chapter 2, the adolescent's acting-out behaviors (in the form of depressive symptomatology) may be a signal that the executive branch of the family is not appropriately executing direction, limits, and support. Work with families within this frame is directed at helping the parents to feel comfortable with their role as parents. The emergence of symptoms is viewed as a temporary condition, and by working together, problem areas can be dealt with and solved.

This approach is often used with families who have successfully negotiated latency with their children, but who have been more unsettled with the emergence of the normative crisis of adolescents. However, concentrating on symptom relief is also used in families that have had a long history of problems (especially around intrafamilial conflict). Working toward symptom relief can be less threatening for these families than it would be to deal with underlying issues such as marital discord, which probably have been long-standing and which feel more hopeless to change. There may also be some secondary gain that does tap into chronic problems: For example, a married couple who is able to agree as parents with regard to rewards and sanctions for their children's behavior may also experience less marital strife. This relief may offer the family some hope that other changes can be realized, thereby possibly decreasing the family's fears of discussing and working on more pervasive problems.

Strategies within this frame involve more direct and behavioral mechanisms for effecting change, such as solution-oriented approaches (e.g., deShazer, 1985; O'Hanlon & Weiner-Davis, 1989) and behavioral contracting. The first goal is to reduce symptoms to solvable behaviors and then to work directly with the family to determine appropriate solutions. Parents are seen as the primary avenue by which the adolescent is stimulated toward forgoing his or her negative behaviors. However, given the developmental concerns of adolescents, their input on some issues is also valued. The following case example illustrates more clearly the specific strategies available when the focus of treatment is on strengthening the parental role, thereby progressing toward symptom relief.

Andy L., a 15-year-old, was brought to an outpatient clinic by his parents, Mr. and Mrs. L. Over the past few months there had been a rapid deterioration in Andy's school performance. He had begun to violate curfew and to be verbally abusive to his parents. Additionally, Andy's mood had been quite labile and he had also recently begun to stay home from school, complaining of vague somatic symptoms. While Andy had been demonstrating increased belligerence in the home situation over the past year, his functioning had deteriorated over the past 5 months, which basically coincided with the sudden illness and death of his maternal grandmother, who lived near the family. Due to the unexpected death, Mrs. L.'s mother's estate had been requiring a great deal of Mr. and Mrs. L.'s time. The parents commented to the therapist that they felt like "hostages in their own home," as every directive they gave to Andy, or any punishments for his negative behaviors were met either by a barrage of verbal and aggressive threats, by threats that he would run away from home, or by an increase in his acting-out behaviors. In order to avoid further temper outbursts and conflict, "so there can be some peace," Mr. and Mrs. L. had recently stopped punishing Andy for his misbehavior, hoping this would give him some relief from all the negative attention and perhaps stimulating him on his own "to clean up his act." However, as Andy's parents backed away, his acting out and avoidant behaviors escalated. He lately had begun to verbalize that the family didn't care about him, as they preferred "their two angels"—namely, his younger sisters, Dana (age 13) and Elizabeth (age 10); and he wondered out loud (in front of his parents) how happy the family would be without all his problems. Feeling demoralized and feeling that they were failures as parents, the family solicited outpatient services. Andy presented himself in the office as sullen and depressed, with his parents looking noticeably anxious. His two sisters seemed uncomfortable also, and they periodically giggled to relieve the tension.

This is an example of a family in which there has been a fairly recent development of symptoms that are closely paired with a traumatic event (i.e., death of grandmother). The parents have abdicated their role ostensibly to stimulate Andy to improve himself, but probably also due to the tremendous strain of dealing with his acting-out behaviors while settling the grandmother's estate. These family members are feeling tired, overwhelmed, and exhausted. The more they feel like "hostages in their home," the more energy is depleted from the executive branch. Additionally, the more Andy feels that they have abandoned him (which may also be a metaphor for the grandmother's sudden death), the more his negative behaviors will increase in order to secure their attention and to forestall the feared abandonment. By strengthening the parental role, the parents help Andy to feel that his needs are met without having to escalate his negative actions, and the parents will feel increased competence, thereby decreasing their hopelessness and giving them energy to deal with their necessary tasks.

In strengthening the parental role, it is often helpful to use a twofold approach: (1) empowering parents and (2) positively affirming a future in which the problems are solved. A helpful structural maneuver in empowering the parents can involve initially meeting with the parents alone during a portion of the session. Especially in families where there is dissension within the parental unit, this gives the parents an opportunity to air their differences and to come to some agreements without broadcasting to the children their difficulties in managing the governing body of the family.

Positively affirming a future with symptom relief involves (a) directing questions toward areas in which the family is currently functioning well (no matter how small), (b) asking family members about how they conceptualize the future when the problems have been solved, and (c) giving attention to areas of agreement and cooperation within the marital unit, as well as among all family members (O'Hanlon & Weiner-Davis, 1989). The following excerpts from the case example further explicate these interventions:

THERAPIST[1]: It sounds from your description that things have been really upsetting lately, with the house being in an uproar. You have told me a lot about the problems Andy has had, and they sound like it has really been difficult for everyone. I was wondering, though, if Andy has followed any of your directions lately? In other words, are there still some areas where you will ask him to do something, and he will comply?

MRS. L.: Well, it really has been pretty awful, everything has been such a struggle, not the least of which is now trying to get him to go to school.

THERAPIST: Well, I am really asking if you can remember anything, no matter how small, of Andy complying with your wishes.

MR. L.: Andy has continued to do his household chores, such as taking out the garbage and cleaning the yard up.

THERAPIST: What do you think is going on with Andy that in all this turmoil he still continues to honor your authority and complete his chores.

ANDY: It is the only way I can get any money; they are so cheap.

MRS. L.: Our kids get an allowance by contributing to the upkeep of the household.

[1]Many of the therapist's questions are adapted from solution-oriented approaches (as discussed in deShazer, 1985; O'Hanlon & Weiner-Davis, 1989).

THERAPIST: So when Andy has a business relationship with you, he tends to honor his side of the bargain.

MR. L.: We are really here talking about something so insignificant. You have to understand that our son is making life a living hell for us even with doing his chores.

THERAPIST: I know I am only talking about a small thing, but I am looking for areas in which Andy does follow your rules, because if we can understand them, perhaps we can generalize that behavior to areas in which he is currently defiant. I am also wondering if there are times when Andy's mood is pleasant, when he is not moody, sullen, or depressed?

MR. L.: Lately, I have only found him impossible to talk to. He is belligerent, unkind, and frequently only talks to us when he is demanding something.

ANDY: You should listen to the way you talk to me. All you ever say is I do everything wrong, you never let me do anything I want to do. I'm the prisoner in my own home.

THERAPIST: (addressing Mr. L.) It sounds like you and Andy have exchanged these words before without you or Andy feeling like things have been resolved. This disagreement seems to be an example where Andy's mood is hostile and disrespectful. I want to return to my question for a minute to see if there are times, when Andy's mood has been less sullen and belligerent.

MRS. L.: Well, it was a long time ago but I must say that I was really proud of Andy at my mother's funeral; he was very pleasant to everyone and really helped a lot. In fact, when he answers the phone or interacts with visitors, he is quite pleasant, he only turns angry at home. Besides his staying home from school a lot, he is pleasant to his teachers. We never hear any complaints except that they are frustrated he is not working up to his potential.

THERAPIST: Again, what I am hearing is Andy has learned what you have taught him in terms of honoring business contracts and treating outsiders with respect. What has fallen by the wayside is treating family members in the same manner. Andy seems to have gotten out of practice, and perhaps we need to build in a more businesslike atmosphere at home in order to assist him in following directions at home as well as he does outside the home.

In concentrating on examples of Andy's positive behaviors, the focus has moved from helplessness and hopelessness about changing the symptoms to increased possibilities for having an impact on his negative behaviors. While the father did express some resistance with accepting the ideas presented by the therapist, toward the end of the session, he did not intrude, maintaining a listening role. Even Andy, whose brief comments periodically served to stir up the turmoil, allowed his parents to make some verbalizations regarding his positive behaviors. However, in some families there will continue to be some opposition to accepting the child as having positive behaviors due to the fact that they have felt so entrenched in the negative interactions. With these families, the therapist may need to spend some time just listening to and allowing the family to vent their frustration. However, once the family is willing to reorient themselves, then it is important for the therapist to begin to work with the parents in order to establish the guidelines for the expectations for their adolescent's behaviors.

Within the home situation, the parents should direct change through setting limits and offering emotional support. With the therapist's guidance, the parents should decide and agree on the positive behaviors that will be reinforced, thereby limiting the complementary negative actions. It is often at this juncture in the treatment session that the therapist should decide whether the parents can come to a fairly quick agreement in front of the children, or whether they need some private time to work out and agree to a plan. Given Andy's propensity to try and get the parents to negatively engage with him, it probably would be helpful for these parents briefly to meet separately. Additionally, it is important in the beginning work with families to assist the family in deciding on a behavior that has the most chance for success. Specifically, the parents often need guidance in not selecting the number one problem that has been resistant to change despite all their energy, as this will only contribute to increased feelings of incompetence and demoralization. Parents should be advised that slow and steady change is more long-lasting than rapid and dramatic change.

THERAPIST: I would like to talk some things over with your parents, so I am going to ask you guys to wait in the waiting room for a short time (the kids leave). I want to spend some time with you both in deciding what should be worked on this week with regard to Andy.

MR. L. :Well, I really can't tolerate Andy staying home from school. I don't really believe he is sick, and I think my wife falls into the trap of worrying about sending him to school if in fact he really is sick.

MRS. L.: I know I am guilty, but I also worry he thinks I don't trust him when I insinuate he may be faking.

THERAPIST: Lately, Andy has not really earned your trust. He has been defying curfew and has been often noncompliant. It is important that you not extend trust without some belief that you won't be taken for a ride. Now you need to let Andy engage in behaviors that will earn back the trust you want to have in him. Because Andy has honored all his recent "business contracts," is there a way we can turn attendance at school into a business relationship?

MR. L.: Well, I am certainly against paying him to go to school. That is a terrible message to give to a kid. He is only in the 10th grade. Am I going to have to pay him for the next two years?

THERAPIST: Mr. L., I am suggesting something a little different. Andy's skipping school is an example of him not following directions, partly because he is angry, and I believe partly because he has some underlying sadness and is being self-defeating. I am only suggesting that perhaps if he is willing to work on beginning to be more compliant and follow your rules, that this behavior can be met with some reward.

MR. L.: Well, really I am against rewarding kids for things they should be doing. If we reward him for this, then every time I ask him to do something, he will be looking for a reward.

THERAPIST: I know it may seem like you are destined to have to reward Andy for each positive behavior, but that doesn't have to be the case. Right now, Andy is out of practice in terms of following through on your directives. All I am suggesting is to get the ball rolling for Andy to have a little external encouragement. As he begins to accept your limits and is respectful, we can make the rewards harder and harder to obtain, ultimately extinguishing the need for the outside encouragement. But things have been so difficult lately that I am wondering whether you are willing to give this a try in order to get things on the right track. In fact, I am only suggesting we try it for a brief period; if it is not working, I will be the first one to want to change things because I am not interested in continuing things that are not working.

MRS. L.: I think we should try it. You know, Jim. (turning to her husband) We have little to lose. Things couldn't get much worse.

MR. L.: (nods in consent) Well what are we talking about?

THERAPIST: Well, we can decide on a reward, or we can negotiate with your son about his ideas, which will probably make it more meaningful for him. You both still retain veto power. For example, just because he wants a car doesn't mean you give it to him. It has to be something reasonable you both can live with.

MR. L.: What happens if Andy doesn't buy into this?

THERAPIST: My preference is to assume that he will. I know that deep down adolescents are not comfortable being in conflict with their parents, and I think Andy also wants to work this out. I initially like to work positively with kids, assuming that they can do it. But if after next week, that isn't the case we can talk about an approach that offers a reward as well as a negative sanction for noncompliance. However, I do want things to change slightly with regard to Andy being allowed to stay at home when he claims he is sick. From now on, Andy should be instructed to go to school, and if the nurse calls once he gets there and complains of sickness, tell her you will only pick him up if he has, in her opinion, a clear medical condition, is vomiting, or is running a fever. Now, if we are in agreement, let's bring the kids back in.

ANDY: I hate to see what is a long time if you think that is a short time, especially with the stupid magazines you have in your waiting room.

THERAPIST: Andy, your parents and I have been discussing the ways you have upheld your end of the bargain and how to extend this to your attending school on a regular basis. It seems that when you have a business relationship with others, you really follow through on things. We were thinking how you can have a business relationship regarding your school attendance.

ANDY: Great, pay me 100 dollars a day and I will go with no problem.

THERAPIST: I am talking about something more realistic, cars, airplanes, and trips to the Bahamas are probably unlikely. If it is difficult to decide, your parents may be able to help you.

ANDY: I want to go out both nights of the weekend until curfew.

THERAPIST: I know from our time before that making curfew was a problem, and I am concerned you will be setting yourself up again to get a lecture from your parents.

ANDY: If they get off my back about telling me all the times I missed curfew before I go out, I will make sure I am in at curfew.

THERAPIST: That means that if you have perfect attendance at school for the week, you want to be able to go out on Friday and Saturday until curfew. Is that acceptable to the two of you? (turning to parents)

MR. L.: Yes, I never wanted to keep Andy in on the weekends. He was just forcing my hand when he came in at one o'clock in the morning. But I will say this, that if you come in late on Friday night you forfeit Saturday night even if you went five days to school.

THERAPIST: It seems to me that Andy is committed to this plan. (turning to Andy) Andy, I think your selection of weekend privileges was excellent because if you also abide by curfew, you will really be moving quite fast in terms of taking back the appropriate responsibilities for someone of your age. Therefore, your father's limit of forfeiting the second night gives you the opportunity to reinforce even further with your parents that you are serious about wanting to earn back your privileges. The last thing for today is to tell Andy the plan for feeling sick.

MRS. L.: Andy, as you know I am not a nurse or a doctor, so I can't tell whether you are really sick or not. Many times lately, you have said you are sick in the morning, and by afternoon, you want to go outside because "you feel fine." From now on, I am going to send you to school and have the nurse verify whether you are sick. If you are, of course, either dad or I will pick you up.

ANDY: (sarcastically) Well that's having a lot of trust in your son!

MRS. L.: Andy, I want to trust you, but lately you have been taking advantage of me, so now you are in a position of needing to prove yourself again.

While it seems very straightforward and even simplistic to the parents involved with their adolescent in a more positive manner, it is a very powerful intervention.

Beginning the process of negotiating yet being firm on certain limits is supportive to adolescents who have feared that ultimately they will be able to engineer their parents' rejection and abandonment. While Andy may not adhere to his bargain the first week, he was willing to agree to and try the contract. Prior to this agreement, the family has not obtained other agreement lately within the household; this agreement gives the family a new experience with Andy. Selecting the school avoidance was a good place to begin because it was of recent inception, thereby making it a less entrenched behavioral symptom. Pairing it with weekend privileges and the curfew (giving some leeway and some limits) was a good metaphor for normative relationships between parents and their teenagers.

It is important to set a positive orientation; thus, often when starting a behavioral contract with an adolescent, negative ramifications are postponed as long as the adolescent is successful (unless the behavior involves very dangerous actions). It is not uncommon, however, for the report from the family the following week to include continued noncompliance on the part of the youngster. It is essential that the clinician get details on how the contract failed. For instance, did one parent collude with the youngster, allowing for only partial compliance. If there is only partial compliance, it is important to ask what is different about the days the contract worked and the days it did not, to discern any patterns of interactions. Frequently, the contract is unsuccessful due to inconsistencies between the parents in enforcing the rules. When the parents demonstrate a united and attentive front, the adolescent at least usually makes some movement toward compliance. For those adolescents in whom the behaviors are more entrenched, adding a negative sanction may become necessary. It is essential that a reward also continue to be available because you want the attention focused on the positive behaviors instead of the negative sanction.

There also are families in which it is difficult to gain agreement from the parents. However, if the clinician is focused on even the smallest example of cooperation between parents, the clinician will find something that can be utilized. With difficult families who are especially overwhelmed by the symptoms, more energy must be directed toward preparing them for being able to exert the proper authority. For example, the clinician may tell parents:

> We are going to need to work together to bring about these changes. Your son's problems have been around for a long time, and I hear that you have been living with all this difficulty for some time. I am wondering what you do and say to yourself before you start a project you know will be especially challenging in order to make more energy available.

It may be necessary to meet with parents alone several times, to prepare them for taking back the appropriate authority they have lost. Even though the adolescent may not be seen during these sessions, the adolescent's world is being enhanced through encouraging more adequate parenting.

There are situations in which empowering the parents is difficult, due to more overt problems in the familial hierarchy. One parent may continue to sabotage efforts, due to the parent's anger toward the other parent. Keeping the adolescent as the focus is viewed as being much safer in these instances. Oftentimes, this situation may necessitate that interventions be directed toward assisting the family in making structural changes. It is important to note that this level of intervention (empowering parents) and even small changes in alleviation of symptoms can have an impact on the overall family structure, and changes in family structure may increase the potential for the family to continue to discern new solutions.

Families Needing Restructuring of the Hierarchy

Adolescent depression may also be the by-product of an arrest of normative development, owing to the adolescent being co-opted into taking on an inappropriate role. Specifically, the depressive symptoms can emerge when the youngster is enlisted by both parents or by one parent to be in a more caregiving role (Sargent, 1989). A caregiving role can be manifested either by what has been termed the "parentified child" or by the adolescent who becomes symptomatic in order to distract the parents from their pain and turmoil. This caregiving position is more than an adolescent can handle in addition to completing the tasks of the particular developmental phase. Thus, energy is depleted from normative growth-facilitating tasks, in order to assist the parent. There is an imbalance in the hierarchy as the adolescent becomes the caregiver for the parents' pain. The symptoms appear as an inappropriate solution to the burden of simultaneously managing the parents' affect and the adolescent's normative developmental crises.

In order to obtain relief of symptoms, the hierarchy promoting this intolerable situation for the child must be corrected. Adolescents need to be released from their caregiving position in order to continue their emotional development. Intervention at this level, however, can be very frightening for families, as the intervention involves changing the patterns of relationships at a time when individual family members are probably feeling most desperate.

Problems with the familial hierarchy are often precipitated by a crisis, such as a separation or divorce, a death in the family, an infidelity, or excessive amounts of situational stress (loss of family income, relocation, or illness). At the time of the crisis, the family may reorganize in a manner that attempts to forestall the change, which is viewed as harmful to family cohesion. For example, in a divorce or separation, a parent may use an adolescent as a confidant, thereby attempting either to minimize the effect of the loss of the partner or to try and continue some connectedness (through the child) with the estranged spouse.

In the short term, the process of changing the family hierarchy to a position that allows for the emotional growth of the adolescent may be threatening to the family, as it may represent further loss in terms of the perceived intimacy in relationships.

In the end, however, the intimacy obtained through inadequate hierarchical relationships can never be satisfactory for either the parent or the adolescent, as it exists at the expense of the necessary growth process. It is only in establishing more appropriate relationships that the closeness and connectedness desired can be actually obtained.

In making interventions on this level, the clinician should be especially respectful of the manner in which the family has reorganized, even though it may be viewed as an inefficient and perhaps harmful pattern of relating. In other words, to collaborate with the family, the clinician must understand the family's world view and must work within that view to reinforce gains already made by the family and to assist in stimulating further areas of modification. If the clinician is able to conceptualize the family's pattern of relating as growing out of mutual caring, then the work becomes reorienting that caring such that individual and family growth can emerge in a more positive context. The following case example illustrates this process.

Sally, age 14 years, was brought to an outpatient office accompanied by Mrs. V., her mother, and Mark, her younger brother (age 12). Mrs. V. had become increasingly concerned about Sally because Sally had begun to be more reclusive in the home, to limit contact with her friends, and to display increased moodiness and hopelessness about the future. Mr. V. had moved out of the house 1½ years earlier, to move in with a woman he had begun to see while he still resided within the family home. His contact with his children was minimal, as his girlfriend resented their existence. The divorce was soon to be finalized. Three years earlier, the family had moved to another state due to the father's job relocation. While Mrs. V. considered moving back to where she had friends and family after her husband left, she thought it would be better to not "once again move the children from their schools, as they were just then getting settled." With few well-established family and friend resources, Mrs. V. experienced a difficult time dealing with the separation. As the children were also quite angry at their father for abandoning them, Mrs. V. found them to be good listeners, especially Sally who "had a way of comforting me when I was really down in the dumps." Mrs. V. was conflicted about finding outside employment, as she felt the children needed some "stability in their lives." However, she had recently made some inquiries into securing a position outside the home, but she was feeling increased guilt due to Sally's growing problems.

Due to the breakup of her marriage and her isolation from her support system, Mrs. V. looked toward the children for comfort and support. The development of symptoms in Sally suggests that she became intimately involved with her mother's burdens, which compromised her ability to sustain interest in more age-appropriate tasks (e.g., pursuing peer relationships). However, it is important to note that there is also another factor in Sally developing symptoms. The children also lost a father, who has been less available to them through the separation. Through Sally's present difficulties, Sally's symptoms not only distracted her mother from the mother's own pain but also served to keep the mother closely connected to her. Fears of abandonment and further rejection (perhaps symbolized by Mrs. V. seeking outside employment) are therefore temporarily forestalled. Therefore, difficulties in the hierarchy (inappropriate use of the children as confidants, the controlling nature of Sally's symptoms) contribute to the suspension of necessary growth within the individual family members and within the family as a whole. The therapeutic work should be directed toward breaking the "log jam" and allowing the growth process to unfold again (Brendler et al., 1989).

In restructuring the hierarchy, the clinician must not buy into the hopelessness that the family cannot survive the changes. The clinician must focus on the part within the individual family members and within the family as a whole that wants to continue to grow and mature. Corrections on the hierarchy can be obtained by working on differentiating the problems from the relationships (alleviating the symptoms). For example, viewing Sally's behavior as noncompliant may motivate her mother to strengthen her parental role, thereby decreasing her interacting with Sally as a peer, especially around emotional issues. Or making overt Sally's role as caregiver of the mother may also prompt Mrs. V. to take back some of her adult responsibilities for dealing with her pain, which again strengthens the hierarchy. These are more straightforward strategies directed at cooperating with the family to make changes. They deal openly and honestly with the problem while the therapist views the symptom as metaphorical of the relationship patterns. The work is framed by starting with the symptom and gently leading the family to understand the placement of the symptom within the family context. The following case excerpts encompass more direct approaches toward restructuring the hierarchy:

THERAPIST: After hearing all that the family has been through, I am impressed with how well you all have coped, given what a difficult time it has been. For example, both kids have continued to do well in school despite all the turmoil. However, it still seems to me that the job of putting things back together is stuck because people are worried about Sally.

MRS. V.: It just seems that we get over one problem and then there is another. Lately I began to worry what will there be next?

THERAPIST: Right now, I was wondering the same thing, but maybe in a different way. What I am wondering is what people will worry about if things did get better with Sally?

MRS. V.: Are you kidding? We would be thrilled! We could go on doing things—like Mark and his basketball—and I would continue to look for a job, and Sally would have lots of friends to do stuff with.

THERAPIST: (turning to the kids) Do you believe your mom that things would really be great, that this would become more of a carefree family?

MARK: I think my mom is always worried about Sally. It would be much better if she came out of her room and joined the world.

THERAPIST: What about you Sally? You have been really quiet today, and I am wondering what you are feeling.

SALLY: I just know that my mom doesn't want a job, and my father is such a jerk for all he has done.

THERAPIST: How do you know that she doesn't want a job?

SALLY: Because she is always complaining she has no skills, and that she has to take a job with people half her age who are jerks.

MRS. V.: Sally, I know I have talked to you about my frustration, but I don't think it is as bad as you make it out to be.

THERAPIST: I am wondering whether in part, Sally has been trying to help you, but in a way that has perhaps created more problems. Let me explain. It is interesting that even though things have been difficult for Sally, her problems got worse when you started to look for a job and to see how hard it was going to be. By having problems, Sally at least wanted to communicate to you that you were important to her and she needed you.

MRS. V.: But I'm not sure that's right because Sally's problems made me feel worse as a mother—totally incompetent, since no matter what I did, she didn't respond.

THERAPIST: I know this may sound strange, and I'm not saying that Sally was totally aware of what she was doing, but in a way I think she wanted to communicate to you that you were needed and special, especially when she heard from you that people did not regard you as important in the work force. I am wondering whether any of this makes sense to you, Sally.

SALLY: I don't know, I just knew she was miserable.

MRS. V.: Yes, but I was upset about how things were going with you. The job hunting was hard but not as important as things going on with you.

THERAPIST: Mrs. V., you have gone through some tough times lately, and I guess it was hard for the kids to see the strengths that you have to have. However, I am wondering whether you can turn to them and give them a message about what it is you can handle.

MRS. V.: I won't lie to you that starting to work isn't hard—especially after going through what I did with dad. But I am ready to see what's out there, and I believe it will be good for me, as maybe I can meet more people in this town, and we can have a little more money for the extra things we have been doing without.

THERAPIST: So one of the things maybe Sally has been missing is that there are some positive aspects of beginning to work.

In reconceptualizing or reframing Sally's problems, the family can begin to talk more openly about the worries and concerns that have been covertly communicated through the pattern of relating around the symptom. If the family accepts the frame—especially the parent—then work can be directed at supporting mother to feel stronger and more adequate in her activities, thereby negating the need for Sally to rescue her. Within the family context, it is helpful for the therapist to offer support to the parent, which can assist in detriangulating the adolescent and reducing the adolescent's burden of taking care of the parent (Sargent, 1989). Restructuring the hierarchy involves both reframing problems within a relationship context and being a supportive figure for the parent or parents in order to release the energy they need to effectively guide and emotionally support the children. With the adolescent's burden of parenting the parents (either through a more parentified stance or a symptom development) decreased, the adolescent can begin to redirect attention to the developmental tasks at hand.

Periodically, families are not available to hear and to reconceptualize problems within a family context. In these families, parents often feel helpless and ineffectual, mostly surrounding their inability to have positive impact on the symptoms. Even if they do see a relationship component to the symptom, they have often felt blocked in effecting more positive connection with others. At times, more indirect strategies may be helpful to unblock these families enough such that they can begin to examine alternative actions. Madanes (1984) has detailed numerous strategies for more paradoxical strategies for stimulating hierarchical change.

One articulated strategy involves inverting the hierarchy if more direct mechanisms for reinforcing appropriate hierarchical positions is not successful. Specifically, Madanes (1984) asserts that if families are not willing to grasp the problem within their present structure, it may be of assistance to dramatize and perhaps center a task on the present family structure. In other words, if parents will not take charge of their lives and that of the families, perhaps they will be more motivated if a task is created that overtly uses the existing family structure. If one conceptualizes that through symptomatic behavior, the adolescents have become in control of the family, then these strategies are designed to make that process overt to the parents (Madanes, 1984). Through the window into the process that is provided (within the task situation), the parents become motivated to take back responsibility and authority. The following strategy was applied to the presented case, due to difficulties in motivating the mother to reaffirm her parental position.

THERAPIST: You know we have talked a lot about the meaning of Sally's behaviors over the past couple of weeks, but you report that things really haven't changed. You have repeatedly told Sally and Mark that you can handle entering the job market, but somehow I'm not sure they believe you. I am really wondering Sally whether you see your mom as being fit to work?

SALLY: I don't know, her attitude seems so poor. She always says to me when I have something hard to do, not to think first that I won't be able to make it, but to think positively. But she needs to think positively herself.

THERAPIST: (to Sally) Perhaps I have been wrong in having your mom tell you how strong she is, maybe she isn't ready. So I am wondering whether if you and Mark were her coach, whether the two of you could groom her to be ready for a job interview.

MRS. V.: This is ridiculous, what could a 14-year-old and a 12-year-old know about looking for a job?

THERAPIST: Well, when you were their age, the job is school, and both of them are doing well at school. So perhaps they can use what they apply there to help you.

SALLY: (more energized by the topic) Well the first thing you have to do is really look through the ads in the paper in a serious way. She looks at the Sunday paper for 3 minutes and then gives up, saying, "There is nothing here for me."

THERAPIST: If you did that with difficult math problems, what would happen?

SALLY: She would send me back into my room until I really could demonstrate to her that I made a serious effort, and then I have to promise I will ask the teacher the question the next day. She is always at the door the next day, and the first thing she asks me is what the teacher said.

THERAPIST: She doesn't let you get away with not knowing and is really teaching you persistence. Perhaps it is time to help her with her own persistence. What I am suggesting is for the next week, mom must spend a full hour analyzing the want ads. At the end of the hour, she must talk to the two of you about what she has found and what plans she has for following it up the next day. She can't leave her study of the ads until you both feel she has given it a true effort and until you are confident that she has a plan for following up or making inquiries of other positions on Monday.

In putting the children in charge of mother's job hunting, the imbalance in the hierarchy is exposed. Mrs. V.'s only credible defense for not following through on this directive is for her to take charge herself of the job-hunting process, thereby dismissing the need for the children. Consequently, if Sally sees more energy on the part of her mother, she may not have to use her symptoms to rescue her from what has been publicized by the mother as a very difficult task. If Mrs. V. is compliant with the task, then Sally is involved in helping her mother in a more positive manner. Either way, the "log jam" is released, allowing for more direct interventions for further strengthening the appropriate hierarchical family positions.

In respecting and collaborating with families in order to effect change, direct and honest strategies are preferable. However, it may be useful to use indirect and paradoxical interventions periodically with families that are having difficulties refocusing their attention from the problem to the possible solutions. Nevertheless, indirect and paradoxical strategies require specific training in order to be effectively and respectfully used. Their utility in unblocking more static patterns of relating are only effective when they are used prudently and judiciously.

Restructuring the hierarchy assists in allowing families to reorganize along patterns that promote the emotional growth of family members. However, symptoms occasionally arise due to some unresolved grief and loss. While the difficulties in working through grief may be complicated by dysfunctional hierarchical relationships, families may need to share and vent feelings before being able to reorganize and change static patterns of relating. Diagnostically, when efforts either to collaborate with the family or to restructure the hierarchy in order to obtain symptom relief are unsuccessful, this may be an important indicator that the family needs to begin treatment with reviewing previous experiences and sharing issues surrounding loss, grief, and possibly even anger.

Families Needing Affective Sharing

Difficulties in family functioning often are precipitated by a loss or a grief experience. Adolescents who are especially sensitive to parental pain may become symptomatic in order to protect a parent from what the adolescent believes is intolerable grief. Their depressive symptoms may be attempts to rescue the parent from feeling sadness and loss. Families do not always enter into therapy at the time of the grief experience. Therefore, when meeting with a family, it is important to conduct a full family history, as some symptomatic behavior may be related to delayed grief reactions on the part of both the parents and the adolescents. In families that present a depressed adolescent member, it is often helpful to inquire directly about the mood of other family members, as the initiation of symptom patterns is often not a spurious process. It is not uncommon for adolescent depression to be modeled from a parent's behavior. Therefore, in helping families to share their grief, it is often helpful to view the depression as being pervasive rather than localized in one individual member.

The goal in helping families to communicate feelings of loss and grief is to provide them with a forum for venting constrained emotions and to give them the opportunity to gain mastery over emotions that often contribute to feelings of being out of control. If the adolescent's behaviors are directed at distracting the parent from personal sadness, the therapy is directed toward helping the parent to label appropriately her or his own feelings, to consequently become acquainted with and to accept these emotions, and to work through problem areas. Within this context, the adolescent not only is released from the burden but also benefits from the parental process of resolving issues because it provides a model for the adolescent for future hurt or loss experiences.

As with the previously mentioned treatment strategies, helping a family to share affect must be done gently and respectfully. Symptoms usually develop because of the fears of directly confronting issues. It is important to honor parental difficulties in sharing emotions by respecting their defensive processes (Sargent, 1989). Moving in too quickly may further reinforce the sense that emotions are dangerous and must be avoided at all costs. Sargent (1989) discusses how to direct interpretations toward the parents initially through consideration of the symptomatic behavior; in this way, the parents seriously attended to these interpretations. The following case example further delineates this strategy, directed at assisting the family in sharing and communicating affect.

Mrs. S. brought her only child, Jeremy (age 17 years), to an outpatient therapist, due to her concerns about his deteriorating school performance, his lack of peer relationships, his repeated complaints of fatigue, and his somatic complaints. After a full physical exam, which was unremarkable, the pediatrician referred Jeremy and his mother for therapy. Mrs. S. related that Jeremy has been a mostly compliant child, "who was easy to raise." Mr. S. had died when Jeremy was 8 years old, so Mrs. S. often had to work two jobs in order to "make ends meet." This reduced her own social sphere, as she was frequently "too busy to be able to go out and meet people." Jeremy was bright, and there was the chance that he could earn a scholarship for college; however, recently his listlessness in the school situation was placing the scholarship in jeopardy. Mrs. S. had grown increasingly angry at Jeremy for compromising his future. But her attempts both to cajole him to apply himself or to threaten him did not have an impact on his recent apathy regarding his future.

This family presented many issues. First, it is not unusual for symptoms to arise at a time of impending separation of family members. This is especially true in families in which there has been a history of unresolved loss. Mrs. S. has really never recovered from the loss of her husband in terms of venturing out to establish new relationships. Jeremy's behavior serves as a metaphor for his mother remaining isolated except to work. Faced with his own emancipation, he makes a similar decision to jeopardize his own opportunity to attend college. However, Jeremy's behavior may also be viewed as protective, as his mother's loneliness may have been lessened due to the presence of Jeremy in the household. Left alone, she may have to face her own isolation and possible unresolved grief at losing her husband. Jeremy's actions assure both his status within the household and her continued status as a mother. Nevertheless, his symptoms exist at the expense of his establishing a more positive future. This family needs assistance in working through previous loss experiences in order to allow the normative developmental processes to unfold. Of primary importance is for Mrs. S. to begin to come to terms with her grief, allowing her to move toward other adults for attention and companionship.

THERAPIST: It is interesting to me that Jeremy is having difficulties making a decision about his future. On the one hand, if he applies himself, he may still be able to earn the scholarship. However, that would mean that he would be leaving, and it may be hard for him to do that.

(Difficulties in separating are attributed initially to Jeremy in order to respect the parent's defenses; however, the interpretations can be applied to both mother and son.)

MRS. S.: You know, all these years I thought of Jeremy leaving to go to college, I thought I would be the one with the hard time seeing him go.

(Even though the mother has not made a statement directly, she intimates that she is also having difficulties dealing with it.)

THERAPIST: So it must be strange for you to be the one to be working so hard to encourage him to do well so he can get the scholarship. You know sometimes when kids have trouble leaving parents, I wonder if there has been some trauma in the past that now gets in the way. In this family, I am wondering how Jeremy dealt with dad's death.

MRS. S.: Jeremy was really great through the whole thing. Mr. S.'s cancer came on very suddenly, and we had less than 4 months from the time he found out 'til the time he died. Most of that time, he was in the hospital, and Jeremy stayed with a neighbor the nights I stayed with my husband in the hospital. The doctors thought he would live longer, and he died suddenly one day just shy of the 4 months. While I told Jeremy that his dad was very sick, I didn't have time to prepare him about how soon the actual death would be. I had even promised (Mrs. S. starts to cry) that I would take him to the hospital the next day to see his dad. It was the hardest thing to do to tell him dad had died before he got to say good-bye.

THERAPIST: It sounds like no one was prepared for how fast it went. I am wondering whether you had some unfinished business you felt bad about?

MRS. S.: I can't really remember, all I remember is how awful it will be to tell my 8-year-old boy about his father. I at least was an adult and had some way of dealing with it. But he was only 8!

THERAPIST: Jeremy, do you remember that time?

JEREMY: I just remember being sad and a lot of people hanging around the house for a couple of days and mom crying. I thought she would never stop.

MRS. S.: Jeremy did become worried, for a period of time after Robert's death, that I would also die. He used to wake up in the middle of the night and come into my room to make sure I was there. But that only lasted a couple of months. He always went to school and had no trouble staying with the babysitter until I came home from work.

THERAPIST: Mrs. S., do you think that in going off to college that Jeremy is once again worried about whether you will be O.K.? He won't have you under his watchful eye.

MRS. S.: I never thought of it like that. I don't think so. Last year, he couldn't wait for college.

THERAPIST: But this year, the reality is so much closer. Perhaps again he thinks you may dissolve into tears.

MRS. S.: Well if that is the case, I wish he would have talked to me instead of goofing off at school.

THERAPIST: You probably would have told him you would be O.K., but he has memories at age 8 that keep on telling him otherwise. You noticed that he wasn't doing so well because of his present behaviors. So behaviors are very powerful ways people can communicate their worries, concerns, and feelings.

MRS. S.: Yes, but I can't change the past. If that is what he needs to go to college, then it is hopeless.

THERAPIST: I am suggesting that you will know that Jeremy is ready to face college because he really will work for his grades. How will he know you are ready for him to go?

MRS. S.: I have been telling him that for the past 3 months. I don't know what more I can do. I know in a way it will be hard to me, but isn't it for every mother, especially when it is their only child?

THERAPIST: You are right; it is hard. I think, however, in this family, it is even harder because all you guys have is each other, and so I think it just needs to be talked about more.

In allowing for some processing of previous experiences, the family can now more directly confront the present separation and its meaning. In talking more openly about it, there is a reduced need for the symptoms within the family context. This family's emotions were fairly accessible, allowing for a more quick refocusing from symptoms to affect. However, some families may experience greater difficulties, and therefore, the therapist may need to continue to frame interpretations within the adolescent's behavior and not move too quickly toward uncovering the parental mask. Ultimately, some recognition on the part of the parent needs to emerge, such that the adolescent does not continue to be burdened by the adult pain. In situations in which the grief is shared (such as the death of a parent), assisting the parent in working through the parent's grief will allow the parent to be more available in helping the child through the trauma.

MAKING A CONTEXT

The foregoing strategies represent interventions useful in helping families overcome adolescent depression. However, they necessitate that the clinician makes adaptations in order to meet the specific needs of the family. Therapy is a difficult process, and articulating strategies only serves to simplify inaccurately the complexity to which the practicing clinician must attend in order to assist families in making a more satisfactory adjustment. Thus, therapeutic interventions must be put forth in a context—a context of respect and acceptance. The clinician must work hard to provide the therapy within the language of the family, which recognizes their pain and honors their resources. Energy must be directed at getting to know the family such that the work done together will not be discarded and discounted.

While family therapy offers families an opportunity to reorganize, in working with an adolescent population, it may also be important in some cases to use additional treatment modalities, such as individual, group, or psychopharmalogical agents. Even though explicating these therapeutic modalities is not within the scope of this book, they do provide the clinician with important mechanisms in facilitating the change process. For example, an adolescent who has been symptomatic for a long time, may develop self-esteem issues that can often be most prudently addressed through individual therapeutic exploration. Additionally, adolescents whose presenting symptoms include poor peer relationships may never feel reintegrated and less depressed until they can establish more adequate peer relationships. A group therapy modality can offer a safe place where relationships with peers can be directly worked on under the supportive guidance of a therapist. Finally, introducing medication may assist in taking the edge off the depression, thereby allowing the adolescent to be available for therapeutic interventions.

Family therapy offers a forum in which families can change together to create a more harmonious existence. It operates from the assumption that every individual is valued and needed to effect change. It views family members as having the resources to heal their wounds and to offer fellow members support. The role of the therapist is conceptualized as a momentary assistant in the life of the family in order to help in dismantling obstacles toward the normative growth process. The family therapist works toward becoming unemployed by the family, assisting them in carrying forth with their own tools to make repairs.

CHAPTER 11

Brief Psychiatric Hospitalization

Case 1

Anne M., age 13 years, was taken to an emergency room of a children's hospital by her mother. The mother reported that Anne had been refusing to go to school for the past 3 days. She also added that Anne had seemed apathetic, lethargic, and she had lately refused to get out of bed. A decrease in appetite was also noted. Anne presented herself to the medical staff as being unkempt, despondent, and tearful. Her only verbalizations were sparse statements of reproach toward her mother for bringing her to the hospital. After a medical clearance had been obtained, the primary physician paged a psychologist on call to assess the degree of depression and the possibility of suicidal risk. After a thorough interview with Anne and her mother and the completion of a behavioral rating form showing many areas of distress, it was determined to place Anne briefly on the inpatient unit for further evaluation.

Case 2

Michael P., age 15 years, had been seen for two sessions in individual psychotherapy on an outpatient basis. His presenting problems had included school failure, poor peer relations, and emotional lability. Before the next scheduled session, his mother phoned the therapist in a panic saying that Michael had come home from school visibly upset and making threatening statements about harming himself and his younger brothers. Although he would not indicate to his mother what had happened in school, he was verbally abusive toward her and began to light fires in the trash cans of the house. The mother was directed, with the father, to bring Michael and the entire family immediately to the therapist's office for an emergency family session. At the meeting, although Michael was still irritable, he was able to relate what had made him so upset and was able to apologize for his actions. Although the therapist had called the various local psychiatric units and hospitals for possible openings, it was decided that the parents could negotiate an around-the-clock observation of Michael and that hospitalization was not needed at this time. The therapist indicated to the parents and to Michael that she would be on call for them and, if necessary, would make the arrangements for any future hospitalization. She reiterated to Michael that they would talk more about the episode during their next scheduled appointment in 2 days.

Case 3

Sharon L., age 17 years, had been living and going to school at a residential treatment center for seriously emotionally disturbed children and adolescents for 2 years. Her initial difficulties included school truancy, alcohol and other drug abuse, rebelliousness toward authority figures, and one suicidal attempt in which she consumed part of her mother's medication. During the past several days, she had become increasingly out of control in her behavior and increasingly aggressive toward peers and staff. This occurred after it was determined that she was pregnant. She would not talk to anyone and kept all the school and mental health professionals at a distance with her anger. At one point, she had to be restrained for her own and others' safety. After several unsuccessful attempts by her therapist and the consulting psychiatrist to interview her, it was decided that a more secure inpatient setting was necessary to care for her physical, as well as emotional, needs. Although the parents were against this plan initially, they were not sure they could handle Sharon, and they reluctantly gave permission to hospitalize her.

The use of psychiatric inpatient settings is a crucial link in the sequence of treatment offered to adolescents who have become a danger to themselves or others, or who have become severely dysfunctional in their behavior (Pfeffer, 1986). As the foregoing case examples illustrate, however, the requirement for a more secure and structured environment can take many forms, and the diversity of referrals is a reflection of this need. For Anne, the suddenness and severity of her depressive symptoms called for a very thorough and detailed evaluation, with as much structure and safety built in that only an inpatient unit could provide. In this case, the mother was also overwhelmed with her own problems and could neither offer much immediate support nor call on family or friends to help. In contrast, Michael's parents, although visibly upset and worried about his safety, as well as their own, were able to mobilize their own resources in a final effort to avoid hospitalization. In a very different context, Sharon could no longer be contained in a loosely structured residential setting, where the safety not only to her, but also to her expected child, was paramount. Hospitalization became the most sensible and potentially lifesaving option to which all staff, and finally her family, agreed. In all of these cases, the input and the condition of the familial support was crucial in making the most informed final decisions.

THE DECISION PROCESS

The decision of whether or not to hospitalize an adolescent depends on the presenting factors, the expressed symptoms, and the family and social support network. In general, the greater the internal and external stressors, the more impulsive or destructive the thoughts and behavior, the more disruptive to the family or other societal system (e.g., school), and the closer the proximity between the crisis and a separation or loss, the greater the reason for the consideration of intensive treatment through temporary hospitalization (Richman, 1986). Due to the high increase in such destructive actions as suicide, drug use, and delinquent activities, a "knee-jerk" response would be to remove all at-risk adolescents from their family and community environment. Hospitalizing an individual usually takes the course of providing a brief evaluative stay or a longer term commitment of time and resources when the behavior and emotional support is more dysfunctional.

Although short-term psychiatric hospitalization can be one of the strongest and most important vehicles in breaking the downward spiral of a chronically depressed or suicidal adolescent, the decision process is complicated and incorporates various systems of family and societal structure. These include such practical matters as family willingness, legal guidelines, and insurance reimbursements. Typical admission criteria focus on whether the adolescent is in a life-threatening situation to her- or himself or to others; whether outpatient intervention has been attempted and determined not successful; whether reality contact is of concern and observation in a restricted setting is essential; and whether social service agencies or the juvenile court is involved. All of these factors contain various implications and assumptions, and all must be considered in making decisions on whether or not hospitalization is warranted. Even in the most difficult of presenting circumstances, hospitalizations can severely disrupt a teenager's life and provide an unnecessary burden for the rest of the adolescent's life. Thus, each admission must be thoroughly evaluated for determination of inclusion.

CRITICISMS OF HOSPITALIZATION

There remains a strong reaction from both the lay and the professional community against removing a teenager from his or her family and familiar surroundings (Haley, 1980; Langsley & Kaplan, 1968). Much of this protest surrounds the concerns that families are often not included in treatment intervention and that additional stress is placed on adolescents when removed from their social milieu. Also, when hospitals are used for primary treatment, it has the potential for setting the tone for future crises (i.e., fostering continual hospitalizations). The use of the psychiatric hospital with adolescents can also exacerbate their already low self-esteem and increase their sense of helplessness and hopelessness because they are often perceived as being both at the end of the road and incurable. Instead of anticipated relief from outside stressors, hospitalization has the potential for increasing teenagers' alienation.

The decision to hospitalize an adolescent must take into account the possible repercussions of an increased sense of isolation from family and friends and the difficulty in reintegrating youths back into their community and school. If the hospitalization severs the ties and does not provide increased alternatives for coping effectively with stressors, then the aloneness and estrangement will only increase. For example, if teenagers are already experiencing school problems, removal from a familiar setting may make their contact with peers more precarious and place them further behind academically. One such alternative is to allow the youth to return to school during the day, as part of the individualized treatment plan (Mirkin, Ricci, & Cohen, 1985). Despite these objections, the psychiatric hospital has become one of the most important sources of treatment and is used the most frequently for severely depressed and suicidal individuals (Pfeffer, 1986).

INCLUDING THE FAMILY

Hospitals vary greatly in their inclusion of the family. Most view the family as merely ancillary for gaining information to have a more complete and insightful understanding of the adolescent. Other less traditional centers of inpatient care use the family as a basis for change, even to the extent of hospitalizing the entire family (Abroms, Fullner, & Whitaker, 1971). If one views the adolescent's misbehavior as an indicator of family problems, the removal of the youth denies access to sorting out those systems within the family that are maintaining the dysfunction. Additionally, if one views the precipitants that have created the crisis of possible hospitalization as a symptom of family expression, then separation, regardless of length, exacerbates the problem and decreases the likelihood for successful change to occur. For instance, when the family has become so rigid in their rejection of independent functioning, where leaving home takes on the perception of disloyalty or of upsetting the family dynamics, the hospitalization will only ensure the maintenance of a position that the child must be monitored (Minuchin, 1974; Mirkin, 1983). In this example, where the family's existence has been threatened by this imposed separation, they are likely to sabotage treatment.

Further, removal of an adolescent disempowers the family even more than the adolescent's misbehavior did. The parents, in a very concrete way, have lost all control of the situation. In attempting to restructure the family in order to strengthen the parental hierarchy, the parents must become the primary avenue of change. Taking away their authority by shifting the control to the unit ward and the residential staff will only increase the family's feeling of ineffectiveness. The nurturance and structure that the parents need to provide is given to the staff and taken even further away from the parents.

Research and clinical experience also report that parental involvement is vital for effective treatment intervention. In a study by Rosenstock and Vincent (1979), parents refusal of treatment caused overall treatment to fail nearly 100% of the time; whereas parental involvement in treatment showed a 64% rate of success. Where a family orientation was the focus in brief hospitalizations, parents and their adolescent children believed that the experience was worthwhile, and improvements were evident (Fineberg, Kettlewell, & Sowards, 1982).

The absence of participation by the parents leaves the teenager still in charge and calling the shots in the parental involvement. Change without family involvement leaves the family vulnerable to escalations in the frequency and intensity of the destructive behavior. From the viewpoint of some family therapists, an admission into a hospital neither rescues the adolescent nor provides a "parentectomy"; rather, it initiates the process of producing structural change to overcome the crisis (Minuchin, 1974). This elevation of the parents being in charge begins with the decision as to whether hospitalization is required. Admission then is used as a first step in intervening on the restructuring of the family instead of the hospitalization being the end goal.

PREPARING FOR ADMISSION

Families and teenagers experience many anxieties when hospitalization is mentioned. There may be internal feelings of guilt and failure that must be confronted, as well as those preconceived notions about a psychiatric hospital that must be addressed. From a parent's view, hospitalization may become a symbol of their own ineffectiveness or failure to meet the emotional needs of the child. For the teenager, the idea of an institution may mean ultimate rejection or punishment for misbehavior.

A critical juncture in the process of admitting an adolescent into an inpatient unit is the need for orienting him or her and the family to the expectations, rules, and guidelines of the therapeutic milieu. Unless there has been considerable preparation for the admission, which is typically not the case, family members will experience considerable anxieties, taking various forms. For adolescents, the fears of meeting new people, of being given unfamiliar tests, of being observed and talked to by mental health professionals (e.g., "shrinks"), and of being separated from family and friends may exacerbate their symptoms and increase their sense of powerlessness. For the family, the unfamiliar territory of the psychiatric hospital may make family members defensive, even to the extent of attempting to prematurely remove the child from the unit. These fears are justified and should be respected.

Orienting the adolescent and family to the hospital milieu communicates to all parties that the professionals involved understand the family's need to be informed and to have some feeling of control. It also promotes a therapeutic alliance and provides a message of joining with the adolescent and the family at the point where they are currently involved. In our own experiences, having an orientation group for the newly admitted adolescent provides a solid base for exploration of questions and feelings. This group meets frequently, emphasizes the identification of staff, and educates the adolescents to the types of tests that they will be expected to take. The smaller orientation group gives the newer admissions the opportunity to address these initial concerns and worries in a manageable format, with individuals that are going through a similar experience. This is especially pertinent to shy, withdrawn individuals who may be fearful of rejection. It also helps those youngsters who may be overwhlemed by their emotions but who do not have the opportunity to express them in a larger group, such as at a meeting of all unit members, many of whom may have been on the unit for several months where other issues of daily living have become more pertinent.

For the family, this orienting phase may take the form of discovering the organizational operation of the unit and the policies that govern visiting privileges, phone calls, weekend passes, and so on. It is helpful to have an orientation booklet to provide to the parents, as their anxiety may interfere with remembering all of the spoken details. It also becomes important to review those questions that may not have been asked, for example, What happens if the youth becomes physically ill? Will restraints or isolation procedures be used? In bringing these subjects into the open, more discussion will likely ensue that will enhance communication between the family members and the treatment team. If handled appropriately, these initial meetings will increase the likelihood of all parties working together instead of against one another.

Another important consideration to address is the likely response of the adolescent. These responses can range from intense anger and the need to retaliate against the parents through guilt-producing behaviors to spontaneous recoveries in order to demonstrate to all parties that it was a terrible mistake to be hospitalized. By signifying to the family that these behaviors are expected, it both provides the family with a framework of thinking about how they will respond to such situations and provides the treatment team with an air of authority and expertise. In this way, the family comes to view the treatment team member as someone "who has been there before" and who can provide alternative options for the family. It also adds one more degree of security that everything will be under control, which can be of great relief to the family. This orientation phase of hospitalization has become of such value that some programs have even begun preadmission home visits to reduce these sources of anxieties (Baldwin & Julien, 1980).

TREATMENT WITHIN THE PSYCHIATRIC HOSPITAL

Inpatient treatment subsumes a wide variety of diagnostic and therapeutic modalities to identify accurately the sources of tension both within and external to the severely depressed or suicidal youth. On admission, the adolescent will usually undergo a series of physiological, as well as psychological, batteries and interviews that will better aid the treatment team to plan for appropriate interventions. In addition to a complete physical, these may include an electroencephalograph (EEG), to rule out abnormal brain activity; an electrocardiograph (EKG), primarily to contraindicate the use of certain medications that may have an effect on heart rhythms; a dexamethasone suppression test (DST), to assess a physiological basis for depression; a mental status exam, to ascertain ego functioning and reality orientation; a comprehensive psychological evaluation to evaluate current intellectual and emotional functioning; an academic screening for educational placement; and (usually) evaluations from the occupational therapy department to delineate strengths and weaknesses of visual–motor functioning, from the audiologist to discover possible information processing dysfunction, and from the art, music, and recreational therapists to determine appropriateness of expanded treatment modalities. Also included is the recording of thorough social and family histories, to have a greater understanding of the origin of disturbance and to plan for aftercare treatment.

Other duties of the hosptial staff involve (a) gathering observations of behaviors from a variety of sources, (b) strengthening and reinforcing appropriate activities of daily living, (c) providing intensive emotional support on a 24-hour-a-day basis, and (d) monitoring treatment effects, including achievement of goal-specific behaviors and medication side effects. This multimodal approach to assessment, diagnosis, and therapy is standard in most psychiatric hospitals for all inpatients.

The careful monitoring within the hospital provides several important functions. It allows for immediate intervention to take place if a child impulsively takes some action that may be life threatening. It also provides a number of sources and opportunities for adolescents to express their varied feelings if they should intensify or become overwhelming. For the teenager in turmoil, this becomes a unique opportunity because the prehospital environment was probably void of or limited in providing such support. Rarely does *anyone* get the chance to have caring individuals available to meet emotional upset at all times of the day and night! The continuity of support also establishes additional controls at a time when the youth is most vulnerable.

The tasks of hospital treatment for the depressed and/or suicidal adolescent are varied, but they mainly focus on (a) protecting the child from further acting out his or her destructive impulses, whether these actions involve continued isolative and noncommunicative behaviors, or actual suicidal gestures, and (b) removing him or her from overwhelming environmental stressors (Pfeffer, 1986). The idea of removing adolescents from their immediate surroundings and stressors also has several implications. Although mixed in with anger and fear due to being placed in an institution, it also brings much relief from the extreme pressures of whatever was happening to the youth at home or in the community that was creating the considerable tension. Additionally, the hospital admission affects the family by creating a new crisis that has to be addressed in a context away from the normal living atmosphere of the home. It forces the family to use its resources not only to examine the reasons for choosing the hospital setting as a respite from further altercation, but also to become instrumental in the change process.

One of the main goals of the hospital treatment team to undertake is to promote a working alliance with the parents and family members (Pfeffer, 1986). It is imperative to underscore the seriousness of the problems and to reiterate the helping function of the hospital. For the therapeutic staff member or members who are working with the family, it is essential to provide whatever assistance the family may need and to evaluate carefully these needs in a therapeutic context; in this way, they can formulate working plans both while the child is in the hospital and upon release. Many adolescents who are presenting severe depression or suicidal ideation have been experiencing extremely conflictual family interactions, where one or more family members may have been abusive, depressed, suicidal, or severely decomposed. Because of the intensity of the parents' own problems, they may not have realized the perceived stressors that the child may have been reacting to or the need for intensive intervention away from the home. Therefore, it is incumbent on the treatment staff to provide time for the parent(s) so that they may sort out their own conflicts in order to take an active part in intervening with their child.

In her work on suicidal children, Pfeffer has conceptualized a series of phases that hospitalized children and adolescents go through before being released (Pfeffer, 1977). Although similar to regular stages of outpatient psychotherapy, where working through problems and considering termination of therapy become essential features, she adds an initial phase that is salient to the expectations and treatment of the hospitalized youngster. In this model, attention must be paid to how the adolescent and family are able to separate and how the individual adjusts to the structured routine of the hospital environment. This concept is very similar to orienting the child and family to this interruption of their lives. It also provides emphasis, though, on directly confronting the youth regarding his or her poor coping choices (i.e., suicidal or isolative behaviors), and it focuses attention on specific alternatives for dealing with stressful circumstances. For example, the treatment team can help the youth to develop a list of more effective means of overcoming unpleasant situations or to construct a contract that encourages the youth to inform the staff of suicidal intentions.

Focus is also placed on forming a therapeutic alliance with the family to counteract any family feelings of ambivalence. This becomes essential so that the potential is minimized for the adolescent to split the interests of the parents and the hospital staff. Pfeffer (1977) has indicated that a direct approach of discussing the seriousness of the suicidal behavior and the possibilities that familial distress were contributing to the actions can obtain the most desirable results. Elaborating on the many aspects of familial stress and the impact it may have on children can provide a framework for direct communication and has the potential for valuable therapeutic insights and behavioral changes. In this way, the participation of the adolescent and his or her family is recognized and rewarded.

The highly structured and monitored setting of the hospital sets the stage for intervening on depressed affect and other associated symptoms, such as low self-esteem, lack of eating or sleeping, and impulsive behaviors. Various therapeutic modalities help depressed youngsters to express their feelings individually and in groups, to elicit more positive aspects of the teenager's living situation, to recognize achievements (no matter how small) in educational or interpersonal activities, and to offer alternatives to coping with feelings of hopelessness or aloneness. Along with these new obtainable skills, the family is also given the opportunity to view their child differently and to enjoy their child's successes and newfound optimism. Through this intensive treatment model, problems are specified, individual treatment plans are introduced and followed through to completion, and goals are accomplished. Because most hospitalizations are limited in time, the primary purpose of hospitalization is stabilization of mood and behavior so that continued destructive actions are no longer occurring. Once these have been stabilized, aftercare plans are introduced to continue the more positive adaptation and to bolster the support system that will intervene as needed during future stressful situations.

PLANNING THE DISCHARGE

Once it has been determined that the adolescent is no longer in need of the hospital, plans for termination are introduced. This usually produces a wide array of intense feelings associated with loss, rejection, and abandonment that are likely to produce increased agitation and sadness. The adolescent may regress to prehospital behavior to display his or her degree of distress. Careful monitoring of impulsive behavior must be implemented by the therapeutic staff, along with alert evaluation of the potential for suicidal behavior. A thorough assessment of the youth's mental status, including preoccupation with death fantasies or with self-destructive ideation, is indicated to determine the degree of depression (Pfeffer, 1986). If the adolescent is demonstrating an extreme reaction to leaving the hospital, plans for discharge may have to be delayed until these strong reactions are resolved. While some regressive behavior is always anticipated in this final phase of hospitalization, if intense symptoms persist, the treatment team must consider the possibility of longer-term hospitalization.

By acknowledging the adolescent's anxiety and discomfort, the treatment team can begin preparation to overcome these feelings by focusing on future plans for placement and for the behaviors that are expected. If a new therapeutic community is recommended, visits can be arranged for both the adolescent and the family. Discussions begin to center around continued improvement and new levels of appropriate behavior. A review of the progress made while in the hospital is also essential to promote improvements in self-esteem and confidence about the future. A way to demonstrate to adolescents that they will be missed is to recreate past times and ask them to leave something behind (e.g., a drawing or poster). By making their need for self-importance overt, it usually bypasses their wanting to leave their personal possessions behind. It also helps them to overcome their fears of losing the people that have become important to them during this unique and stressful time.

If a decision has been made to return the adolescent to his or her family, much work still remains. Guidelines must be established in order for each family member, including the returning adolescent, to feel secure about the future. For instance, who will the family contact or what will they likely do if the adolescent begins another self-destructive course? These kinds of open discussions help overcome initial fears and anxieties and help solidify the perception that the parents will once again be in charge of their children's care. Continuation of some types of treatment also need to be discussed. If medication has been implemented, contact must be made with the physician who will be monitoring the dosage. Additionally, the family must decide who among the family members will be responsible to provide the medication during the scheduled times. It is essential to involve the continuing-care therapist during the final phase of inpatient treatment to ensure that an appropriate mental health provider has a thorough understanding of the precipitants of the hospitalization and the work that has been completed. Sometimes, it becomes necessary to work with the adolescent's school, if all confidentialities are upheld, to strengthen the social network and help the adolescent adjust to the extended absence.

It can be especially comforting to all parties concerned and can maximize their personal resources if hospital staff carefully plans for and educates the adolescent and family about their next phase of treatment outside the confines of the hospital setting. This is especially crucial for adolescents who are at high risk for acting out their worries and concerns through life-threatening gestures.

It is hoped that the following case example clarifies and explores (a) the goals for the treatment team, (b) the hospital experience for the adolescent, (c) the types of behaviors associated with depression, and (d) the various treatment modalities that are usually introduced.

Case Example

Arlene T., age 14, was voluntarily admitted into the adolescent unit of a private psychiatric hospital after repeated episodes of running from home, school truancy, and an apparent suicide attempt (taking an overdose of aspirin). She presented herself to the treatment team as sullen, somewhat agitated, and disheveled in personal hygiene. Reports from the unit staff indicated that Arlene was tearful when confronted and was experiencing difficulties sleeping. During some group meetings with her peers, she described many feelings of hopelessness and helplessness, as her parents were recently divorced, and she felt abandoned and rejected. In attempting her attention-seeking activities of running and staying away from school, she had hoped her parents would come together to rescue her; instead, it took an overdose and an emergency-room hospitalization to see her parents together again. In this, she was satisfied. However, her pervasive sense of powerlessness, her self-degrading remarks, her poor peer relations, and her marked poor sense of self-esteem indicated that her problems had been long-standing.

In initial interviews with the parents, her father described Arlene as angry and resentful and always seeking attention and sympathy from others. It was evident that he was annoyed about what had happened and did not understand why Arlene would have to resort to such extreme measures to receive what she wanted. This was the first time that he had ever been involved with the mental health system, and he was reticent to disclose much information. He had thought that he had done a respectable job in providing for the family, but they always wanted more than he could provide, both emotionally and financially. After 17 years of marriage, he felt he could no longer live within the household.

The mother, in contrast, had always suspected that Arlene had underlying problems. She was more articulate in expressing her concerns about Arlene's actions and identified with Arlene's feelings of apathy and depression—something she had experienced briefly during the divorce. However, she needed to get back on her feet quickly in order to protect herself and Arlene, but she seemed to forget the impact that the divorce would have on her child. The mother indicated that Arlene had always been a sensitive and caring child and that perhaps she had mistakenly used Arlene too often for her own support when feeling upset. She now felt guilty about the events leading to the hospitalization and wanted to take full responsibility for Arlene's present situation.

Because the hospital was composed of a multidisciplinary treatment team that provided a broad range of services, including individual, group, and family therapies, in addition to expressive, activity, and occupational modalities, it was essential to specify the various approaches required when developing a treatment plan—that is, how to actively intervene on behalf of Arlene and her family to effectively overcome the current crisis and to devise a plan that would be agreeable after the hospitalization.

The clinician in charge of the case needed to articulate a conceptual framework that would make sense (a) in the context of the hospital, (b) to the therapeutic staff, and ultimately (c) to the parents if indeed they were going to take charge of Arlene's life after the brief hospitalization. This becomes especially important in multidisciplinary settings where each therapist is expecting to make some impact on the child.

The individual treatment goals for working with Arlene were to improve her personal hygiene, to enhance her self-esteem, to lessen her self-degrading thoughts and comments, to provide alternative reasoning for her perceived failures, to broaden her expression of emotion, and to improve her interpersonal relationships. In order to intervene effectively on each stated goal, Arlene was placed in a social skills training group and an art therapy group, to facilitate prosocial behaviors and to offer her a wider range of communication alternatives. Her individual therapy would attempt to counteract her negative and pessimistic viewpoints by challenging her logic and providing alternative options with which to view both success and failure, as well as to initiate rewards for prosocial interactions.

In helping to determine the direction to take in working with the family, it was deemed beneficial to conceptualize their problems and treatment strategies in terms of units (i.e., the individual and the dyads and triads within the family configuration). For instance, Arlene's behavior could be viewed in the context of a protective stance to guard the mother from expressing her own distress about the circumstances surrounding the divorce. The mother's decision to focus on work and not deal with her own depression may have given the signal to Arlene that she needed to do something extreme (i.e., the suicide attempt), so that the mother would receive the safe outlet of a therapeutic relationship without having to immediately acknowledge her own pain. Another way to view their relationship would be that Arlene's sacrificial actions were parallel to her mother's decision to place her feelings on hold in order to provide for herself and for her daughter. An additional, more concrete hypothesis would be that Arlene was just trying to distract the mother so the mother would not brood and would have to refocus her energy on Arlene. That is, Arlene's suicidal gesture has provided a framework of what is to be focused on and talked about and in what kind of setting.

A similar working hypothesis was made for the father and for Arlene's relationship to him. For instance, Arlene may have felt that the father was so distant from her that an extreme measure was necessary in order to receive the attention that she sought from him. Another possible view of their relationship would consider Arlene's action as an attempt of overcoming her own sense of helplessness and feelings of guilt surrounding her perceived involvement in the divorce. In the suicidal attempt, she viewed the action as a desperate gesture to involve the father in her life once again.

Sometime in the zeal for caring for the child, especially in a hospital setting, it is sometimes forgotten that the remainder of the child's social system must be taken into account in order to initiate lasting remedial change. Thus, not only should detailed accounts be gathered regarding the precipitating events, but also contacts should be initiated, with family approval, for historical records from school, physicians, and mental health professionals. Because a suicide attempt usually increases the number of professional helpers involved with the case, it has the potential for creating more confusion and anxiety from all participants. The already complex network of persons involved with the adolescent (e.g., extended family members and peers) may increase to include school officials and the referral person or agency. For successful intervention to occur, these individuals must be included into the therapeutic scheme in some manner. Making contact with all concerned individuals initially increases the likelihood that any goals or changes that are accomplished will be maintained once the hospitalization is completed. For Arlene, this became crucial in planning for her aftercare in regard to parental custody, placement alternatives, and available supporting services after discharge.

Although the hospital admission relieved some of the immediate pressures on Arlene and her parents, the action did not entirely exonerate them from responsibility. In determining whether to reestablish Arlene back into her family and home community, it became incumbent on the treatment team to restructure the family hierarchy in such a way as to empower the parents to manage any future problems themselves. If the parents could not be engaged within the treatment alliance, they would remain powerless to maintain change or to help intervene on future episodes of conflict or of acting-out behaviors. Thus, one of the initial goals was to encourage the parents to set rules for future home visits and to begin negotiating with each other their behavioral expectations of Arlene once she left the confines of the hospital.

During the initial phase of her treatment, Arlene was timid and fearful of her new surroundings. Her participation in the orientation group allowed her the opportunity to ventilate her fears and made her more cognizant of her surroundings. She was able to relay some of her frustrations in small groups or on a one-to-one basis, but she found the large unit meetings particularly difficult and did not add much to the discussions in that setting. She was quick to befriend one of the senior nursing staff, but she tended to keep others at a safe distance with her uncaring facade and her irritability. These actions did not allow her the opportunity to become emotionally involved with the milieu. At one point, she attempted to run away, but she was coerced to return. She then tried to obtain sympathy from her peers by focusing on her past failure and her home situation, but with little success.

Reports from the psychiatric and psychological evaluations portrayed Arlene as being of average intelligence, but lacking in insight and displaying marked feelings of worthlessness and excessive guilt. Her perceptual processes were viewed as being concrete and overly constricted. This had the potential of leaving her vulnerable to distorting incoming information and translating the world in an idiosyncratic and unconventional manner. In turn, this contributed to impaired judgment and inconsistency in her behavior. Scores on two depression scales were significantly elevated, as was her DST, suggesting a biological basis for her depression. A diagnosis of dysthymia was provided. A trial of antidepressant medication was recommended and implemented.

Arlene's initial family sessions were volatile, as she experienced divided loyalties for her two parents. She was distractible and became provocative during the sessions, ignoring both her parents and the directives issued by the therapist. The parents became increasingly annoyed and frustrated. Sometimes, Arlene would react angrily toward the mother, at other times, her verbal onslaught would be directed at the father. In this way, the parents could not resolve their responsibilities toward her and gave Arlene an escape from her own conflicts. When this was finally pointed out to her, Arlene was relieved, and she was able to participate and express her concerns more openly. The parents were also more willing to negotiate with each other, but their overriding anger at each other began to surface, and a decision was made to see each separately with Arlene.

As her initial anxiety began to subside, Arlene became more invested in reaching out to her peers and to the adult staff. To promote this positive change, the staff acknowledged these prosocial behaviors and encouraged her to increase her participation in all aspects of her daily living. Reports from her individual and group therapists also indicated this increased activity. In one of her drawings during art therapy, she was able to suggest renewed hope about the future. She graphically portrayed herself as being involved in school and athletic events, whereas before her drawings were barren and constricted. She was also beginning to focus on the positive aspects of herself, and this was reflected by improved personal hygiene. Although there were times when she would feel saddened by the events in her life, there was no evidence of continued suicidal thoughts, and her impulsiveness also subsided.

At this point, aftercare plans became salient to her treatment. The parents had agreed that the mother would continue being the primary caregiver for Arlene. Although Arlene was still fearful of losing her parents' love and was protective of them, she began to accept their separation and divorce with greater understanding. She no longer saw her misbehavior as effective in bringing her parents together. She was able to express her feelings of insecurity to her father, who reinforced the notion that he would be available to her whenever she needed to see him. Contact was made with a therapist in the community who would continue the family meetings in a similar fashion. This therapist was allowed to come into the hospital for the final sessions, to gain a clearer understanding of the family dynamics and of what had transpired during the hospitalization. This was especially important so that the new therapist could gain an appreciation of the rules that had been established for Arlene to return home.

During this final phase of treatment, Arlene went out of her way to seek more support and reassurance from the staff. Her uncertainties about herself began to resurface, and her difficulties in concentration increased, leaving her feeling estranged from others. The separation from staff also produced similar to the feelings of loss that she had experienced when her parents separated. However, she was more available to hear these fears reflected to her from her various therapists. Her sadness about leaving the unit was handled by the unit staff and peers by encouraging her to contact them whenever she felt the need and by conveying to her that she would be missed and remembered. Arlene was finally able to leave, feeling increased optimism and hopefulness about her future.

CONCLUDING REMARKS

Hospitalization has clearly become a high-priority treatment alternative for the health and mental health community who are increasingly confronting dysfunctional families and out-of-control teenagers. This is certainly true in life-threatening cases. Hospitals have become highly visible to the lay community, especially with television advertisements making parents aware of their parental responsibility when the child's behavior has dramatically changed and the fear of suicide or substance abuse is suspected. "Come to us before it's too late," is the usual message, and insurance companies back up this claim, as they view the hospital as a first-line prevention strategy by underwriting 100% of the stay.

The controversies surrounding this decision have been delineated in this chapter. The decision process is multifaceted, and the pressure from various sources (e.g., general practitioners or social and juvenile services) is enormous. The disadvantages as well as the advantages have been set forth herein. It is strongly believed and scientifically supported that without parental involvement from the beginning, success with any particular adolescent can be only minimal, with the expectation of a high degree of recidivism.

The hospital setting does offer the adolescent an opportunity for safety and a thorough evaluation. It also presents opportunities for treatment staff to observe the teenager's reactions and responses to a variety of treatment modalities. In addition, it allows for a time out from familial and environmental stressors and permits changes to occur in order to broaden the external support system and to enhance communication among all parties involved with the adolescent. Preparing to leave the hospital has also been shown to involve much careful planning and involvement. It is a crucial time both for adolescents and their families, as old fears begin to reemerge, and for the treatment team, who must assess whether change has generalized to continue outside of the structured environment and whether safety will be maintained. The clinical example at the end of the chapter illustrated the various phases that an adolescent may go through while hospitalized, and it clarified the many available interventions that are typically used in diagnosing and treating a depressed adolescent.

CHAPTER 12

Residential Treatment Centers

CASE 1

Bill F., 14 years old, was admitted into a residential treatment center due to social withdrawal, poor personal hygiene, low self-esteem, and family difficulties. Problems with Bill were first noticed in second grade, when he suffered from academic deficiencies (despite above-average intelligence) and physical awkwardness, which produced peer ridicule. By age 11, he exhibited facial tics, stuttering, nightmares, ritualistic behaviors, suicidal ideation, and rapid mood changes—from withdrawal and depression to sudden violent outbursts. Upon returning from a year out of the United States, where his functioning had improved, he was hospitalized in a private psychiatric facility, due to an exacerbation of the aforementioned symptoms. Reports indicated that he engaged in distorted thinking, as well as being at risk for self-destructive behaviors. Long-term residential placement was recommended. He stayed for several years, benefitting from the structure, the antidepressant medication, and the various therapies that were offered to him.

CASE 2

Gail S., 16 years old, was admitted into a residential treatment program due to a deterioration of her behavior at a group home, where she had lived for a year after a brief hospitalization for suicidal ideation and self-destructive behaviors (e.g., carving words in her arm with hot scissors). She was judged to have not yet established a personal identity, and she had tremendous internal fears and little feeling of self-worth. She tended to gravitate toward peers with drug problems, although she was not a user. She was attractive, intelligent, and creative, yet she had been underachieving for a number of years. She had adopted a general stance of nonconformity, feeling disillusioned and frustrated. She tended to withdraw from social contact, and she acknowledged experiencing much anxiety in social situations. Her parents had divorced when she was young, and both of them had remarried. After the divorce, she remained with her mother for a number of years, then she lived with her father after the remarriages. After 9 months in the treatment program, with much attention focused on her family relationships and her personal expression of wants and needs, she was able to return home and enroll in a program for gifted students.

CASE 3

Joe R., 15 years old, was admitted into a residential treatment program due both to agressive and destructive behaviors in his home and to expressions of suicidal ideation. He had also been having school-related problems, which included loss of interest in extracurricular activities and declining grades. There was no known history of substance abuse. He had two previous hospitalizations in a private facility and was then transferred to a state facility for continued treatment and placement recommendations. His parents had divorced, and neither could tolerate the strain of his inconsistent and volatile behavior. He entered the extended residential program on medication for depression (Tofranil), anxiety (Stelazine), and explosiveness (Tegretol). He initially presented himself as shy and socially awkward and unable to modulate his emotions. He appeared suspicious and untrusting of others and seemed to have minimal emotional resources in which to deal with daily stressors. Although he was able to respond positively to the structure of the residence and the school and to follow basic guidelines, he still expressed much rage, especially toward his parents. After showing some positive gains and with the gradual removal of his medication, attempts were made to place him in a summer job. However, he perceived the daily responsibilities as overwhelming and began to experience severe withdrawal and irritability. At that point in his treatment, he left the community to live with relatives.

THE OPTION OF RESIDENTIAL TREATMENT

Troubled adolescents, especially those who have long-standing depressive disorders or who may be suicidal, place an inordinate strain on families and schools. Often, intensive intervention is required that necessitates at least a partial break from the family. Because hospitalization tends to be brief due to economic constraints and the need for placement in the least restrictive environment, other treatment alternatives must be considered. Although this is usually viewed as a last resort because of the longer physical separation from the family household and the inability of social service, juvenile, and educational systems to fund such placements, it can have a major positive impact on the adolescent and the family when all systems are involved and communication is well coordinated. A wide variety of residential treatment programs across the country serve adolescents with a broad range of emotional disturbance. These programs also encompass a vast range of treatment philosophies and behavioral objectives that either include or exclude family participation. In making recommendations to a residential program, mental health professionals need to be well informed of these differences when attempting to find a suitable match for the client who may need these extended services.

Separating adolescents from their families is not a simple choice, nor is it always effective. Several crucial questions require much information and clarification (DeSisto & Koltz, 1985):

1. Should the adolescent be separated from the family at this time?
2. What has been happening up to now that would warrant extended separation (e.g., What other interventions have been attempted? Were any of these successful? What new stressors have entered the picture?)
3. What type of program would be a good match for this individual and this family?
4. In looking at the entire picture, approximately how long should the separation be?

The answer to the preceding questions may depend more on the philosophy of the referring agencies and individuals than on the needs of the adolescent or the family's personal resources. Many may view the choice of long-term separation appalling, while others may see it as an opportunity to begin the individuation process. Both sides are usually adamant about their convictions. Removing a youth from the home often stigmatizes the parents as failures. Some argue that it increases the sense of powerlessness already felt strongly by the overly burdened family. It also has the possibility of producing even greater feelings of alienation and rejection in the adolescent. However, the additional input provided to the family by numerous sensitive and caring professionals and the lessened strain of daily fighting may in fact be the prescription of choice for many problematic situations.

The adolescent and family who find themselves at this crossroads have usually run the gamut of services, often on both an outpatient and an inpatient basis. Up to this point, all therapeutic interventions have proved largely ineffective for the degree of dysfunction. Whatever is maintaining the disturbance has not been addressed or successfully altered. Only a comprehensive program of therapeutic and educational services can provide the opportunity for change. Some parents may react extremely negatively toward such recommendation, while others may coerce the system to remove the adolescent. Some parents may feel that no matter how terrible the emotional conditions in their home, they must take care of their own problems—not give them to a stranger. They are usually paralyzed in their ambivalence to let go of the child whose problematic behaviors may be functionally overshadowing the other problems in the family. Also, many parents try to manipulate the system in such a way as to rid themselves of the burden of dealing with problematic children without financial expense to themselves. Mental health professionals involved in such a choice must be prepared for any number of possible reactions.

Whatever the reactions of the parents, it is the adolescent who has continued to increase and intensify his or her actions in order to signal the need for enhanced intervention. Threats of suicide or running away from home become common, alcohol or other drug use increase, changes in appearance become extreme, and strongly expressed emotional reactions become increasingly frequent. At this point, the adolescent has effectively taken control of the daily functioning of the family and seems to be holding the family members as hostages. It can be described as a time when everyone is "walking on eggshells." There is a sense of helplessness, with few answers available to overcome the feelings. It is during these crises that at least temporary separation should be considered in order to provide time for effective change to occur and to become internalized. These messages by the adolescent tell everyone involved that only intensive intervention can help. These youths, such as the ones described in the initial section of this chapter, let people know that they are not ready to change, to remain in, or to return to their family home.

Not many parents can admit failure or acknowledge that their resources in dealing with their adolescent are exhausted. Parents have much at stake, including their own feelings of competence, as well as strong feelings of love and guilt. How can parents say that they are no longer capable of taking care of their child? Another factor for parents is giving custodial management of their child over to an agency that is unknown and that may not share similar values or concerns. For some families, although the endless attempts at intervention remain ineffective, they still insist that someone can help. It is these families that, although usually resistant to change, have a large investment in correcting their child. They may or may not participate in the change process, but they are the ones who are most taxing to the mental health professional with their endless calls and demands for crisis interventions.

Investigating the possibilities of residential treatment can be time consuming and painstaking. There are usually many agency resistances and restrictions regarding the type and length of stays. If the family is in a position of gaining help through educational advocates or lawyers, they will usually be better served. With this type of support behind them, additional treatment options become available. Without someone looking after the rights of the family and child, options are limited, and placement is usually defined by the agency that has been involved in the case. The variety of settings and services available, whether the setting or service is totally restricted and therapeutic or has a broad educational and vocational component, makes the selection process even more difficult. Within similar institutions, there are also a diversity of differences in the type of treatment philosophies and the number of qualified professionals. Another major difference is the type of adolescent that is typically encountered in the setting, whether most are seriously emotionally disturbed, learning disabled, antisocial, or lower functioning. Finally, the extent and the kind of involvement of the family are of great significance in selecting an appropriate match for the child.

THE ESTABLISHMENT OF RESIDENTIAL TREATMENT CENTERS

There is a long history of residential placement for the treatment of seriously emotionally disturbed children and adolescents (Barker, 1974). When multiple interventions have been attempted with little success, they seem the natural choice as a last resort for intensive, 24-hour care to take effect in order to provide a chance for the youth and the family. The choice becomes even more clear when the youngster has been maintained in a dysfunctional family system where the stressors have been overwhelming to everyone involved.

However, like any attempt at resolving a complex situation, there is no easy answer. For every so-called positive step taken, there are both practical and theoretical drawbacks to placing an individual into residential treatment (Barker, 1988). For example, even the additional treatment may not make a noticeable difference in the adolescent's behavior. Also, teenagers may become overly dependent on the structure and treatment. They may incorporate additional maladaptive behaviors learned from the other residents. The possibility of abandonment by their family is always a concern. Finally, whether funded privately or publicly, long-term placement is expensive.

From a theoretical perspective, behaviors by children and adolescents are highly context dependent. Although competent treatment staff may be able to control behaviors and reduce conflict and dangerous outbursts, the changes may not generalize to the home environment. Also, teenagers may not be able to internalize either different moral values and new modes of behavior in isolation from their previous environment, or it may take years to accomplish. Even from a family systems perspective, commitment to treatment in a facility may be problematic; teenagers will usually accept the separation as their fault, which often increases their sense of guilt and alienation and may exacerbate their problems. It is also a bit paradoxical that family work will take place when the youngster is being cared for on a daily basis by others. Also, the idea that institutionalization has lost its favor in society means that much disappointment has been faced in the past and funding sources are no longer willing to support the settings such that optimal treatment can occur.

Whittaker (1979) has pointed to several areas of concern that have altered the form of residential care. First, he emphasized the importance of continuity of care. By this, he proposed that all services must be coordinated in terms of all major systems that interact with the youth. This means that much interaction must take place among the family, the peer group, the school, the aftercare health and mental health professionals, and the community. He concluded that adequate treatment that will produce change cannot take place in isolation.

Second, the kinds of treatment offered should benefit the family in addition to the adolescent. The family must be instrumental in change. More work with the family should be provided than merely parent training. This can take the form of parent and multiple family support groups, and active parent participation in treatment objectives.

Third, the treatment center and the referring agencies should come to terms with their own philosophies and realize that no single viewpoint will meet all the needs of the troubled youth and family. The programs themselves must also quantitatively demonstrate their effectiveness in treatment and must be able to share their strategies for intervention in an understandable manner to the outside world.

Further measures to promote success in residential treatment approaches have also been advocated (Barker, 1988). The planning of a discharge date should commence with the admission into any program. Goals should be well-defined and clearly articulated to all concerned parties (including residential staff, school personnel in both the treatment center and the youth's home school, the referring agencies involved), and to all family members, as well as to the adolescent being placed. Communication breakdowns are often the cause of unnecessary delays in aftercare planning and of extended stays. By thinking in terms of outcome and desired results, everybody can work in unison toward similar results. Both Haley (1976) and Madanes (1981) have illustrated how therapeutic strategies presuppose the existence of clear treatment objectives.

Also, the goals of treatment must consider what behaviors will replace those that are being corrected or reduced. That is, what desirable behaviors can the adolescent incorporate that will replace responses in situations that currently produce negative reactions? By clearly stating alternative behaviors in a direct fashion, both the adolescent and the family can see that things can be different. In addition, it gives the family members the opportunity to discuss the possible ramifications that changes in behavior may have on their routine functioning. Another way to present this would be in terms of discovering why the family has not considered the desired changes or what has impeded them in successfully overcoming the problems. It also becomes important to discover the function of the expressed emotions. That is, some behaviors can be appropriate in certain situations to keep the family functioning in its unique way; thus, one needs to consider desired change within the unique family context. Another avenue to pursue is how long will it take for the desired changes to occur. Addressing this question provides a timetable for change and implies that success will occur.

Other considerations for treatment planning revolve around the involvement of the family and the message they are given. From the beginning of treatment, problems should be stated in the family context, and not as only occurring within the adolescent. As much as possible, the parents should be involved in the decision making and the problem solving, no matter how minor. This is essential in getting cooperation, and it can take place in the residence (e.g., the parents might be called to coordinate a special incentive program) or in crisis situations (e.g., the parents should be considered in planning to briefly hospitalize a suicidal teenager). Even though many residential programs operate 7 days a week, all efforts should be made to promote frequent visits home. If these visits are contingent on behavior, this gives the signal that only well-behaved children are welcome (Barker, 1988). Again, the focus on treatment should be on the family system and not on the individual teenager. Finally, periodic individual progress reviews can be instrumental in keeping all interested parties informed in a timely manner. With the involvement of governing bodies, such as the Joint Commission on Accreditation of Health Care Organizations (JCAHO) and Medical Assistance, this is usually done routinely every 30 to 60 days.

MULTIPLE-FAMILY GROUPS

Removing adolescents from their families is a major disruption, and there are many pitfalls that can further damage the vulnerability of the already disorganized family system. In order to overcome these potential problem areas, a therapeutic environment that includes the family's active involvement is crucial. One way to promote this concept of integrated and coordinated treatment is to hold multiple-family groups. These groups comprise two or more families that meet with one or two therapist(s) who serve as facilitator(s) much as other kinds of group therapies do. This allows the families to be a concerted part of their teenagers' change and to learn effective ways for this change to be maintained.

There seems no better way to reduce the feelings of isolation, to challenge misperceptions, and to learn more effective alternative behaviors than in therapeutic groups for families. The multiple-family group empowers all family members by the help that is given each other. It is also a platform where the focus is on normalcy and on self-help (Paul & Paul, 1985). It allows for dialogue between generations, which enhances autonomy for the adolescent members. This becomes crucial in their lives at the time of leaving home, and having the opportunity for validation and consensus of their thoughts and feelings can be enormously beneficial. It also allows the parents to experience their teenager's growth without becoming alarmed by the possibility of feeling abandoned. It is a developing process that is being experienced by many different people, and the support that is provided by other families allows the parents to let go and learn to negotiate this important stage of separation–differentiation. In addition to the extra support, the context is safe. The mixture of numerous parents and teenagers overcomes the natural and often negative battlegrounds that are usually established over clothes, curfew, and so on. By providing input from many sources, impasses are overcome more easily and flexibility in negotiating differences of opinion becomes the standard.

The multiple-family group is a complex system. In the beginning, everyone is a stranger, with only few commonalities. What evolves is like a symphony orchestra, with an enhanced repertoire of communication skills that is a vitally important source of nutrients for the depressed adolescent and family (Koman, 1985). While the final product may still be imperfect, the process of negotiating and realigning structural family patterns becomes the basis for change and for improved functioning.

The leader(s) as conductor directs the group toward resolution of the many presented problems. This is done by actively intervening on both the content and the process of the ongoing group. The leader(s) assumes responsibility for promoting harmony between comfort and discomfort for the individuals, the families, and the group as a whole. Within this context, the leader(s) does not simply restate the presenting problems, but initiates solution-oriented themes.

The inclusion of families in group treatment has come of age and is a major part of integrating the various components of a well-planned residential treatment program. All aspects and advantages of family therapy can be found when family groups are formed, with the advantage of increased input and feedback. In a larger context, fights within the dyad or triad of the family lose their momentum, and the support and benefit to the individual family group is enhanced geometrically by the sharing of experiences and information in dealing with the larger system. Even if a single family is stuck in maladaptive ways of responding to one another, the larger group adds a vast array of resources and caring actions that often is able to meet the needs of the individual adolescent or family. Under the supportive umbrella of the group, the individual responsibility and vulnerability are relieved temporarily, and new, instructive learning occurs. With this protection, individual family members are more likely to take risks in expressing themselves and be more willing to try out new roles and behaviors without fear of scrutiny or rejection. (See Laquer, 1972, and Paul, Bloom, & Paul, 1981 for a comprehensive review of how this change occurs in multiple-family groups.)

The adolescent has a unique contribution to provide to the overall structure of the group, and in return much learning is reciprocated. As Leichter and Schulman (1968) have noted, adolescents can relate to and understand family problems, sometimes quite deeply. This is perhaps because the adolescent has been playing a key role in the family turmoil and is perceptive to the central dynamics. It is also typical that the adolescents have already been exposed to intensive therapeutic experiences of group training in the residential program before family groups are established, and this makes them most eager to initiate meaningful interactions in an open and genuine manner. This, in turn, has the effect of reducing the tension and the defensiveness experienced by the adult members.

Usually, it is one of the adolescents focusing on another peer that begins the dialogue. Through this initial confrontation, change begins to take place. Because adolescents are readily available to act out their individual symptoms or their family dilemmas, they often spur their own confrontations with their emotional outbursts or their refusal to participate. These set the tone for the group's work and offer live drama and rehearsal of flexible ways to negotiate more effective methods to relate fears, anger, and frustrations. As the group is confronted by these behaviors and forced to work on solutions to the expressed behaviors and emotions, a cohesiveness emerges that results in commonality and competence. This gives adolescents a new status. Whereas they may have been viewed as the main source of conflict in the family, they now can be viewed as making positive contributions to the group of which the family is one part.

The multiple-family group provides a forum whereby adolescents can be heard and appreciated for their contributions while being held responsible for their own actions. While this is occurring, the parents in the group no longer have to feel stigmatized for their teenager's difficulties or to feel isolated in their failures. They can once again feel competent as they receive support for the stresses they all can identify with on a daily basis. As this reciprocity is maintained, the process of overcoming long-standing dysfunctional patterns of interacting can proceed for the adolescent, as well as for the family.

RETURNING HOME

As residential programs differ in philosophy, resources, and treatment modalities, so do they differ on when and how troubled adolescents should return to their home environments. Some will recommend a less structured alternative residence, such as a group home or a foster home, as a transitional step toward the family home, whereas another may want to return the adolescent directly to the family home. Other programs may include special schools that will allow the teenager to return on a daily basis to provide continued educational and clinical interventions during school hours. Most will have a formal process that is built into the structure of the program that will gradually wean the adolescent from the strictly supervised environment to more independent functioning.

Timing is always a factor in planning a discharge. Many adolescents, especially when their depressed mood lifts, seem on the surface to be working and responding to the expectations of the program quite adequately, but they may not be ready to deal with whatever dynamics were maintaining their symptoms at home. Oftentimes, the family members at home have not had enough time to adjust to whatever changes the adolescent was trying to make, and they still cannot tolerate the additional stress of their returning son or daughter. Even when short vacations seem to have gone well, the thought of longer stays is sometimes overwhelming to all concerned. Therefore, the therapist and other staff, as well as the adolescent and the family, must be prepared for the ambiguity and impasses that might occur in attempting a discharge. Additionally, even the best plans for a return home can backfire as anxieties mount and fears of failure develop. This is a time when the expectations must be clear and the lapses in behavior anticipated. Too many times, the adolescent's or the family's behavior regresses to the point of seeming that a successful return home could never occur. Education and plans for intervention when brief crises arise are instrumental in beginning the transition away from the residential program.

Even when old behavioral and interactional patterns begin to develop during the transitional phase, learning that has occured is often sufficient to deal with the stress. The adolescent and the family have now learned enough new responses that they can intervene effectively without having to depend on others to resolve the crisis. The parents are in a position of control and can now tolerate what they could not tolerate before. The adolescent, although fearful of being out of control again, can accept the consequences of the parent's actions. There is no longer a feeling of impotence or hopelessness.

REGIONAL INSTITUTE FOR CHILDREN AND ADOLESCENTS (RICA)

The following is a description of one such residential program that has been considered a model treatment center. It combines a broad system of clinical, residential, and educational care that is found too infrequently among the choices in placements. Its advantages have been maintained by the support of the community as well as the dual funding sources that operate its daily functioning. Its emphasis on family involvement and on active participation by parents makes it stand apart from most similarly conceived programs. Its quality is also ensured through its highly professional and caring staff. The following description is adapted from a critique that profiled several residential and day treatment programs for seriously emotionally disturbed youths across the country (Isaacs & Goldman, 1985). (Also, the authors of this book had the opportunity to work full-time for this facility for nearly 4 years before leaving to work in their current positions.)

Description

Located in Rockville, Maryland, RICA is a residential and day treatment facility that is operated jointly by the State of Maryland's Department of Health and Mental Hygiene and the Department of Education of Montgomery County. The program has the capacity for 100 daytime students, from grades 1 to 12, and 80 adolescent residential students. Included in the residential component is an eight-bed evaluation unit for adolescents who have been placed by the juvenile courts for comprehensive psychological, educational, social, and psychiatric evaluations. RICA—Rockville, one of three RICAs in the state, was established out of a community concern that the needs of their severely emotionally disturbed children and youths were not being met. Also, many youths with severe personality disorders or adjustment reactions to adolescence were being placed out of state. The RICAs would be an alternative that could bring these youths back to the state, to be served along with their families.

The RICA complex is a one-story brick structure containing a large educational and clinical unit with therapy rooms, including space for art, music, and dance therapies; professional conference rooms; administrative offices; classrooms; vocational and crafts workshops; a gymnasium; an infirmary; and a cafeteria. This central building is connected to three cottages, which house the residential students. Each cottage has three or four units, with eight youths per unit. Each unit has its own contained living room for recreation and socializing. A central living space is also provided in each cottage for residents to meet and participate in supervised activities. An outdoor recreational area is adjacent to these buildings.

Because it is a dually funded program, RICA has an extensive staff and a larger administrative structure than similar residential treatment programs. A chief executive officer (CEO) oversees the daily operations of the program and the staff of approximately 180 state employees. Reporting to the CEO are a medical director, an assistant superintendent, an associate administrator for residential nursing services, and the principal of the school. The school principal supervises about 65 educational staff members, along with a small administrative staff, all of whom are Montgomery County employees. The medical director supervises the psychiatric staff, a full-time pediatrician, and the clinical services staff. A clinical management position was formed to supervise the team leaders and the direct therapeutic activities. The assistant superintendent is responsible for housekeeping, food service, plant management, and staff procurement. Reporting to the head of residential services are the chief nursing supervisors for the three cottages, the nursing and residential staff, and the activities coordinator. These senior administrative staff meet regularly as an executive management group, to discuss issues pertaining to management of the various programs.

The program treats children and adolescents with a wide range of emotional problems. The overwhelming majority have had previous outpatient therapies; about one half have been in special education programs; approximately one third have been in psychiatric hospitals; and about one fourth have been in out-of-state placements. Additionally, about 40% have had juvenile court involvement. The two most predominant diagnoses in recent years have been conduct disorder and dysthymia, although an increasing number of youths have been characterized as suffering from borderline personalities and thought disturbances. Most of the youths have at least average intellectual levels and are not actively a threat to themselves or others.

All referrals to RICA are reviewed by both the clinical and the school staff, to determine the appropriateness of the youth for placement. All referrals must have already had a current assessment and diagnostic workup. On admission, each individual is assigned to one of several multidisciplinary teams. A primary therapist, who serves as case manager, as well as individual and family therapist, is then assigned to the youth. In addition to this person, who is either a Ph.D. psychologist, a master's level social worker (MSW or LCSW), or a master's level nurse clinical specialist (MSN), a school and a residential advocate are also assigned. A psychiatrist assigned to each team serves as supervisory consultant to the primary therapist and other members of the treatment team; this person prescribes and monitors medication, if needed, and is available for emergencies. The first month of treatment is focused on obtaining a clinical and educational picture of the child in order to serve his or her needs. An individualized treatment plan (ITP) is developed by the representatives from each component of the program and is then discussed with the family. The plans are updated at 15-day intervals for the first 2 months, then at 30- to 90-day intervals thereafter, depending on the child's situation.

The caseload for each primary therapist varies from 4 to 10 children and adolescents, depending on the various other administrative duties performed. Several different modalities of treatment are offered to each child and family. Each primary therapist sees the student in formal individual therapy at least once per week. It is often the case that the therapist sees the student informally during crises, which are many. The primary therapist also meets on a weekly basis with the families, to focus on weekend visits and enhance family functioning and communication. It is the expectation of the facility that weekend visits for residential students are mandatory, to promote independence and to practice at home what is learned during the week at the residence.

Small-group therapies are also a vital component of the treatment process. There are often focused on special topics, such as the problems of facing late adolescence, of being children of alcoholics and other substance abusers, and of being adopted children. Expressive therapists also provide group formats to broaden the base of communication to include nonverbal areas. Families are also provided an assortment of therapeutic modalities. Parent education and parent support groups are instrumental in supplying information to the families regarding normal and abnormal behavior and how to deal with difficult situations. The sharing of experiences is also extremely helpful in allowing the families to reduce their feelings of aloneness and stress. Multifamily groups are also held, to provide a format in which different families can exchange ideas and see how each functions in a unique but similar manner.

The residential program is designed to provide a 24-hour therapeutic environment. There are no locked units or rooms. Staff assigned to the residential units communicate daily with the clinical and school staff and with the residential coordinators. They also participate in all treatment planning, monitor the behaviors (through a progressive behavioral system—described later in this chapter), monitor the students' activities when not in school, and mediate during times of crises. The daily activity schedule attempts to provide a balance of free and structured times, of private and social times, of accountability and individual responsibility, and of skill development and nonpressured activities. All residential students join together for evening activities and weekend activities if not able to go home.

The educational component is fully staffed with faculty and administrators hired by the county. The school meets for a full day throughout the academic year. There is also a modified summer program that incorporates both academic and experiential activities (e.g., an "Adventure Bound" program). The school program serves both residential and daytime students whose needs cannot be met in regular school or who require less restrictive, special education settings. The county provides bus transportation for the daytime students. The primary purpose of the school is to provide both academic and therapeutic intervention in order that the students can return to their respective home schools. Therapeutic services are provided to all students during the school day, as well as during after-school hours. The teaching staff instructs the students according to the county curriculum, but it is individually tailored to meet the needs and the grade level of each student in the program. Within 2 months after admission to the program a detailed individualized educational plan (IEP) is developed by the homeroom teacher and the teacher advisor, specifying behavioral and academic goals. The IEP attempts to complement the ITP, and to ensure this coordination, weekly meetings are held between the school and the clinical staffs.

An important feature of the school program is preparing students for their return to their regular home school. An appointed "mainstreaming specialist" handles this process by making the appropriate arrangements with the personnel in the home schools. The mainstreaming process is gradual and begins in increments, with the students attending their home schools for one or two periods before increasing their class schedules only after proven successes. Support is provided to the students by all staff, in addition to being placed in a mainstream support group with other students going through the process of leaving RICA and returning to their home schools. During these groups, which are co-led by the mainstream specialist and by one of the primary therapists from the clinical staff, many of the initial fears are overcome, and many problems are solved through an exchange of ideas among all participants. During this process of mainstreaming, the student's progress is monitored as the mainstream specialist visits the school sites frequently, and written and oral feedback is exchanged between the RICA staff and the home schools.

Another important element of the RICA program is the development of interviewing and job skills through vocational placements. This allows the students to enhance their independent skills, as well as to build self-esteem. Within RICA, students are offered opportunities in industrial arts, offset printing and graphics, business education, and food service. As part of the progressive behavioral system, after reaching certain levels by engaging in specified behaviors, students become eligible to work within the school program. (This system is described in a subsequent paragraph.) Job placements are designed to be appropriate to the student's maturity and interest level. In addition, community jobs have become available in a variety of settings in nearby research firms, in fast-food restaurants, and in other small businesses and social service agencies. These real-world experiences provide both the opportunity for beginning job training and the basis for future employment.

RICA attempts to monitor the progress of students' and family functioning by using a number of pencil and paper devices provided to the staff (to evaluate students) and to families at regular intervals: (a) the Achenbach Child Behavior Checklist (Achenbach & Edelbrock, 1983), which provides an overview profile of a child's behavior, delineates his or her strengths and weaknesses, and makes comparisons against normal populations by age and sex grouping; (b) the Pupil Observation System, a 41-item questionnaire designed to assess improvements in 15 areas of basic skills and behaviors, which is completed by clinical, school, and residential staff several times during the year; and (c) the Family Assessment Device (Epstein, Baldwin, & Bishop, 1983), a 60-question instrument given to all family members at intake and annually, which analyzes the family system on seven dimensions of functioning pertaining to emotional and physical health problems, according to the McMaster Model of Family Functioning.

The behavioral management "levels" system developed at RICA is used as a highly structured, objective treatment modality that creates a format for helping students to increase the frequency of adaptive, age-appropriate behavior and to reduce the incidence of immature and inappropriate behavior. For success, the students attempt to progress systematically through a series of seven levels, in addition to a baseline period. Progress is determined by attaining a certain number of successful days without exceeding the number of unsuccessful days characteristic for each level. Consistent reinforcement and feedback is provided as the students move up each successive level. Through increased privileges, the students are expected to increase their motivation and decision-making abilities.

The levels system provides daily feedback and information to students and staff and is integrated into the entire structure of the RICA program. Each student enters the system on an orientation level. This is a 10- to 14-day period during which a baseline is taken of the student's positive and negative behaviors, as defined and tallied on the daily interaction sheet (DIS) (see Figure 12.1). For students to demonstrate a successful day, they must meet the criterion of totaling higher positives and lower negatives than they showed on their established baseline. This baseline is reevaluated as needed in order to focus on the students achieving success in the program. The behaviors on the DIS were selected on the basis that a high rate of positive behaviors and a low rate of negative behaviors are typically associated with successful adjustment in the real world. They are standard behaviors (e.g., positively interacting with others, ignoring the inappropriate behaviors of others, staying on task) that anyone would have to exhibit to succeed

Name ______ Date ______

Level ______ S ______ U ______

School Per Interval Avg. Pos. ______ Neg. ______

Residential Per Interval Avg. Pos. ______ Neg. ______

RICA — ROCKVILLE
DAILY INTERACTION SHEET (DIS)

Key to marking target behaviors

Positive:
- P – Positive Interaction
- C – Cooperative
- I – Ignoring
- **B – Behavior Goal (I.B.G.)**
- V – Verbal Assertion

Negative:
- D – Distraction
- A – Aggression
- U – Uncooperative
- L – Location
- P.C. – Physical Contact

PERIOD	Positive Baseline ____	Total	Negative Baseline ____	Total
Wake-up	P C I B V		D A U L PC	
Breakfast	P C I B V		D A U L PC	
School Prep	P C I B V		D A U L PC	
Homeroom	P C I B V		D A U L PC	
Period 1 ☐	P C I B V		D A U L PC	
Period 2 ☐	P C I B V		D A U L PC	
Period 3 ☐	P C I B V		D A U L PC	
Period 4 ☐	P C I B V		D A U L PC	
Period 5 ☐	P C I B V		D A U L PC	
Period 6 ☐	P C I B V		D A U L PC	
Homeroom	P C I B V		D A U L PC	
Lunch	P C I B V		D A U L PC	
A.M. / School Totals				

School: S U Daily Status ______

PERIOD	Positive Baseline ____	Total	Negative Baseline ____	Total
Level	P C I B V		D A U L PC	
Free Time	P C I B V		D A U L PC	
Comm	P C I B V		D A U L PC	
Study	P C I B V		D A U L PC	
Dinner	P C I B V		D A U L PC	
Activity 1	P C I B V		D A U L PC	
Activity 2	P C I B V		D A U L PC	
Activity 3	P C I B V		D A U L PC	
Quiet Hour	P C I B V		D A U L PC	
Bedtime	P C I B V		D A U L PC	
Late Night	P C I B V		D A U L PC	
Late Night	P C I B V		D A U L PC	
P.M. / Residence Totals				
A.M. / School Totals				
DAILY TOTALS				

Individual Behavior Goal (I.B.G.)

Increase ______

Decrease ______

School comments to parents: ______

Signature:

Parental comments to school: ______

Signature:

Total Positive Baseline		Total Negative Baseline	
Total Successful Days		Total Unsuccessful Days	

PROGRESS NOTES

NIGHT: Reporter & Title ______

DAY: Reporter & Title ______

EVENING: Reporter & Title ______

Figure 12.1 Example of Daily Interaction Sheet (DIS) used at RICA-Rockville.

in a less restrictive environment. An individual behavior goal is also selected for the students to focus on specific troublesome behaviors.

At the end of each school day, the students are provided with a tally of their scores. This determines their daily status in regard to evening privileges or consequences. Privileges take the form of engaging in planned or informal activities, and consequences include being restricted to the cottage, the unit, or the room. Advancement to Level 5 within the system serves as a signal to the entire program that the student is ready to plan for the transition to live at home, for being mainstreamed into a less restrictive school program, or for other major changes in the program. A formal meeting is held to facilitate this planning.

Case Summary

Rachel B., 16 years old, was admitted into residential treatment after the last of four brief psychiatric hospitalizations extending over a 3-year period. Her first hospitalization occurred following an overdose of over-the-counter sleeping pills, in addition to her manifesting such behaviors as shaving her head for no apparent reason and being preoccupied with horror and sadistic films. Her other hospitalizations centered on continued oppositional behaviors, chronic truancy from a special education school, and self-injurious actions (e.g., burning herself with cigarettes). One previous attempt at a residential program had failed, due to elopement and various suicidal ideation and gestures. On entering her latest placement, her initial Axis I diagnoses were dysthymia, oppositional defiant disorder, and schizoid disorder of adolescence.

During the first 4 months of her placement, she was able to be maintained adequately. She was respectful of limits, followed directives appropriately, and was able to demonstrate improved school performance. She also made steady progress in the behavioral management system. Her behavioral objectives included increased positive interactions with staff and peers, decreased isolative and withdrawing behaviors, and increased appropriate verbalizations of emotions.

In weekly individual therapy session, Rachel was initially quite guarded and avoided emotionally charged material. While she had some difficulty even identifying various feeling states, she had even further problems disclosing any external or internal events that precipitated either her repetitive suicidal crises or her anger and depression. For the most part, she could only identify her current residential placement as contributing to any feelings of sadness, anger, or hopelessness. Yet, her more acute suicidal ideation surfaced when plans were being formalized for her transition home and when she was to go home for an extended vacation. This necessitated another brief hospitalization.

While Rachel did seem to manifest a considerable degree of depression, it appeared that her suicidal ideation was also a product of feelings of anger that she directed onto herself. Additionally, the timing of her repetitive suicidal ideation also seemed somewhat manipulative in nature, as it served to push both her family and treatment staff to consider at least a temporary alternative placement. During the course of her treatment, it was difficult to explore this issue further, as her history of serious suicidal attempts and her poor problem-solving skills necessitated that she not be confronted on these actions without the ability to ensure her safety should she decide to push the limits. Therefore, uncovering the underpinnings of her depression, anger, and manipulative behavior within an unsecured residential setting was extremely difficult and potentially hazardous.

Rachel's parents, for their part, very consistently attended scheduled family sessions. Both parents seemed to express genuine love and care about their daughter and demonstrated a willingness to work with the school and clinical staff during her stay. The parents were in agreement to work toward their daughter's return to their home. The sessions primarily focused on planning for her return and working on intrafamilial communication as it concerned Rachel's verbalizing her thoughts and feelings to her parents. Another central issue that was discussed entailed securing Rachel's medication such that her access was limited only to times when her parents dispensed the particular dosage at the appointed hour. This was crucial because Rachel had admitted that she had access to her medication and had thoughts of taking it during her last suicidal episode. Despite frequent reminders about securing the medication, Rachel's subsequent access to her medication seemed to suggest some minimization or some resistance to acknowledge the severity of her continued problems and impulsivity on the part of her parents.

Strong support during this time came from a parents group that was initiated. This gave the parents a safe environment in which to ventilate their concerns to other interested parents in a similar situation, and it provided feedback and appropriate confrontation about their particular way of responding to their daughter's threats. The group also solidified the two parents in their attempt to present a unified front to Rachel when preparing to make new rules within their living situation. The extra input created an optimistic outlook for them by providing an almost infinite number of alternative ideas regarding child-rearing practices that were produced from the group and the clinicians. It also gave the parents a more realistic view of their daughter by seeing the impact that inappropriate behaviors can have in influencing the stress on parents and on the living situation. This alone had a dramatic effect on their marriage.

On returning to the residential program after her most recent hospitalization, Rachel began to acknowledge the intensity of her emotions and how they interfered with her progress. Although she still tended to dichotomize her feelings into rage or sadness, and at times, she made veiled threats toward herself, she made progress in her ability to reach out to staff and peers. This created a more relaxed atmosphere between her and the entire residential program. However, one disastrous weekend at home caused a temporary slide in her progress, leaving her parents discouraged, angry, and disappointed. After this, she began to withdraw from them, which caused a major split. She also became emotionally fragile and required a lot of approval and support to overcome this setback. For example, she was sensitive to any slights about her character and became easily discouraged. She also became very depressed during the next 2 months, which culminated in a superficial suicidal gesture.

Considerable therapeutic intervention from her therapist and from residential and school staff focused on Rachel gaining control over her past and dealing with the present in a more honest and direct fashion; through this intervention, she was able to allay her anxiety and stabilize her behavior. She again began to work her way up the behavioral levels system. Her parents also began to show renewed signs of being comfortable with Rachel, which added considerably to her feeling supported. She was then placed in group therapies, one verbal and one art, to broaden her base of support and to expand her interpersonal repertoire. A home contract was constructed during family sessions, which gave the parents more perceived control over Rachel and allowed her more independence. With these multiple interventions, Rachel became more spontaneous in talking about the anger and competition she experienced toward her mother. She acknowledged wanting to be the powerful figure in the family, and that her past negative, impulsive behaviors were shortsighted attempts at protecting herself and her father from the mother's authority.

Once Rachel became more interpersonally accessible and more capably maintained appropriate behavior, a transition home was again discussed. Although she remained prone to bouts of depression, her weekends at home were successful with no major incidents, as were extended home vacations. The transitional period, which lasted for several months, was somewhat rocky, but it was successful. Both Rachel and her parents were able to work through this difficult period and began to renegotiate their respective wants and needs as housemates and as parents and child. Rachel also began to extend her relationships with peers outside of the treatment center even though she was still in the school's day program. With continued success and therapeutic support provided by the clinical and school staff, Rachel was able to begin successful mainstreaming to her home school.

Future Directions

A recent article in the American Psychologist cited a survey taken by schools in the 1940s showing that their main problems involved students running in the halls, chewing gum, talking out of turn, wearing inappropriate clothes, and getting out of line (Kean, 1989). In contrast, an identical survey taken in the 1980s identified pregnancy, alcohol and other drug abuse, venereal disease, suicide, unemployment, child abuse, rape, assault, and gang warfare as the salient issues that were impeding educational progress. Even though teenagers have been castigated by philosophers for centuries (see quotes by Socrates, circa 400 B.C., speaking of youth as "tyrants," or carvings 4,000 years old suggesting that civilization will be doomed if the "actions of our younger generations are allowed to continue"), few would have envisioned the problems that make the teenage years of today so tumultuous. The period of adolescence has always seemed to be an accurate reflection of the changing morals and values of society, and adolescents themselves seem to react to these varying challenges and pressures, sometimes creatively, sometimes destructively.

As the pendulum of the societal structure has changed, we have placed more emphasis on the study and treatment of adolescents as a separate entity. This focus over the past decades has evolved to also include a family systems perspective of emotional disturbance. Few clinicians today are actively advocating for "parentectomies" as a solution to the myriad of problems that their young patients–clients are presenting. Those mental health professionals who work with troubled adolescents are also finding that much of their time is being devoted to strengthening family communication and the parental hierarchy, advocating for appropriate services on behalf of parents and their children in the public schools, and consulting in the schools and communities to establish preventive programs for teenage suicide and pregnancy. Without this support from the broader context, few programs or individual treatments could be effective to overcome the difficult and challenging problems being confronted by today's adolescents.

However, this active involvement by therapists does not preclude the individual within the context. Even recent family therapy conventions (e.g., the Family Therapy Networker convention held in Washington, D.C. during March, 1989 entitled "The Self in the Family System") are acknowledging the need to rethink and refine the strategies that have been so efficient and effective for family therapists. This is especially pertinent to the treatment of depression, for which so many useful and viable therapeutic strategies have been forthcoming. These multimodal techniques, stemming from advances in how the entire spectrum of health and mental health disciplines view the problem, offer considerable help for the direct service professional.

As we approach the last decade of the 20th century, there is a radically changing mental health system that is beset by budget constraints, by outside agencies determining the length of treatment, by rapidly progressing diagnostic techniques, by sophisticated research methodology that makes it necessary frequently to update diagnostic nomenclature, and by pharmacological agents that are allowing individuals in distress to overcome severe feelings of depression and anxiety more rapidly. Within this changing climate, there is also a need for clinicians to feel that they are making knowledgeable decisions in their treatment approaches and to have at their disposal state-of-the-art diagnostic instruments and therapeutic techniques. Clinicians working with adolescents are often confronted with the arduous task of assessing behavior that may have multiple etiologies and many disguises. On top of this is an environment, in either the family, the school, or the community, that is not willing or ready to accept changes, either positive or negative, from an adolescent who has been expressing distress that has caused considerable problems. Much of this resistance is understandable when stress and anxiety are heightened and exasperation is the general feeling.

Many disciplines have unique contributions to provide to the understanding and treatment of depression in our young people, but too few individuals and organizations have the time or the desire to communicate this information in an integrated and palatable manner, which could then be translated into workable formulas. In compiling and writing this book and in our continuing daily practices, we have attempted to acknowledge the need and the difficulty of discovering effective therapeutic strategies to relieve the emotional tension between depressed adolescents and their families. As more and more information is being disseminated in both the scientific and the popular media about the effects of adult depression and how it has interfered with work productivity, family preservation, and the enjoyment of life, more attention and effort should be directed toward the considerable loss of emotional and intellectual growth and development that occurs when teenagers become depressed. Not only is there a present loss of achievement and skill attainment occurring, but it is also having an impact on their future and the future of society. Adolescent depression is not only an individual and family problem, but it is also a problem for all of society.

There is much to be said about working with troubled adolescents. Many view it not only as a test of one's patience, but also as a measure of one's perseverance and creativity. Clinicians are often challenged on several levels of intrapsychic and interpersonal conflict created by the expressed symptoms of emotionally disturbed youth. However, few practitioners actually want to work with adolescents because of their impulsivity, enormous need for gratification, lack of insight, limited coping mechanisms, rage, emotional volatility, and sometimes insulting remarks. Additionally, when depressive symptoms are evident, this further limits the access to potentially helpful and healthy responses that could help to overcome many of their problems. This places clinicians in a variety of roles with which they may not be entirely comfortable, but which they must take on if they are to be successful in their work. We hope that this book has created a niche for itself in making the practitioner more aware both of the issues, strategies, instruments, and programs that are available for understanding and working therapeutically with adolescents and of the need to find solutions for them and their families.

References

Abraham, K. (1912). Notes on the psychoanalytic investigation and treatment of manic–depressive insanity and allied conditions. In K. Abraham (Ed.), *Selected papers* (pp. 137–156). London: Hogarth Press.

Abramson, L. Y., Alloy, L. B., & Metalsky, G. I. (1988). The cognitive diathesis–stress theories of depression: Toward an adequate test of the theories' validities. In L. B. Alloy (Ed.), *Cognitive processes in depression.* New York: Guilford.

Abramson, L. Y., Seligman, M. E. P., & Teasdale, J. (1978). Learned helplessness in humans: Critique and reformulation. *Journal of Abnormal Psychology, 87*, 49–74.

Abroms, G., Fullner, C., & Whitaker, C. (1971). The family enters the hospital. *American Journal of Psychiatry, 127*, 1363–1370.

Achenbach, T. M. (1988). Integrating assessment and taxonomy. In M. Rutter, A. H. Tuma, & I. S. Lann (Eds.), *Assessment and diagnosis in child psychopathology*. New York: Guilford.

Achenbach, T. M., & Edelbrock, C. S. (1983). *Manual for the child behavior checklist and revised child behavior profile.* Burlington, VT: Thomas M. Achenbach.

Ackerman, N. W. (1970). Adolescent problems: A symptom of family disorder. In N. W. Ackerman (Ed.), *Family process* (pp. 203–213). New York: Basic Books.

Aldridge, D. (1984). Family interaction and suicidal behaviors: A brief review. *Journal of Family Therapy, 6*, 309–322.

Aldridge, D., & Dallos, R. (1986). Distinguishing families where suicidal behavior is present from families where suicidal behavior is absent. *Journal of Family Therapy, 8*, 243–252.

Aldridge, D., & Rossiter, J. (1984). A strategic assessment of deliberate self-harm. *Journal of Family Therapy, 6*, 113–129.

Alloy, L. B., Abramson, L. Y., Metalsky, G. I., & Hartlage, S. (1988). The hopelessness theory of depression: Attributional aspects. *British Journal of Clinical Psychology, 27*, 5–21.

Alloy, L. B., Clements, C., & Kolden, G. (1985). The cognitive diathesis–stress theories of depression: Therapeutic implications. In S. Reiss & R. Bootzin (Eds.), *Theoretical issues in behavior therapy*. New York: Academic Press.

American Psychiatric Association. (1987). *Diagnostic and statistical manual of mental disorders* (3rd ed., rev.). Washington, DC: Author.

Andreasen, W. C., Rice, J., Endicott, J., Coryell, W., Grove, W. M., & Reich, T. (1987). Familial rates of affective disorder. *Archives of General Psychiatry, 44*, 461–469.

Anthony, E. J. (1970). Two contrasting types of adolescent depression and their treatment. *Journal of the American Psychoanalytic Association, 18*, 841–859.

Apter, A., Bleich, A., Plutchik, B., Mendelson, S., & Tyano, S. (1988). Suicidal behavior, depression, and conduct disorder in hospitalized adolescents. *Journal of the American Academy of Child and Adolescent Psychiatry, 27*, 696–699.

Asarnow, J. R., Carlson, G. A., & Guthrie, D. (1987). Coping strategies, self-perceptions, hopelessness, and perceived family environments in depressed and suicidal children. *Journal of Consulting and Clinical Psychology, 53*, 361–366.

Baldwin, P. J., & Julien, S. A. (1980). Nursing of adolescents in a psychiatric inpatient setting. In J. Howe (Ed.), *Nursing care of adolescents* (pp. 487–510). New York: McGraw-Hill.

Barker, P. (1974). History. In P. Barker (Ed.), *The residential psychiatric treatment of children*. New York: Halstead.

Barker, P. (1988). The future of residential treatment for children. In C. E. Schaefer & A. J. Swanson (Eds.), *Children in residential care: Critical issues in treatment* (pp. 1–16). New York: Van Nostrand Reinhold.

Barkley, R. A. (1988). Child behavior rating scales and checklists. In M. Rutter, A. H. Tuma, & I. S. Lann (Eds.), *Assessment and diagnosis in child psychopathology*. New York: Guilford.

Barnard, C. P., & Corrales, R. G. (1979). *The theory and technique of family therapy*. Springfield, IL: Charles C. Thomas.

Barnett, P. A., & Gotlib, I. H. (1988). Psychosocial functioning and depression: Distinguishing among antecedents, concomitants, and consequences. *Psychological Bulletin, 104*, 97–126.

Beck, A. T. (1967). *Depression: Clinical, experimental, and theoretical aspects*. New York: Hoeber.

Beck, A. T. (1976). *Cognitive therapy and the emotional disorders*. New York: International Universities Press.

Beck, A. T., Rush, A. J., Shaw, B. F., & Emery, G. (1979). *Cognitive therapy of depression*. New York: Guilford.

Becker, R. E., Heimberg, R. G., & Bellack, A. S. (1987). *Social skills training treatment for depression*. New York: Pergamon.

Bemporad, J. (1978). Critical review of the major concepts of depression. In S. Arieti & J. Bemporad (Eds.), *Severe and mild depression*. New York: Basic Books.

Berkovitz, I. (1981). Feelings of powerlessness and the role of violent actions in adolescents. In S. Feinstein, J. Looney, A. Schwartzberg, & A. Sorosky, *Adolescent psychiatry: Developmental and clinical studies* (Vol. 9). Chicago: University of Chicago Press.

Berkowitz, D. (1987). Adolescent individuation and family therapy. In J. C. Coleman (Ed.), *Working with troubled adolescents: A handbook*. London: Academic Press.

Bernstein, G. A., & Garfinkel, B. D. (1986). School phobia: The overlap of affective and anxiety disorders. *Journal of the American Academy of Child Psychiatry, 25*, 235–241.

Bloom, M. (1980). *Adolescent parental separation*. New York: Gardner.

Blos, P. (1979). *The adolescent passage*. New York: International Universities Press.

Blotcky, A. D. (1984). A framework for assessing the psychologic functioning of adolescents. *Developmental and Behavioral Pediatrics, 5*, 74–77.

Boszyormenyi-Nagy, I., & Framo, J. L. (1965). *Intensive family therapy*. New York: Harper & Row.

Boszyormenyi-Nagy, I., & Spark, G. (1973). *Invisible loyalties*. New York: Harper & Row.

Bowen, M. (1966). The use of family theory in clinical practice. *Comprehensive Psychiatry, 7*, 345–374.

Bowen, M. (1972). Principles and techniques of multiple family therapy. In J. Bradt & C. Moynihan (Eds.), *Systems therapy*. Washington, DC: Groome Child Guidance Center.

Bowlby, J. (1973). *Separation: Attachment and loss*. New York: Basic Books.

Bradburn, N. M. (1977). The measurement of psychological well-being. In J. Elinson et al. (Eds.), *Health goals and health indicators*. Washington, DC: American Association for the Advancement of Science.

Brady, J. P. (1984). Social skills training for psychiatric patients: I. Concepts, methods, and clinical results. *Occupational Therapy in Mental Health, 4*, 51–68.

Brendler, J., Silver, M., Haber, M., & Sargent, J. (1989, March). *Explosive families: Breaking the symptomatic cycle*. Paper presented at the annual symposium of the Family Therapy Networker, Washington, DC.

Brown, G. M., Johnston, R., & Mayfield, D. (1979). The 24 hour dexamethasone suppression test in a clinical setting: Relationship to diagnosis, symptoms and response to treatment. *American Journal of Psychiatry, 136*, 543–547.

Brown, G. W., & Harris, T. (1978). *Social origins of depression*. New York: Free Press.

Bryant, C. (1984). Working for families with dysfunctional children: An approach and structure for the first therapy interview. *Child and Adolescent Social Work, 1*, 102–117.

Burns, D. (1980). *Feeling good: The new mood therapy*. New York: Morrow.

Caille, P. (1982). The evaluation phase of systemic family therapy. *Journal of Marital and Family Therapy, 8*, 29–39.

Cantwell, D. P. (1983). Depression in childhood: Clinical picture and diagnostic criteria. In D. P. Cantwell & G. A. Carlson (Eds.), *Affective disorders in childhood and adolescence: An update*. (pp. 3–18). New York: Spectrum.

Carlson, G. A., & Cantwell, D. P. (1979). A survey of depressive symptoms in a child and adolescent psychiatric population. *Journal of the American Academy of Child Psychiatry, 18*, 587–599.

Carlson, G. A., & Garber, J. (1986). Developmental issues in the classification of depression in children. In M. Rutter, C. E. Izard, & P. B. Read (Eds.), *Depression in young people*. New York: Guilford.

Chiles, J. A., Miller, M. L., & Cox, G. B. (1980). Depression in an adolescent delinquent population. *Archives of General Psychiatry, 42*, 696–702.

Cicchetti, D., & Schneider-Rosen, K. (1984). Toward a transactional model of childhood depression. *New Directions for Child Development, 26*, 5–27.

Clarkin, J. F., & Glazer, H. I. (Eds.). (1981). *Depression: Behavioral and directive intervention strategies*. New York: Garland Press.

Clarkin, J. F., Haas, G. L., & Glick, I. D. (1988). Inpatient family intervention. In J. F. Clarkin, G. L. Haas, & I. D. Glick (Eds.), *Affective disorders and the family* (pp. 134–152). New York: Guilford.

Coles, R. (1983). Alienated youth and humility for the professions. In L. Arnold (Ed.), *Preventing adolescent alienation.* Lexington, MA: D.C. Heath & Co.

Constantine, L. L. (1978). Family sculpture and relationship mapping techniques. *Journal of Marriage and Family Counseling, 4*, 13–23.

Constantine, L. L. (1986). *Family paradigms: The practice of theory in family therapy.* New York: Guilford.

Contes, R. M. (1967). The family crises and the impulsive adolescent. *Archives of General Psychiatry, 17*, 64–71.

Costello, A. J., Edelbrock, C., Kalas, R., Kessler, M. D., & Klaric, S. H. (1982). *The NIMH Diagnostic Interview Schedule for Children (DISC).* Unpublished interview schedule, Department of Psychiatry, University of Pittsburgh.

Costello, A. J., & Angold, A. (1988). Scales to assess child and adolescent depression: Checklists, screens, and nets. *Journal of the American Academy of Child and Adolescent Psychiatry, 27*, 726–737.

Covi, L. (1986). The depressive syndromes: An overview. *Journal of Psychotherapy and the Family, 2*, 41–77.

Cromwell, R., Fournier, D., & Kvebaek, D. (1980). *The Kvebaek family sculpture technique.* Jonesboro, TN: Pilgrimage Press.

Crumley, F. E. (1982). The adolescent suicide attempt: A cardinal symptom of a serious psychiatric disorder. *American Journal of Psychotherapy, 36*, 158–165.

Cytryn, L., & McKnew, D. H. (1972). Proposed classification of childhood depression. *American Journal of Psychiatry, 129*, 140–155.

Cytryn, L., McKnew, D. H., & Bunney, W. E., Jr. (1980). Diagnosis of depression in children: A reassessment. *American Journal of Psychiatry, 137*, 22–25.

Davis, L., Geikie, G., & Schamess, G. (1988). The use of genograms. *International Journal of Group Psychotherapy, 38*, 190–209.

deShazer, S. (1984). The death of resistance. *Family Process, 23*, 11–21.

deShazer, S. (1985). *Keys to solution in brief therapy.* New York: W. W. Norton.

deShazer, S., Berg, I. K., Lipchik, E., Nunnally, E., Molnar, A., Gingerich, W., & Weiner-Davis, M. (1986). Brief therapy: Focused solution development. *Family Process, 25*, 207–221.

DeSisto, M., & Koltz, N. (1985). The role of the family in residential treatment. In M. P. Mirkin, & S. L. Koman, *Handbook of adolescents and family therapy* (pp. 127–148). New York: Gardner.

Digdon, N., & Gotlib, I. H. (1985). Developmental considerations in the study of childhood depression. *Developmental Review, 5*, 162–199.

Duhl, F., Kantor, D., & Duhl, B. (1973). Learning, space and action in family therapy. In D. Block (Ed.), *Techniques of family psychotherapy.* New York: Grune & Stratton.

Dweck, C. S., & Reppucci, N. D. (1973). Learned helplessness and reinforcement responsibility in children. *Journal of Personality and Social Psychology, 25*, 109–116.

Edelbrock, C., & Costello, A. J. (1988). Structured psychiatric interviews for children. In M. Rutter, A. H. Tuma, & I. S. Lann (Eds.), *Assessment and diagnosis in child psychopathology.* New York: Guilford.

Ellis, A. (1985). Cognition and affect in emotional disturbance. *American Psychologist, 40,* 471.

Emde, R. N., Harmon, R. J., & Good, W. V. (1986). Depressive feelings in children: A transactional model for research. In M. Rutter, C. E. Izard, & P. B. Read (Eds.), *Depression in young people,* New York: Guilford.

Emery, G., Bedrosian, R., & Garber, J. (1983). Cognitive therapy with depressed children and adolescents. In D. P. Cantwell & G. A. Carlson (Eds.), *Affective disorders in childhood and adolescence—An update.* New York: Spectrum.

Endicott, J., & Spitzer, R. L. (1978). A diagnostic interview: The Schedule for Affective Disorders and Schizophrenia. *Archives of General Psychiatry, 35,* 837–844.

Epstein, N. B., Baldwin, L. M., & Bishop, D. S. (1983). The McMaster Family Assessment Device. *Journal of Marital and Family Therapy, 9,* 171–180.

Erickson, M. T. (1987). *Behavior disorders in children and adolescents.* Englewood Cliffs, NJ: Prentice-Hall.

Erikson, W. H. (1968). *Identity: Youth and crisis.* New York: W. W. Norton.

Everstine, D. S., & Everstine, L. (1983). *People in crisis.* New York: Brunner/Mazel.

Ferster, C. B. (1965). Classification of behavioral pathology. In L. Krasner & L. P. Ullmann (Eds.), *Research in behavior modification: New developments and implications* (pp. 6–26). New York: Holt, Rinehart and Winston.

Ferster, C. B. (1973). A functional analysis of depression. *American Psychologist, 28,* 857–870.

Fineberg, B., Kettlewell, P., & Sowards, S. (1982). An evaluation of adolescent inpatient services. *Journal of Orthopsychiatry, 52,* 337–345.

Fish, L. S., & Piercy, F. P. (1987). The theory and practice of structural and strategic family therapies: Adelphi study. *Journal of Marital and Family Therapy, 13,* 113–125.

Fishman, H. C. (1983). Reflections on assessment in structural family therapy. In J. C. Hansen & B. P. Keeney (Eds.), *Diagnosis and assessment in family therapy* (pp. 63–82). Rockville, MD: Aspen.

Fishman, H. C. (1988). *Treating troubled adolescents.* New York: Basic Books.

Fogarty, T. F. (1976). System concepts and the dimensions of self. In P. J. Guerin, Jr. (Ed.), *Family therapy: Theory and practice* (pp. 144–153). New York: Gardner.

Freud, S. (1917). Mourning and melancholia. In *The standard edition of the complete psychological works of Sigmund Freud* (Vol. 20). London: Hogarth.

Friedman, R. C., Corn, R., Aronoff, M. S., Hurt, S. W., & Clarkin, J. F. (1984a). The seriously suicidal adolescent: Affective and character pathology. In H. S. Sudak, A. B. Ford, & W. B. Rushforth (Eds.), *Suicide in the young* (pp. 209–226). Boston: John Wright-PSG.

Friedman, R. C., Corn, R., Aronoff, M. S., Hurt, S. W., & Clarkin, J. F. (1984b). Family history of illness in the seriously suicidal adolescent: A life cycle approach. *American Journal of Orthopsychiatry, 54,* 390–397.

Gabel, S., Oster, G. D., & Butnik, S. M. (1986). *Understanding psychological testing in children: A guide for health professionals.* New York: Plenum.

Garber, J. (1984). The developmental progression of depression in female children. In D. Cicchetti & K. Schneider-Rosen (Eds.), *Developmental approaches to childhood depres-*

sion: A special edition of new directions for child development. San Francisco: Jossey-Bass.

Geller, B., Chestnut, E. C., Miller, M. D., Price, D. T., & Yates, E. Y. (1985). Preliminary data on DSM-III associated features of major depressive disorder in children and adolescents. *American Journal of Psychiatry, 142*, 643–644.

Gershon, W. S., Targum, S. D., Kessler, L. R., Mazure, C. M., & Bunney, W. E., Jr. (1977). Genetic studies and biologic strategies in the affective disorders. *Progress in Medical Genetics, 2*, 101–164.

Gibbs, J. T. (1981). Depression and suicidal behavior among delinquent females. *Journal of Youth and Adolescence, 10*, 159–167.

Gispert, M., Wheeler, K., Marsh, L., & Davis, M. S. (1985). Suicidal adolescents: Factors in evaluation. *Adolescence, 20*, 753–762.

Gittelman-Klein, R. (1977). Definitional and methodological issues concerning depressive illness in children. In J. G. Schulterbrandt & A. Raskin (Eds.), *Depression in childhood* (pp. 69–85). New York: Raven Press.

Gjerde, P. F., Block, J., & Block, J. H. (1988). Depressive symptoms and personality during late adolescence: Gender differences in the externalization–internalization of symptom expression. *Journal of Abnormal Psychology, 97*, 475–486.

Goldsmith, J. D., & McFall, R. M. (1975). Development and evaluation of an interpersonal skill-training program for psychiatric inpatients. *Journal of Abnormal Psychology, 1*, 51–58.

Gotlib, I. H., & Colby, C. A. (1987). *Treatment of depression: An interpersonal systems approach*. New York: Pergamon.

Greuling, J., & DeBlassie, R. R. (1980). Adolescent suicide. *Adolescence, 15*, 589–601.

Haley, J. (1963). *Strategies of psychotherapy*. New York: Grune & Stratton.

Haley, J. (1976). *Problem-solving therapy*. San Francisco: Jossey-Bass.

Haley, J. (1980). *Leaving home: The therapy of disturbed young people*. New York: McGraw-Hill.

Haley, J. (1984). *Ordeal therapy*. San Francisco: Jossey-Bass.

Hammen, C., Adrian, C., & Hiroto, D. (1988). A longitudinal test of the attributional vulnerability model in children at risk for depression. *British Journal of Clinical Psychology, 27*, 37–46.

Hammen, C., Mayol, A., deMayo, R., & Marks, T. (1986). Initial symptom levels and the life-event–depression relationship. *Journal of Abnormal Psychology, 95*, 114–122.

Harpin, R. E., Liberman, R. P., Marks, I., Stern, R., & Bohannon, W. E. (1982). Cognitive-behavior therapy for chronically depressed patients: A controlled pilot study. *The Journal of Nervous and Mental Disease, 170*, 295–301.

Hawton, K. (1982). Attempted suicide in children and adolescents. *Journal of Child Psychology and Psychiatry and Allied Disciplines, 23*, 497–503.

Herjanic, B., & Campbell, W. (1977). Differentiating psychiatrically disturbed children on the basis of a structured interview. *Journal of Abnormal Child Psychology, 5*, 127–134.

Herjanic, B., & Reich, W. (1982). Development of a structured psychiatric interview for children: Agreement between child and parent on individual symptoms. *Journal of Abnormal Child Psychology, 10*, 307–324.

Hirschfeld, R. M. A., Klerman, G. L., Chodoff, P., Korchin, S., & Barrett, J. (1976). Dependency–self-esteem–clinical depression. *Journal of the American Academy of Psychoanalysis, 4*, 373–388.

Hoberman, H. M., & Garfinkel, B. D. (1988). Completed suicide in children and adolescents. *Journal of the American Academy of Child and Adolescent Psychiatry, 27*, 689–695.

Holden, C. (1986). Youth suicide: New research focuses on a growing social problem. *Science, 233*, 839–841.

Hollinger, P. C., & Offer, D. (1981). Perspectives on suicide in adolescence. *Research in Community & Mental Health, 2*, 139–157.

Isaacs, M. R., & Goldman, S. K. (1985). *Profiles of residential and day treatment programs for seriously emotionally disturbed youth.* Washington, DC: Alpha Center.

Jacob, T., & Tennenbaum, D. L. (1988). Family assessment methods. In M. Rutter, A. H. Tuma, & I. S. Lann (Eds.), *Assessment and diagnosis in child psychopathology.* New York: Guilford.

Jacobson, E. (1943). Depression: The Oedipus complex in the development of depressive mechanisms. *Psychoanalytic Quarterly, 12*, 541–560.

Jarrett, R. B., & Rush, A. J. (1985). Psychotherapeutic approaches to depression. In J. O. Cavenar (Ed.), *Psychiatry* (Vol. 1), Philadelphia: J. B. Lippincott.

Jenkins, H. (1981). Can I (let you, let me) leave? Therapy with the adolescent and his family. *Journal of Family Therapy, 3*, 113–138.

Journal of the American Academy of Child Psychiatry. (1988). 27 (6), November.

Kandel, D. B., & Davies, M. (1982). Epidemiology of depressive mood in adolescents: An empirical study. *Archives of General Psychiatry, 39*, 1205–1212.

Kantor, D., & Lehr, W. (1975). *Inside the family: Toward a theory of family process.* San Francisco: Jossey-Bass.

Kaplan, H. B., Robbins, C., & Martin, S. (1983). Antecedents of psychological distress in young adults: Self-rejection, deprivation of social support and life events. *Journal of Health and Social Behavior, 24*, 230–244.

Kaplan, S. L., Hong, G. K., & Weinhold, C. (1984). Epidemiology of depressive symptomatology in adolescents. *Journal of the American Academy of Child Psychiatry, 23*, 91–98.

Karpman, S. (1968). Fairy tales and script drama analysis. *Transactional Analysis Bulletin, 7*, 39–43.

Kazdin, A. E. (1988). Childhood depression. In E. J. Mash & L. G. Terdal (Eds.), *Behavioral assessment of childhood disorders* (2nd ed., pp. 157–196). New York: Guilford.

Kazdin, A. E., Esveldt-Dawson, K., & Matson, J. L. (1984). The effects of instructional set on social skills performance among psychiatric inpatient children. *Behavior Therapy, 14*, 413–423.

Kazdin, A. E., & Petti, T. A. (1982). Self-report and interview measures of childhood and adolescent depression. *Journal of Child Psychology and Psychiatry, 23*, 437–457.

Kaslow, N., Rehm, L., & Siegel, A. (1984). Social-cognitive correlates of depression in children. *Journal of Abnormal Child Psychology, 12*, 605–620.

Kean, T. H. (1989). The life you save may be your own: New Jersey addresses prevention of adolescent problems. *American Psychologist, 44*, 828–830.

Kendall, P. C., Pelligrini, D., & Urbain, E. S. (1981). Approaches to assessment for cognitive behavioral interventions with children. In P. C. Kendall & S. D. Hollon (Eds.), *Assessment strategies for cognitive-behavioral interventions.* New York: Academic.

Kerfoot, M. (1979). Parent–child role reversal and adolescent suicidal behavior. *Journal of Adolescence, 2*, 337–343.

Kerfoot, M. (1987). Suicidal behavior in adolescents. In J. C. Coleman (Ed.), *Working with troubled adolescents* (pp. 187–202). New York: Academic.

Klerman, G. L. (1982). Practical issues in the treatment of depression and mania. In E. S. Paykel (Ed.), *Handbook of affective disorders.* New York: Guilford.

Klerman, G. L., Weissman, M. M., Rounsaville, E. S., & Chevron, E. S. (1984). *Interpersonal psychotherapy of depression.* New York: Basic Books.

Kolvin, I., Berney, P., & Bhate, R. (1984). Classification and diagnosis of depression in school phobia. *British Journal of Psychiatry, 145*, 347–357.

Koman, S. L. (1985). Conducting short-term inpatient multiple family groups. In M. P. Mirkin & S. L. Koman (Eds.), *Handbook of adolescents and family therapy* (pp. 173–192). New York: Gardner.

Koman, S. L., & Stechler, G. (1985). Making the jump to systems. In M. P. Mirkin & S. L. Koman (Eds.), *Handbook of adolescents and family therapy* (pp. 3–20). New York: Gardner.

Konopka, G. (1983). Adolescent suicide. *Exceptional Children, 49*, 390–394.

Kovacs, M. (1982). *The Interview Schedule for Children (ISC).* Unpublished interview schedule, Department of Psychiatry, University of Pittsburgh.

Kovacs, M. (1983). *The Children's Depression Inventory: A self-rated depression scale for school-aged youngsters.* Unpublished manuscript, Department of Psychiatry, University of Pittsburgh.

Kovacs, M. (1989). Affective disorders in children and adolescents. *American Psychologist, 44*, 209–215.

Kovacs, M., & Beck, A. (1977). The wish to die and wish to live in attempted suicides. *Journal of Clinical Psychology, 33*, 361–365.

Kovacs, M., Paulauskas, S. L., Gatsonis, C., & Richards, C. (1988). Depressive disorders in childhood: III. A longitudinal study of comorbidity with and risk for conduct disorders. *Journal of Affective Disorders, 15*, 205–217.

Kreider, D. G., & Motto, J. A. (1974). Parent–child role reversal and suicidal states in adolescence. *Adolescence, 33*, 365–370.

Kwiatkowska, H. Y. (1978). *Family therapy and evaluation through art.* Springfield, IL: Charles C. Thomas.

Landau-Stanton, J., & Stanton, D. (1985). Treating suicidal adolescents and their families. In M. P. Mirkin & S. L. Koman (Eds.), *Handbook of adolescents and family therapy* (pp. 309–328). New York: Gardner.

Landgarten, H. B. (1981). *Clinical art therapy: A comprehensive guide.* New York: Brunner/Mazel.

Langsley, D. G., & Kaplan, D. M. (1968). *The treatment of families in crisis.* New York: Grune & Stratton.

Lapouse, R. (1966). The epidemiology of behavior disorders in children. *Journal of Affective Disorders of Children, 3,* 594–599.

Laquer, H. P. (1972). Multiple family therapy. In A. Ferber, M. Mendelsohn, & A. Napier (Eds.), *The book of family therapy* (pp. 618–636). New York: Jason Aronson.

Lefkowitz, M. M., & Burton, N. (1978). Childhood depression: A critique of the concept. *Psychological Bulletin, 85,* 716–726.

Lefkowitz, M. M., & Tesiny, E. P. (1985). Depression in children: Prevalence and correlates. *Journal of Consulting and Clinical Psychology, 53,* 647–656.

Leichter, E., & Schulman, G. L. (1968). Emerging phenomena in multi-family group treatment. *International Journal of Group Psychotherapy, 18,* 58–69.

Lesse, S. (Ed.) (1988). *What we know about suicidal behavior and how to treat it.* New York: Jason Aronson.

Lewinsohn, P. M. (1974). A behavioral approach to depression. In M. M. Friedman & R. J. Katz (Eds.), *The psychology of depression: Contemporary theory and research.* Washington, DC: Winston/Wiley.

Lewinsohn, P. M. (1975). The behavioral study and treatment of depression. In M. Hersen, R. M. Eisler, & P. M. Miller (Eds.), *Progress in behavior modification* (Vol. 1). New York: Academic Press.

Lewinsohn, P. M., & Arconad, M. (1981). Behavioral treatment of depression: A social learning approach. In J. F. Clarkin & H. I. Glazer (Eds.), *Depression: Behavioral and directive intervention strategies* (pp. 33–67). New York: Garland.

Lewis, M. (1982). Adolescent psychic structure and societal influences: A psychosocial model. In S. C. Feinstein, J. Looney, A. Schwartzberg, & A. Sorosky (Eds.), *Adolescent psychiatry: Developmental and clinical studies* (Vol. 10). Chicago: University of Chicago Press.

Lewis, M., & Lewis, D. (1981). Depression in childhood: A biopsychosocial perspective. *American Journal of Psychotherapy, 35,* 356–362.

Loarder, P., Burck, C., Kinston, W., & Bentovim, A. (1982). A method for organizing the clinical description of interaction: The family interaction summary format. In F. W. Kaslow (Ed.), *International book of family therapy.* New York: Brunner/Mazel.

Madanes, C. (1981). *Strategic family therapy.* San Francisco: Jossey-Bass.

Madanes, C. (1984). *Behind the one-way mirror.* San Francisco: Jossey-Bass.

Madanes, C. (1985). The prevention of rehospitalization of adolescents and young adults. In M. P. Mirkin & S. L. Koman, *Handbook of adolescents and family therapy* (pp. 207–222). New York: Gardner.

Madanes, C. (1986). Integrating ideas in family therapy with children. In H. C. Fishman & B. L. Rosman (Eds.), *Evolving models for family change* (pp. 183–203). New York: Guilford.

Matson, J. L. (1986). Treatment outcome research for depression in mentally retarded children and youth: Methodological issues. *Psychopharmacology Bulletin, 22*, 1081–1085.

McGee, R., & Williams, S. (1988). A longitudinal study of depression in nine-year-old children. *Journal of the American Academy of Child and Adolescent Psychiatry, 27*, 342–348.

McGoldrick, M., & Gerson, R. (1985). *Genograms in family assessment*. New York: W. W. Norton.

McIntire, M. S., Fine, P., & Fain, P. R. (1984). Early indicator of self-destructive behaviors in children and adolescents: Primary detection by pediatricians. In H. S. Sudak, A. B. Ford, & W. B. Rushforth (Eds.), *Suicide in the young* (pp. 259–270). Boston: John Wright-PSG.

McPherson, S. R., Brackelmanns, W. E., & Newman, L. E. (1977). Stages in the family therapy of adolescents. In J. F. McDemott & S. L. Harrison (Eds.), *The psychiatric treatment of the child*. New York: Jason Aronson.

McWhirter, J. J., & Kigin, T. J. (1988). Depression. In D. Capuzzi & L. Golden (Eds.), *Preventing adolescent suicide*. Muncie, IN: Accelerated Development.

Mezzich, A. C., & Mezzich, J. E. (1979). Symptomatology of depression in adolescence. *Journal of Personality Assessment, 43*, 267–275.

Minuchin, S. (1974). *Families and family therapy*. Cambridge: Harvard University Press.

Mirkin, M. P. (1983). The Peter Pan syndrome: Systematic approaches to short-term inpatient treatment of anorexia nervosa. *International Journal of Family Therapy, 5*, 289–295.

Mirkin, M. P., Ricci, R. J., & Cohen, M. D. (1985). A family and community systems approach to the brief psychiatric hospitalization of adolescents. In M. P. Mirkin, & S. L. Koman (Eds.), *Handbook of adolescents and family therapy*. New York: Gardner.

Mishne, J. M. (1986). *Clinical work with adolescents*. New York: Free Press.

Molin, R. S. (1986). Covert suicide and families of adolescents. *Adolescence, 21*, 177–184.

Molnar, A., & deShazer, S. (1987). Solution-focused therapy: Toward the identification of therapeutic tasks. *Journal of Marital and Family Therapy, 13*, 349–358.

Moreno, J. L. (1946). *Psychodrama*. New York: Beacon.

Morrison, G. C., & Smith, W. R. (1975). Emergencies in child psychiatry: A definition. In G. C. Morrison (Ed.), *Emergencies in child psychiatry: Emotional crises of children, youth and their families* (pp. 13–20). Springfield, IL: Charles C. Thomas.

Munton, A. G., & Antaki, C. (1988). Causal beliefs amongst families in therapy: Attributions at the group level. *British Journal of Clinical Psychology, 27*, 91–97.

National Mental Health Association Information Center. (1986).

National Adolescent Student Health Survey. (1988, August 16). Washington Post.

Nelson, T. S., Fleuridas, C., & Rosenthal, D. M. (1986). The evolution of circular questions: Training family therapists. *Journal of Marital and Family Therapy, 12*, 113–127.

Nichtern, S. (1982). The sociocultural and psychodynamic aspects of the acting-out and violent adolescent. In S. C. Feinstein, J. Looney, A. Schwartzberg, & A. Sorosky (Eds.), *Adolescent psychiatry: Developmental and clinical studies* (Vol. 10). Chicago: University of Chicago Press.

Nurnberger, J. I., & Gerson, E. S. (1982). Genetics. In E. S. Paykel (Ed.), *Handbook of affective disorders* (pp. 109–125). New York: Guilford.

O'Hanlon, W. H., & Weiner-Davis, M. (1989). *In search of solutions.* New York: W. W. Norton.

Oster, G. D., Caro, J. E., Eagen, D. R., & Lillo, M. A. (1988). *Assessing adolescents.* New York: Pergamon.

Oster, G. D., & Gould, P. (1987). *Using drawings in assessment and therapy: A guide for mental health professionals.* New York: Brunner/Mazel.

Overmier, J. B., & Seligman, M. E. P. (1967). Effects of inescapable shock upon subsequent escape and avoidance learning. *Journal of Comparative and Physiological Psychology, 63*, 28–33.

Packard, V. (1983). *Our endangered children: Growing up in a changing world.* Boston: Little, Brown.

Papp, P., & Imber-Black, E. (1989, March). *Developing themes in family treatment.* Paper presented at the annual symposium of the Family Therapy Networker, Washington, DC.

Paul, B. B., & Paul, N. L. (1985). Outpatient multiple family group. In M. P. Mirkin & S. L. Koman (Eds.), *Handbook of adolescents and family therapy* (pp. 161–172). New York: Gardner.

Paul, N. L., Bloom, J. D., & Paul, B. B. (1981). Outpatient multiple family group therapy: Why not? In L. Wolberg & M. Aronson (Eds.), *Group and family therapy.* New York: Brunner/Mazel.

Peterson, A., & Hamburg, B. (1986). Adolescence: A developmental approach to problems and psychopathology. *Behavior Therapy, 17*, 480–499.

Peterson, C., & Seligman, M. E. P. (1984). Causal explanations as a risk factor for depression: Theory and evidence. *Psychological Review, 91*, 347–374.

Petzel, S., & Riddle, M. (1981). Adolescent suicide: Psychosocial and cognitive aspects. In S. C. Feinstein, J. Looney, A. Schwartzberg, & A. Sorosky (Eds.), *Adolescent psychiatry: Developmental and clinical studies* (Vol. 9). Chicago: University of Chicago Press.

Pfeffer, C. R. (1977). Psychiatric hospital treatment of suicidal children. *Suicide and Life-Threatening Behavior, 8*, 150–160.

Pfeffer, C. R. (1984). Clinical assessment of suicidal behavior in children. In H. S. Sudak, A. B. Ford, & W. B. Rushforth (Eds.), *Suicide in the young* (pp. 171–182). Boston: John Wright-PSG.

Pfeffer, C. R. (1985). Self-destructive behavior in children and adolescents. *Psychiatric Clinics of North America, 8*, 215–226.

Pfeffer, C. R. (1986). *The suicidal child.* New York: Guilford.

Pfeffer, C. R. (1988). The family system of suicidal children. In P. S. Lesse (Ed.), *What we know about suicidal behavior and how to treat it* (pp. 407–422). New York: Aronson.

Puig-Antich, J. (1986). Psychobiological markers: Effects of age and puberty. In M. Rutter, C. E. Izard, & P. B. Read (Eds.), *Depression in young people: Developmental and clinical perspectives* (pp. 341–381). New York: Guilford.

Puig-Antich, J., & Chambers, W. (1978). *The Schedule for Affective Disorders and*

Schizophrenia for School-Aged Children. Unpublished interview schedule, New York State Psychiatric Institute.

Puig-Antich, J., & Gittelman, R. (1982). Depression in childhood and adolescence. In E. S. Paykel (Ed.), *Handbook of affective disorders* (pp. 379–392). New York: Guilford.

Quinn, W. H., Newfield, N. A., & Protinsky, H. O. (1985). Rites of passage in families with adolescents. *Family Process, 24,* 101–111.

Rado, S. (1928). The problem of melancholia. *International Journal of Psychoanalysis, 9,* 420–438.

Range, L. M., Goggin, W. C., & Steede, K. K. (1988). Perception of behavior contagion of adolescent suicide. *Suicide and Life-Threatening Behavior, 18,* 334–341.

Rapoport, J. L., & Ismond, D. R. (1984). *DSM-III training guide for diagnosis of childhood disorders.* New York: Brunner/Mazel.

Rehm, L. P. (1977). A self-control model of depression. *Behavior Therapy, 8,* 787–804.

Reynolds, W. M. (1984). Depression in children and adolescents: Phenomenology, evaluation and treatment. *School Psychology Review, 13,* 171–182.

Reynolds, W. M. (1987). *Reynolds Adolescent Depression Scale.* Odessa, FL: Psychological Assessment Resources.

Richman, J. (1979). The family therapy of attempted suicide. *Family Process, 18,* 131–142.

Richman, J. (1984). The family therapy of suicidal adolescents: Promises and pitfalls. In H. S. Sudak, A. B. Ford, & W. B. Rushforth (Eds.), *Suicide in the young* (pp. 393–406). Boston: John Wright-PSG.

Richman, J. (1986). *Family therapy for suicidal people.* New York: Springer.

Richman, J., & Rosenbaum, M. (1970). Suicide: The role of hostility and death wishes from the family and significant others. *American Journal of Psychiatry, 126,* 128–131.

Rie, H. E. (1966). Depression in childhood: A survey of some pertinent contributions. *Journal of the American Academy of Child Psychiatry, 5,* 653–685.

Robins, D. R., Alessi, N. E., Cook, S. C., Poznanski, E. O., & Yanchyshyn, G. W. (1982). The use of diagnostic criteria (RDC) for depression in adolescent psychiatric inpatients. *Journal of the American Academy of Child Psychiatry, 21,* 251–255.

Robins, E., & Guze, S. (1972). Classification of affective disorders. In T. A. Williams, M. M. Datz, & J. A. Shield (Eds.), *Recent advances in the psychobiology of depressive illness.* Washington, DC: U.S. Government Printing Office.

Rochlin, G. (1959). The loss complex. *Journal of the American Psychoanalytic Association, 7,* 299–316.

Rosenstock, H., & Vincent, K. (1979). Parental involvement as a requisite for successful adolescent therapy. *Journal of Clinical Psychiatry, 40,* 132–134.

Rosenthal, N. E., Carpenter, C. J., James, S. P., Parry, B. L., Rogers, S., & Wehr, T. (1986). Seasonal affective disorder in children and adolescents. *American Journal of Psychiatry, 143,* 356–358.

Rosenthal, N. E., Sack, D. A., Gillin, J. C., Lewy, A. J., Goodwin, F. K., Davenport, Y., & Mueller, P. S. (1984). Seasonal affective disorder: A description of the syndrome and preliminary findings with light therapy. *Archives of General Psychiatry, 41,* 72–80.

Rosenthal, R. H., & Akiskal, H. S. (1985). Mental status examination. In M. Hersen & S. M. Turner (Eds.), *Diagnostic interviewing* (pp. 25–52). New York: Plenum.

Rotheram-Borus, M. J., & Trautman, P. D. (1988). Hopelessness, depression, and suicide intent among adolescents. *Journal of the American Academy of Child and Adolescent Psychiatry, 27*, 700–704.

Rubin, J. A. (1978). *Child art therapy*. New York: Van Nostrand Reinhold.

Rutter, M. (1986). The developmental psychopathology of depression: Issues and perspectives. In M. Rutter, C. E. Izard, & P. B. Read (Eds.), *Depression in young people: Developmental and clinical perspectives* (pp. 3–32). New York: Guilford.

Rutter, M. (1988). Depressive disorders. In M. Rutter, A. H. Tuma, & I. S. Lann (Eds.), *Assessment and diagnosis in child psychopathology*. New York: Guilford.

Sargent, J. (1987, March). *Treating suicidal adolescents*. Paper presented at the annual symposium of the Family Therapy Networker, Washington, DC.

Sargent, J. (1989, March). *Depression and the family*. Paper presented at the annual symposium of the Family Therapy Networker. Washington, DC.

Satir, V. (1972). *Peoplemaking*. Palo Alto, CA: Science & Behavior.

Saylor, C. F., Finch, A. J., Jr., Spirito, A., & Bennett, B. (1984). The Children's Depression Inventory: A systematic evaluation of psychometric properties. *Journal of Consulting and Clinical Psychology, 52*, 955–967.

Seligman, M. E. P. (1975). *Helplessness: On depression, development, and death*. San Francisco: Freeman.

Seligman, M. E. P., Abramson, L. Y., Semmel, A., & von Baeyer, C. (1979). Depressive attributional style. *Journal of Abnormal Psychology, 88*, 242–247.

Seligman, M. E. P., & Maier, S. P. (1967). Failure to escape traumatic shock. *Journal of Experimental Psychology, 74*, 1–9.

Seligman, M. E. P., & Peterson, C. (1986). A learned helplessness perspective on childhood depression: Theory and research. In M. Rutter, C. E. Izard, & P. B. Read (Eds.), *Depression in young people: Developmental and clinical perspectives* (pp. 223–249). New York: Guilford.

Seminars in Adolescent Medicine. (1986). December.

Senior, N. (1988). Families of suicidal and nonsuicidal self-mutilating adolescents. *Family Therapy, 15*, 31–37.

Shaffer, D. (1985). Depression, mania and suicidal acts. In M. Rutter & L. Hersov (Eds.), *Child and adolescent psychiatry: Modern approaches* (2nd ed.). Oxford: Blackwell.

Shafii, M., Carrigan, S., Whittinghill, J. R., & Derrick, A. (1985). Psychological autopsy of completed suicide in children and adolescents. *American Journal of Psychiatry, 142*, 1061–1064.

Siassi, I. (1984). Psychiatric interviews and mental status examinations. In G. Goldstein & M. Hersen (Eds.), *Handbook of psychological assessment* (pp. 259–275). New York: Pergamon.

Sobel, B. (1982). Art therapy and strategic family therapy. *American Journal of Art Therapy, 21*, 23–31.

Spitz, R. (1945). Hospitalism: An inquiry into the genesis of psychiatric conditions in early childhood. *Psychoanalytic Study of the Child, 1*, 53–75.

Spitz, R. (1946). Anaclitic depression. *Psychoanalytic Study of the Child, 2*, 313–342.

Statistical Bulletin. (1987, October–December).

Stierlin, H. (1975). Family therapy with adolescents and the process of intergenerational reconciliation. In M. Sugar (Ed.), *The adolescent in group and family therapy* (pp. 194–204). New York: Brunner/Mazel.

Stierlin, H., Rucker-Embden, I., Wetzel, N., & Wirsching, M. (1980). *The first interview with the family.* New York: Brunner/Mazel.

Strauss, C. C., Last, C. G., Hersen, M., & Kazdin, A. E. (1988). Association between anxiety and depression in children and adolescents with anxiety disorders. *Journal of Abnormal Child Psychology, 16*, 57–68.

Strober, M. (1983). Clinical and biological perspectives on depressive disorders in adolescence. In D. P. Cantwell & G. A. Carlson (Eds.), *Affective disorders in childhood and adolescence: An update* (pp. 97–105). New York: Spectrum.

Strober, M., & Carlson, G. A. (1982). Bipolar illness in adolescents with major depression. *Archives of General Psychiatry, 39*. 549–555.

Strober, M., Green, J., & Carlson, G. (1981). Utility of the Beck Depression Inventory with psychiatrically hospitalized adolescents. *Journal of Consulting and Clinical Psychology, 49*, 482–483.

Sudak, H. S., Ford, A. B., & Rushforth, N. B. (1984). *Suicide in the young*. Boston: John Wright-PSG.

Teichman, Y. (1986). Family therapy of depression. *Journal of Psychotherapy and the Family, 2*, 9–39.

Thase, M. E., Hersen, M., Bellack, A. S., Himmelhoch, J. M., Kornblith, S. J., & Greenwald, D. P. (1984). Social skills training and endogenous depression. *Journal of Behavior Therapy & Experimental Psychiatry, 15*, 101–108.

Tishler, C. L., & McKenry, P. C. (1982). Parental negative self and adolescent suicide attempts. *Journal of the American Academy of Child Psychiatry, 29*, 404–408.

Trad, P. V. (1987). *Infant and childhood depression: Developmental factors.* New York: Wiley.

Usin, W., Asber, M., Bertilsson, L., & Sjoqvist, F. (Eds.). (1984). *Advances in biochemical psychopharmacology: Vol. 39. Frontiers in biochemical and pharmacological research in depression.* New York: Raven.

Wattenberg, E. (1986). The fate of baby boomers and their children. *Social Work, 58*, 20–28.

Watzlawick, P. (1984). *The invented reality*. New York: W. W. Norton.

Weiner, I. B. (1980). Psychopathology in adolescence. In J. Aselson (Ed.), *Handbook of adolescent psychology*. New York: Guilford.

Weiner-Davis, M. (1987, October). *Solution-oriented therapy: A wellness approach.* Paper presented at the annual meeting of the American Association for Marriage and Family Therapy, Chicago.

Weiner-Davis, M., deShazer, S., & Gingerich, W. (1987). Building in pretreatment change to construct the therapeutic solution: An exploratory study. *Journal of Marital and Family Therapy, 13*, 359–363.

Weins, A. N., & Matarazzo, J. D. (1983). Diagnostic interviewing. In M. Hersen, A. E. Kazdin, & A. S. Bellack (Eds.), *The clinical psychology handbook* (pp. 309–328). New York: Pergamon.

Weiss, B., & Weisz, J. R. (1988). Factor structure of self-reported depression: Clinic-referred children versus adolescents. *Journal of Abnormal Psychology, 97*(4), 492–495.

Weissman, M. M., Orvaschel, H., & Padian, N. (1980). Children's symptom and social functioning self-report scales: Comparison of mothers' and children's reports. *Journal of Nervous and Mental Disease, 168*, 736–740.

Weltner, J. S. (1985). Matchmaking: Choosing the appropriate therapy for families at various levels of pathology. In M. P. Mirkin & S. L. Korman (Eds.), *Handbook of adolescents and family therapy*. New York: Gardner.

Whittaker, J. (1979). *Caring for troubled children.* San Francisco: Jossey-Bass.

Wilkes, T. C. R., & Rush, A. J. (1988). Adaptations of cognitive therapy for depressed adolescents. *Journal of the American Academy of Child and Adolescent Psychiatry, 27*, 381–386.

Wirt, R. D., Lachar, D., Klinedinst, J. K., & Seat, P. D. (1977). *Multidimensional description of child personality: A manual for the Personality Inventory for Children.* Los Angeles: Western Psychological Services.

Wodarski, J. S., & Harris, P. (1987). Adolescent suicide: A review of influences and the means for prevention. *Social Work, 32*(6), 477–481.

Wright, J. H., & Beck, A. T. (1983). Cognitive therapy of depression: Theory and practice. *Hospital and Community Psychiatry, 34*, 1119–1127.

Yapko, M. D. (1988). *When living hurts: Directives for treating depression.* New York: Brunner/Mazel.

Youngren, M. A., & Lewinsohn, P. M. (1980). The functional relationship between depression and problematic interpersonal behavior. *Journal of Abnormal Psychology, 89*, 333–341.

Zis, A. P., & Goodwin, F. K. (1982). The amine hypothesis. In E. S. Paykel (Ed.), *Handbook of affective disorders* (pp. 175–190). New York: Guilford.

Author Index

Subject Index

(continued from front)

Handbook of Research Methods in Clinical Psychology *edited by Philip C. Kendall and James N. Butcher*

A Social Psychology of Developing Adults *by Thomas O. Blank*

Women in the Middle Years: Current Knowledge and Directions for Research and Policy *edited by Janet Zollinger Giele*

Loneliness: A Sourcebook of Current Theory, Research and Therapy *edited by Letitia Anne Peplau and Daniel Perlman*

Hyperactivity: Current Issues, Research, and Theory (Second Edition) *by Dorothea M. Ross and Sheila A. Ross*

Review of Human Development *edited by Tiffany M. Field, Aletha Huston, Herbert C. Quay, Lillian Troll, and Gordon E. Finley*

Agoraphobia: Multiple Perspectives on Theory and Treatment *edited by Dianne L. Chambless and Alan J. Goldstein*

The Rorschach: A Comprehensive System. Volume III: Assessment of Children and Adolescents *by John E. Exner, Jr. and Irving B. Weiner*

Handbook of Play Therapy *edited by Charles E. Schaefer and Kevin J. O'Connor*

Adolescent Sexuality in a Changing American Society: Social and Psychological Perspectives for the Human Service Professions (Second Edition) *by Catherine S. Chilman*

Failures in Behavior Therapy *edited by Edna B. Foa and Paul M.G. Emmelkamp*

The Psychological Assessment of Children (Second Edition) *by James O. Palmer*

Imagery: Current Theory, Research, and Application *edited by Anneés A. Sheikh*

Handbook of Clinical Child Psychology *edited by C. Eugene Walker and Michael C. Roberts*

The Measurement of Psychotherapy Outcome *edited by Michael J. Lambert, Edwin R. Christensen, and Steven S. DeJulio*

Clinical Methods in Psychology (Second Edition) *edited by Irving B. Weiner*

Excuses: Masquerades in Search of Grace *by C.R. Snyder, Raymond L. Higgins and Rita J. Stucky*

Diagnostic Understanding and Treatment Planning: The Elusive Connection *edited by Fred Shectman and William B. Smith*

Bender Gestalt Screening for Brain Dysfunction *by Patricia Lacks*

Adult Psychopathology and Diagnosis *edited by Samuel M. Turner and Michel Hersen*

Personality and the Behavioral Disorders (Second Edition) *edited by Norman S. Endler and J. McVicker Hunt*

Ecological Approaches to Clinical and Community Psychology *edited by William A. O'Connor and Bernard Lubin*

Rational-Emotive Therapy with Children and Adolescents: Theory, Treatment Strategies, Preventative Methods *by Michael E. Bernard and Marie R. Joyce*

The Unconscious Reconsidered *edited by Kenneth S. Bowers and Donald Meichenbaum*

Prevention of Problems in Childhood: Psychological Research and Application *edited by Michael C. Roberts and Lizette Peterson*

Resolving Resistances in Psychotherapy *by Herbert S. Strean*

Handbook of Social Skills Training and Research *edited by Luciano L'Abate and Michael A. Milan*

Institutional Settings in Children's Lives *by Leanne G. Rivlin and Maxine Wolfe*

Treating the Alcoholic: A Developmental Model of Recovery *by Stephanie Brown*

Resolving Marital Conflicts: A Psychodynamic Perspective *by Herbert S. Strean*

Paradoxical Strategies in Psychotherapy: A Comprehensive Overview and Guidebook *by Leon F. Seltzer*

Pharmacological and Behavioral Treatment: An Integrative Approach *edited by Michel Hersen*